PERSIAN GRAMMAR

PERSIAN GRAMMAR

BY

ANN K. S. LAMBTON

O.B.E., B.A., PH.D., D.LIT.

Professor of Persian in the
University of London

CAMBRIDGE
AT THE UNIVERSITY PRESS
1967

Published by the Syndics of the Cambridge University Press
Bentley House, 200 Euston Road, London, N.W.1
American Branch: 32 East 57th Street, New York, N.Y. 10022

First Edition 1953
Reprinted with corrections 1957
1960
1961
1963
1967

Printed in Great Britain
at the University Printing House, Cambridge
(Brooke Crutchley, University Printer)

CONTENTS

PART I

PART II

The Arabic Element

PREFACE

This work is intended primarily to meet the needs of the student of the Persian language of the present day, but it is hoped that it will also serve as an introduction to the student who wishes to read the classics.[1] The first part is devoted to a description of the main Persian grammatical forms and their use, without reference to their historical development. These forms have been arranged into classes according to their grammatical function. The terminology used is the traditional grammatical terminology of English. These classes do not necessarily correspond exactly with similar classes in English; as in English, some words belong to more than one class. Exact definitions of the various classes have not been given and an exhaustive division into sub-classes has not been attempted. Part II describes the main Arabic forms used in Persian, a knowledge of which is indispensable for the student of Persian. A standard Arabic grammar should be consulted for a more detailed description of these forms. The usages described in this work are those current unless the contrary is stated. In many cases these do not differ from the Classical Persian usage. It should be remembered that language is in a constant state of flux: on the one hand there is a tendency to drop certain expressions and words or to restrict their meaning, while on the other 'slang' expressions are being constantly incorporated into the literary language. No attempt has been made to include in this work words and expressions which are not already so incorporated. The student should beware of using 'slang expressions' in literary contexts. There is, moreover, a vagueness of usage in Persian; and the student should also beware of supposing that the forms set out in the grammar are always

[1] Literary Persian (Farsi), as its name implies was originally the dialect of the province of Fars, the Persis of the Greeks. It can historically be divided into three main periods: (*a*) Old Persian, represented by the Achaemenid cuneiform inscriptions; (*b*) Middle Persian, represented chiefly by the Zoroastrian 'Pahlavi' books, the Sasanian inscriptions and the Manichaean texts recently discovered in Central Asia; and (*c*) New Persian, by which is understood the literary language of Mohammadan times written in the Arabic script. This work is concerned with Modern Persian, which term is used to mean the language of the present day. Incidental references will be found to Classical Persian, the earliest extant examples of which belong to the tenth century A.D. Broadly speaking the term Classical Persian covers the whole Islamic period down to, and perhaps even including, Qajar times. The best period of Persian prose is, however, considered to be the pre-Mongol period. Lastly, occasional references will be found to Colloquial Persian, which is a form of spoken Persian. This work is not intended to be a complete description of modern colloquial idiom.

strictly adhered to. A transcription has been used to indicate pronunciation. The pronunciation given is that of Tehran. No attempt has been made to describe local variations of this. An English—Persian and Persian—English vocabulary for the convenience of the student will be published as a separate volume, but it is not intended that these vocabularies should enable him to dispense with the use of a dictionary. A full description of all words is not given: for this the student must refer to a dictionary. Further, the meanings given are those in current use, which, in many cases, differs from the classical usage.

It remains for me to record my gratitude to Professor A. J. Arberry, Professor H. W. Bailey, and Mr N. C. Sainsbury, for reading through the manuscript and making valuable suggestions, to Professor J. R. Firth for his advice on the use of phonetic symbols in the transcription and for help in the preparation of Appendix VI, and to Mr N. C. Sainsbury for proof-reading.

My thanks are also due to the School of Oriental and African Studies who made a subvention towards the publication of this work.

Lastly I should like to record my appreciation of the care which the Cambridge University Press have bestowed on the production of the book.

A. K. S. L.

July 1952

INTRODUCTION

1. Persian is written in the Arabic script, which is read from right to left. The letters پ *p*, چ *c*, ژ *ʒ* and گ *g* were added by the Persians to the Arabic alphabet. For the complete Persian alphabet see para. 5 below.

2. Vowels:

i approximating to the vowel in the English word 'beat' and represented by ی in the Arabic script, e.g.

بید *bid*, willow-tree.

e approximating to the vowel in the English word 'bed' and not represented in the Arabic script, e.g.

به *beh*, better.

a intermediate between the vowels in the English words 'bed' and 'bad' and not represented in the Arabic script, e.g.

بد *bad*, bad.

a approximating to the vowel in the English word 'barred' and represented by ا in the Arabic script, e.g.

باد *bad*, wind.

o rather more rounded than the vowel in the English word 'book' and not represented in the Arabic script, e.g.

بردن *bordan*, to carry.

u approximating to the vowel in the English word 'booed' and represented by و in the Arabic script, e.g.

بود *bud*, he, she or it was.

i, *e* and a are front vowels; *a*, *o* and *u* back vowels. *i*, *a* and *u* are longer than *e*, a and *o*. The latter group, namely *e*, a and *o*, are slightly prolonged when followed by two consonants in the same syllable, but their articulation time, even when thus prolonged, is less than that of *i*, *a* or *u*.

A vowel approximating to the vowel in the English word 'bit' is heard in a few words, notably شش *ʃeʃ* 'six' (except in the expression شش و بش *ʃeʃ o beʃ* 'six and five' used in backgammon, when the vowel of شش approximates to the *e* of the English word 'bed'). This vowel belongs, as regards articulation time, to the group *e*, a and *o*. Its occurrence, however, is so rare that it has not been thought necessary to represent it in the transcription by a separate symbol, and it will accordingly be transcribed *e*.

In a few words ا followed by ن represents a vowel intermediate between *a* and *o*. Its articulation time is also intermediate between that of *a* and *o*. Again, its occurrence is not so common that it has been thought necessary to represent it by a separate symbol (see Lessons v, para. 2 and xiv, para. 2).

See also Introduction to Part II.

3. The formation of the vowels is shown in the following diagram. In this diagram the tongue positions of the vowels are compared with those of the eight cardinal vowels.[1] The dots indicate the position of the highest point of the tongue.

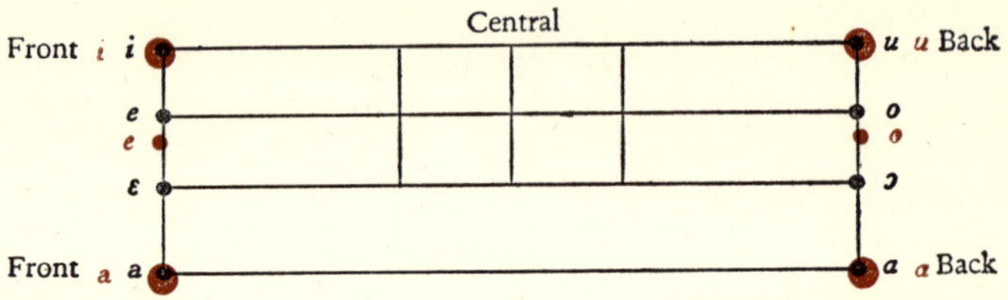

Cardinal vowels: black. Persian vowels: red.

4. Diphthongs. These are *e͡ɩ*, *a͡ɩ*, *u͡ɩ*, *o͡u* and *ɑ͡ɩ*. The starting-point and direction of the diphthongs is shown in the following diagram. *e͡ɩ* and *a͡ɩ* are represented in the Arabic script by ـَی; *u͡ɩ* by وی, *ɑ͡ɩ* by ای and *o͡u* by ـَو. In the transcription the diphthongs are shown by a ligature mark; thus in گوی *gu͡ɩ* 'ball' the *u͡ɩ* represents a diphthong whereas in گوئی *gui* 'thou sayest' *u* and *i* are separate vowels.

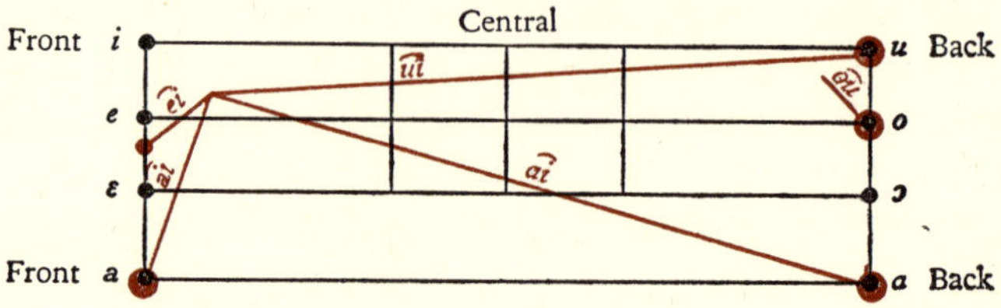

Cardinal vowels: black. Persian diphthongs: red.

[1] The cardinal vowels are fixed vowel sounds which have fixed tongue positions and known acoustic qualities. Their sounds are recorded in Linguaphone, No. DAJO 1/2 H.M.V. B 804.

5. THE ALPHABET. The majority of the letters of the alphabet have four forms, which are used according to the position of the letter in the word. These forms are initial, medial, final joined and final unjoined. The letters ا, د, ذ, ر, ز, ژ and و cannot join the following letter, hence the existence of two final forms, one joined and the other unjoined. The medial and final joined forms of ا, د, ذ, ر, ز, ژ and و are thus identical as also are their initial and final unjoined forms. The term 'initial' is used to cover the case not only of a letter in an initial position in a word, but also of a medial following one of the letters which cannot join the following letter. The table overleaf shows the various forms of the letters, and gives their Persian names, phonetic description and transcription. The system adopted is a 'transcription' and not a 'transliteration', one symbol being used for all letters having the same sound. Thus ث, س and ص are all transcribed by *s*.[1]

6. The sign ء is known as *hamze*. In Persian words it only occurs in a medial position and is written over a bearer, thus ئ. It is a grammatical mark indicating that there is a junction of vowels and it will not be represented in the transcription, e.g.

پائیز *paiz*, autumn.

It performs this function in the following cases also:

(*a*) Between the Present Stem of a verb if this ends in a vowel and the personal endings of the 2nd pers. singular and plural and the 1st pers. plural, e.g.

میگوئی	*migui*, thou sayest.	میائی	*miai*, thou comest.
میگوئید	*miguid*, you say.	میائید	*miaid*, you come.
میگوئیم	*miguim*, we say.	میائیم	*miaim*, we come.

(*b*) Between a word ending in ا *a* or و *u* and the Indefinite ی *-i* (see Lesson I, para. 2 (*c*) below), e.g.

پاروئی *parui*, a spade.

دانائی *danai*, a wise man.

(*c*) Between the final ا *a* or و *u* of a word and the suffixed Abstract ی *-i* (see Lesson X), e.g.

زناشوئی *zanaʃui*, matrimony.

توانائی *tavanai*, power, strength.

[1] An exception is made in the case of غ and ق, which are transliterated as *ɣ* and *q* respectively.

Name	Final unjoined	Final joined	Medial	Initial	Tran-scription	Phonetic description	Remarks
alef	ا	ـا	ـا	ا	—	*alef*, or *alef hamze* as it is properly known, represents at the beginning of a word a glottal plosive and may be vowelled *e*, *a* or *o*. In a medial or final position it represents the vowel *a*. E.g. امروز *emruz* 'to-day', اسب *asb* 'horse', افتاد *oftad* 'he fell', باد *bad* 'wind', ما *ma* 'we'	The vowel ***a*** in an initial position is written آ and known as *alef madde*, e.g. آب *ab* 'water' *alef* is written before the vowels ی *i* and و ***u*** at the beginning of a word, e.g. این *in* 'this', او ***u*** 'he'
be	ب	ـب	ـبـ	بـ	*b*	Voiced bilabial plosive	
pe	پ	ـپ	ـپـ	پـ	*p*	Voiceless aspirated bilabial plosive	
te	ت	ـت	ـتـ	تـ	*t*	Voiceless aspirated dental plosive	See also ط below. ت (and ط) differ from the English *t*, which is alveolar
se	ث	ـث	ـثـ	ثـ	*s*	Voiceless alveolar fricative	See also س and ص below
jim	ج	ـج	ـجـ	جـ	*j*	Voiced post-alveolar plosive	=*j* in the English word 'John'
cim	چ	ـچ	ـچـ	چـ	*c*	Voiceless post-alveolar fricative	=*ch* in the English word 'church'

he hoti	ح	ـح	ـحـ	حـ	*h*	Glottal fricative	English students should be careful to give *h* (whether this is ح or ه below) its full value in a final position, e.g. صبح *sobh* 'morning', راه *rah* 'road', and also when followed immediately by another consonant, e.g. شهر *ʃahr* 'town'
xe	خ	ـخ	ـخـ	خـ	*x*	Voiceless velar uvular with scrape	Approximating to the *ch* in the Scottish word 'loch'
dal	د	ـد	ـد	د	*d*	Voiced dental plosive	د differs from the English *d*, which is alveolar
zal	ذ	ـذ	ـذ	ذ	*z*	Voiced alveolar fricative	See ز, ض and ظ below
re	ر	ـر	ـر	ر	*r*	Voiced alveolar with weak roll or tap	
ze	ز	ـز	ـز	ز	*z*	Voiced alveolar fricative	See ذ above and ض and ظ below
ʒe	ژ	ـژ	ـژ	ژ	*ʒ*	Voiced post-alveolar fricative	=*j* in the French word 'jour'
sin	س	ـس	ـسـ	سـ	*s*	Voiceless alveolar fricative	See ث above and ص below
ʃin	ش	ـش	ـشـ	شـ	*ʃ*	Voiceless post-alveolar fricative	=*sh* in the English word 'show'
sad	ص	ـص	ـصـ	صـ	*s*	Voiceless alveolar fricative	See ث and س above
zad	ض	ـض	ـضـ	ضـ	*z*	Voiced alveolar fricative	See ذ and ز above and ظ below
ta	ط	ـط	ـطـ	طـ	*t*	Voiceless aspirated dental plosive	See ت above
za	ظ	ـظ	ـظـ	ظـ	*z*	Voiced alveolar fricative	See ذ, ز and ض above

Name	Final unjoined	Final joined	Medial	Initial	Tran-scription	Phonetic description	Remarks
a͡in	ع	ع	ع	ع	ʿ	Glottal plosive	ع is a glottal plosive and is represented in the transcription by ʻ.[1] It corresponds to the check in the voice substituted for *t* in Cockney and other dialects in such words as ʻbottleʼ, ʻwaterʼ, etc., e.g. بعضی *ba*ʿ*zi* ʻsomeʼ, وضع *vaz*ʿ ʻsituationʼ. In an initial position when it is followed immediately by a vowel it is omitted from the transcription, e.g. عمر *omr* ʻlifeʼ. The combination of ع preceded by *a* and followed by *i* tends to become *a͡i*, e.g. سعی *sa͡i* ʻeffortʼ
γe͡in	غ	غ	غ	غ	*γ*	Voiced or voiceless uvular plosive according to phonetic context	See ق below
fe	ف	ف	ف	ف	*f*	Voiceless labio-dental fricative	
qaf	ق	ق	ق	ق	*q*	Voiced or voiceless uvular plosive according to phonetic context	غ and ق are not differentiated by most speakers. Both are pronounced as a voiceless uvular plosive (formed by the back of the tongue coming into contact with the rearmost part of the soft palate), unless between two back vowels when they tend to be pronounced as a voiced uvular plosive

kaf	ك	ـك	كـ	ـكـ	*k*	Voiceless aspirated palatal or velar plosive according to phonetic concontext	ك *k* and گ *g* (see below) are palatal if followed by a front vowel, i.e. *i*, *e* or *a* or the diphthong *ei͡*, or in a final position (whether in a word or syllable). In other contexts ك *k* and گ *g* are velar. The palatal *k* and *g* are not found in English. They are made by the front of the tongue, excluding the tip, coming against the hard palate
gaf	گ	ـگ	گـ	ـگـ	*g*	Voiced palatal or velar plosive according to phonetic context	See ك above. ك *k* and گ *g* followed by ا *a* are written كا and گا respectively
lam	ل	ـل	لـ	ـلـ	*l*	Voiced alveolar lateral	ل *l* followed by ا *a* is written لا
mim	م	ـم	مـ	ـمـ	*m*	Voiced nasal bilabial	
nun	ن	ـن	نـ	ـنـ	*n*	Voiced nasal alveolar	ن *n* if followed by ب *b* in the same word is pronounced *m* and will be so represented in the transcription, e.g. انبار *ambar* 'store'
vav	و	ـو	و	ـو	*v*	Voiced labio-dental fricative	و can be a consonant, vowel or diphthong. After an initial خ *x* in Persian words it is not pronounced, e.g. خواستن *xastan* 'to want'. Exceptions to this are خوب *xub* 'good', خون *xun* 'blood', خوك *xuk* 'pig', خوشه *xuʃe* 'a cluster of grapes', خوزستان *xuzestan* 'Khuzistan'
					u	See para. 2 above	
					ou͡	See para. 4 above	

[1] See Introduction to Part II for the use of this sign to transcribe a medial or final *hamze* in Arabic words.

Name	Final unjoined	Final joined	Medial	Initial	Tran-scription	Phonetic description	Remarks
							In the words دو *do* 'two', تو *to* 'thou', and بوته *bote* 'bush' the و is pronounced *o* (see para. 2 above) In words derived from Turkish و is also sometimes pronounced *o*, thus دوشك (توشك) *doʃak* 'mattress', تومان *toman* 'ten rials', توتون *totun* 'tobacco'. يورتمه *yortme* 'trotting, trot'
he havaz	ه	ـه	ـهـ	هـ	*h*	Glottal fricative	See ح above. In a final position in certain words when preceded by the vowel *e*, ه is not pronounced. This will be called the 'silent' *h*. This is the case when ه represents a verbal, adjectival or nominal suffix, e.g. گفته *gofte* 'said', نامه *name* 'letter', ماهه *mahe* 'monthly'. The ه of نه *na* 'no' and بله *bale* 'yes' is not pronounced. See also Introduction to Part II, para. 11
ye	ى	ـى	ـيـ	يـ	*y* *i* *e͡i*, *a͡i*	Semi-vowel See para. 2 above See para. 4 above	In certain contexts ى represents the *ezafe* and is pronouned *ye* (see Lesson II, para. 7)

(*d*) Between a word ending in ا *a* or و *u* and the Relative ى *-i* (see Lesson VIII), e.g.

...کتابهائیکه *ketabhai ke*, the books which....

...آدم پرروئیکه *adame porrui ke*, the bold (brazen) man who....

7. Over the 'silent' *h* a *hamze* represents:

(*a*) The Indefinite ى *-i*, e.g.

نامهٔ *namei*, a letter.

(*b*) The 'Adjectival' ى, e.g.

سرمهٔ *sormei*, dark blue.

(*c*) The personal ending of the 2nd pers. sing., e.g.

گفتهٔ *goftei*, Thou hast said.

(*d*) The *ezafe* (see Lesson II, para. 6), in which case it is represented in the transcription as *ye*, e.g.

نامهٔ من *nameye man*, my letter.

8. For the *hamze* in Arabic words see the Introduction to Part II, paras. 8 and 9.

9. The following orthographic signs exist, but are not in common use:

ـَ *fathe*=a.

ـِ *kasre*=e.

ـُ *zamme*=o.

ـّ *tašdid*, used to mark a doubled consonant.

ـْ *sokun* or *jazm*, used to show a consonant is not vocalized.

These signs are placed above or below the letter to which they refer, e.g.

دَر *dar*, door.

کِشْت *kešt*, cultivation.

پُر *por*, full.

The student should note that although the sign *tašdid* is rarely used the doubling of a consonant should be strictly observed in pronunciation (except in a final position).

Reading Exercise

آب *ab* water	آش *aʃ* stew	آن *an* that	با *ba* with	تا *ta* until	پا *pa* foot
جا *ja* place	تو *tu* in	رو *ru* on	بی *bi* without	کی *ki* who (interrog.)	باج *baj* tribute
باد *bad* wind	بار *bar* time	باز *baz* open	باغ *baɣ* garden	باك *bak* fear	بال *bal* wing
بام *bam* roof	بود *bud* he was	بوم *bum* soil	بیخ *bix* root	بید *bid* willow	بیش *biʃ* more
بیل *bil* spade	بیم *bim* fear	پاس *pas* watch	پاك *pak* clean	پوچ *puc* futile	پود *pud* weft
پوك *puk* rotten	پول *pul* money	پیت *pit* petrol-tin	پیچ *pic* corner	پیر *pir* old	پیش *piʃ* before
پیل *pil* elephant	پیه *pih* lard	تاج *taj* crown	تار *tar* guitar	توپ *tup* ball	تور *tur* net
تیر *tir* arrow	تیز *tiz* sharp	تیغ *tiɣ* thorn	جام *jam* cup	جان *jan* soul	جاه *jah* rank
جوب *jub* irrigation channel	جور *jur* kind, sort	جوش *juʃ* boiling	جیب *jib* pocket	جیغ *jiɣ* scream	چاپ *cap* print
چاق *caq* fat	چال *cal* pit	چاه *cah* well	چوب *cub* wood	چون *cun* when	چیت *cit* calico
چین *cin* pleat	حال *hal* state	حین *hin* time	خار *xar* thorn	خاص *xas* special	خال *xal* mole

خام	خان	خواب	خواه	خوب	خون
xam	*xan*	*xab*	*xah*	*xub*	*xun*
raw	khan	sleep	whether	good	blood
خیس	خیش	داد	دار	داغ	دام
xis	*xiʃ*	*dad*	*dar*	*daɣ*	*dam*
soaked	plough	justice	gallows	hot	snare
دود	دور	دوش	دوغ	دیر	دیگ
dud	*dur*	*duʃ*	*duɣ*	*dir*	*dig*
smoke	far	shoulder	sour milk	late	cauldron
دین	دیو	ذات	راز	رام	ران
din	*div*	*ʒat*	*raʒ*	*ram*	*ran*
religion	demon	nature	secret	tame	thigh
راه	روح	رود	روز	ریش	ریگ
rah	*ruh*	*rud*	*ruʒ*	*riʃ*	*rig*
road	soul	river	day	beard	sand
زاغ	زود	زور	زیج	زیر	زین
ʒaɣ	*ʒud*	*ʒur*	*ʒij*	*ʒir*	*ʒin*
magpie	early	force	almanac	under	saddle
ساق	سال	سان	سوت	سود	سور
saq	*sal*	*san*	*sut*	*sud*	*sur*
shank	year	parade	whistle	benefit	feast
سیخ	سیر	سیم	شاخ	شاد	شام
six	*sir*	*sim*	*ʃax*	*ʃad*	*ʃam*
skewer	garlic	silver	branch	happy	supper
شور	شوم	شیر	صاف	طاق	طول
ʃur	*ʃum*	*ʃir*	*saf*	*taq*	*tul*
brackish	ill-omened	lion	pure	portico	length
طین	عود	عید	غار	غاز	غول
tin	*ud*	*id*	*ɣar*	*ɣaʒ*	*ɣul*
clay	lute	holiday	cave	goose	ghoul
فاش	فال	فام	فیل	قاب	قیر
faʃ	*fal*	*fam*	*fil*	*qab*	*qir*
divulged	omen	colour	elephant	plate	pitch
کاج	کاخ	کار	کال	کام	کان
kaj	*kax*	*kar*	*kal*	*kam*	*kan*
pine	pavillion	work	unripe	desire	mine

کاه	کوچ	کور	کول	کوه	کیف
kah	*kuc*	*kur*	*kul*	*kuh*	*kif*
straw	migration	blind	shoulder	mountain	bag
گاو	گاه	گور	گوش	گول	گیج
gav	*gah*	*gur*	*guʃ*	*gul*	*gij*
ox	place	tomb	ear	deceit	giddy
گیر	لات	لاش	لاف	لال	لور
gir	*lat*	*laʃ*	*laf*	*lal*	*lur*
caught	vagabond	carrion	boast	dumb	whey
لیف	مات	مار	ماش	مال	ماه
lif	*mat*	*mar*	*maʃ*	*mal*	*mah*
fibre	checkmate	snake	a kind of pulse	possessions	moon
موم	میخ	میز	میش	میل	نام
mum	*mix*	*miz*	*miʃ*	*mil*	*nam*
wax	nail	table	ewe	rod	name
نان	ناو	نور	نیز	نیش	نیل
nan	*nav*	*nur*	*niz*	*niʃ*	*nil*
bread	ship	light	also	sting	indigo
نیم	وام	هوش	هیچ	ایل	این
nim	*vam*	*huʃ*	*hic*	*il*	*in*
half	debt	intelligence	nothing	tribe	this
یاس	یار	یال	رأس	شأن	یأس
yas	*yar*	*yal*	*ra‘s*	*ʃa‘n*	*ya‘s*
lilac	helper	mane	head	dignity	despair
دَور	ذَوق	شَوق	فَوج	خَیر	سَیل
do͡ur	*zo͡uq*	*ʃo͡uq*	*fo͡uj*	*xe͡ir*	*se͡il*
round	taste	enthusiasm	battalion	good	flood
صَیف	عَیب	مَیل			
se͡if	*e͡ib*	*me͡il*			
summer	fault	inclination			

PART I

LESSON I

The Indefinite ی -*i*. The Personal Pronouns. The Demonstrative Pronouns.

1. There is no definite or indefinite article in Persian.[1] Broadly speaking, a noun becomes indefinite by the addition of ی -*i*, e.g.

کتاب *ketab*, (the) book.

کتابی *ketabi*, a book.

2. (*a*) If the noun ends in the 'silent' *h* preceded by *e*, the Indefinite ی -*i* is not written. The sign ـٔ known as *hamze* is written over the 'silent' *h*,[2] e.g.

پنجره *panjare*, (the) window.

پنجرهٔ *panjarei*, a window.

The sign ـٔ is usually omitted in writing, the reader being expected to know from the context whether the word is definite or indefinite. (See also para. 15 (*e*) below.)

(*b*) The Indefinite ی -*i* is not added to a word ending in ی *i*; thus صندلی *sandali* is used to mean '(the) chair' or 'a chair'.

(*c*) If the noun ends in ا *a* or و *u* a *hamze* over a bearer is inserted between the final ا *a* or و *u* and the Indefinite ی -*i* to mark the transition between the final long vowel of the noun and the Indefinite ی -*i*. It will not be represented in the transcription, e.g.

پا *pa*, (the) foot.

پائی *pai*, a foot.

پارو *paru*, (the) wooden spade.

پاروئی *parui*, a wooden spade.

[1] The student must not expect the application of the terms 'definite' and 'indefinite' in Persian to correspond exactly with their application in English.

[2] Words ending in ه *h* take the Indefinite ی in the usual way, e.g.

راه *rah*, (the) road.

راهی *rahi*, a road.

3. If two or more nouns are joined by و *va* 'and' and are indefinite, the Indefinite ى *-i* is added to the final one only, the group being regarded as a syntactical whole, e.g.

کتاب و مداد و قلمی بمن داد *ketab va medad va qalami be man dad*, He gave a book, a pencil and a pen to me.

4. A noun qualified by the Interrogative Adjective چه *ce* 'what' usually takes the Indefinite ى *-i*, e.g.

چه کتابی *ce ketabi*, what book?

5. The Indefinite ى *-i* never carries the stress.

6. Persian has no inflexions. When a *definite* noun is the direct object of the verb, this is marked by the addition of the suffix را *-ra*, e.g.

کتابرا بمن داد *ketabra be man dad*, He gave the book to me.

But

کتابی بمن داد *ketabi be man dad*, He gave a book to me.[1]

7. If more than one definite noun forms the direct object of the verb, these are regarded as a syntactical whole, and the را *-ra* is placed after the final noun, e.g.

مداد و قلمرا بمن داد *medad va qalamra be man dad*, He gave the pen and the pencil to me.

8. را *-ra* never carries the stress.

9. The Personal Pronouns are:

من	*man*, I.	ما	*ma*, we.
تو	*to*,[2] thou.	شما	*ʃoma*, you.
او	*u*, he, she.[3]	ایشان	*iʃan*, they.[4]

[1] There is a third possibility, namely:

کتاب بمن داد *ketab be man dad*, He gave a book to me.

Here there is no differentiation of number or particularization, whereas in the example above کتابی *ketabi* implies 'some book or other' or 'a particular book, from among the class of articles known as book'. See also Lesson XII, para. 1 (*a*) (iii) and para. 3.

[2] For the pronunciation of تو *to* see Alphabetical Table in Introduction.

[3] There is no gender in Persian. Different words are used to differentiate between male and female animals, or the words نر *nar* or نره *nare* 'male' and ماده *made* 'female' are added before or after the name of the animal, which in the latter case takes the *ezafe*.

[4] See also Lesson XIV, para. 1 (*a*).

وی *vei* is an alternative form to او *u* but is seldom used in Colloquial Persian.

The Demonstrative Pronoun آن *an* 'that' is used to mean 'it'. Its plurals آنها *anha* and آنان *anan* are used in Colloquial and Literary Persian respectively in place of ایشان *iʃan* 'they'.

10. The Personal Pronouns are by their nature definite and consequently take را *-ra* when the direct object of a verb. من *man* 'I' followed by را *-ra* contracts into مرا *mara* 'me' and تو *to* 'thou' into ترا *tora* 'thee'.

11. If the grammatical subject of a sentence is a personal pronoun, this is implicit in the verb and is not usually expressed separately unless it is desired to lay special emphasis on the pronoun.

12. آن *an* 'that' and این *in* 'this' may be either Demonstrative Pronouns or Demonstrative Adjectives. As Demonstrative Pronouns they stand alone, e.g.

آن چیست *an cist*, What is that?

این چیست *in cist*, What is this?

آن *an* and این *in* when used as pronouns may mean 'the former' and 'the latter' respectively.

When used as Demonstrative Adjectives آن *an* and این *in* precede the noun they qualify, e.g.

آن کتاب *an ketab*, that book.

این میز *in miz*, this table.

13. آیا *aya* is a particle used to introduce a question which does not contain an interrogative word, e.g.

آیا این کتاب است *aya in ketab ast*, Is it this book?

In conversation questions which do not contain an interrogative word are usually indicated by a rising intonation at the end of the sentence (see Appendix VI) rather than by the use of آیا *aya*.

14. The normal word order in simple sentences is Subject (unless this is contained in the verb), Object, Indirect Object, Extension, Verb.

15. The following orthographical points should be noted:

(*a*) آن *an* 'that' is frequently joined to the following word, provided the initial letter of this is a consonant, e.g.

آنکتاب *an ketab*, that book.

(*b*) The preposition به *be* 'to' is usually joined to the following word, the final ه of به *be* being omitted, e.g.

بمن *be man*, to me.

The following combinations should be noted:

باین *be in*, to this.

بآن *be an*, to that.

باو *be u*, to him, to her.[1]

(*c*) The initial *alef* of است *ast* 'he, she or it is' can be omitted, the ست being joined to the preceding word, provided the final letter of this is not the 'silent' *h*, e.g.

این کتابست *in ketab ast*, This is the book.

If the preceding word ends in ا *a* or و *u*, the initial *alef* of است *ast* is always omitted and the *a* of *ast* elided, e.g.

آنجاست *anjast*, He, she or it is there.

اوست *ust*, It is he, it is she.

Similarly, if است *ast* follows the word تو *to* 'thou' the initial *alef* of است *ast* is sometimes dropped and the *a* of *ast* elided, e.g.

توست *tost*, It is thou.

If است *ast* follows a word ending in ی *i*, the initial *alef* of است *ast* is usually dropped and the *a* of *ast* elided, e.g.

کتابیست *ketabist*, It is a book.

(*d*) چه *ce* 'what' followed by است *ast* is written چیست and pronounced *cist*, e.g.

این چیست *in cist*, What is this?

(*e*) If a noun ending in the 'silent' *h* is made indefinite ای can be written after the word in place of the *hamze* over the 'silent' *h* (see para. 2(*a*) above), e.g.

پنجره‌ای *panjarei*, a window.

[1] Some writers insert a د *d* between the preposition به *be* and آن *an* این *in*, او *u*, and ایشان *iʃan*, e.g.

بدان *bedan*, to that.

بدین *bedin*, to this.

بدو *bedu*, to him, to her.

بدیشان *bediʃan*, to them.

If such a noun is followed by است *ast* 'is' the *alef* of است *ast* is omitted, e.g.

پنجره‌ایست *panjareist*, It is a window.

16. Word stress falls on the final syllable of nouns and pronouns. Stress is marked in the transcription by an upright stroke preceding the syllable which carries the stress, e.g.

کتاب *ke'tab*, book.
صندلی *sanda'li*, chair.
شما *ʃo'ma*, you.

As stated above, neither the Indefinite ی *-i* nor را *-ra* carries the stress, thus

کتابی *ke'tabi*, a book.
کتابرا *ke'tabra*, the book (acc.).

Vocabulary

این *in*, this.
آن *an*, that; it.
جا *ja*, place.
اینجا *inja*, here.
آنجا *anja*, there.
کجا *koja*, where?
من *man*, I.
تو *to*, thou.
او *u*, he, she.
ما *ma*, we.
شما *ʃoma*, you.
ایشان *iʃan*, they.
آنها *anha*, those; they.
میز *miz*, table.
صندلی *sandali*, chair.
کتاب *ketab*, book.
مداد *medad*, pencil.
قلم *qalam*, pen.
کاغذ *kaɣaz*, paper.
پنجره *panjare*, window.
پا *pa*, foot.
پارو *paru*, a kind of wooden spade.
چیز *ciz*, thing.
چه *ce*, what?
به (بـ) *be*, to.
و *va*, and.
یا *ya*, or.
است *ast*, he, she or it is.
نیست *nist*, he, she or it is not.
داد *dad*, he, she or it gave.
دید *did*, he, she or it saw.
بله *bale*, yes.
نخیر *naxeir*, no.
آیا *aya*, an interrogative particle (see para. 13 above).

Exercise 1

کتاب اینجاست — مداد آنجاست — آن میز است و این صندلی است — این
قلم است — کجاست — اینجا نیست — این چیست — این کتابی است — چه
کتابی است — کتابی بمن داد — قلمرا بمن داد — شمارا کجا دید — اورا اینجا
دید — این مدادرا بمن داد — میز و صندلی و کتابرا دید — مداد و قلمرا باو
داد — میز و صندلی‌را بشما داد — مارا دید — صندلی اینجا نیست

Exercise 2

1. This is the book. 2. He saw a book. 3. Where did he see the pen and the pencil? 4. He gave a book to me. 5. Here is the table. 6. What is this? 7. This is a pen. 8. He gave the pen and the pencil to you. 9. The book is here and the pencil is there. 10. What is that? 11. That is a chair. 12. Where did he see the book? 13. He saw it here. 14. He saw you.

LESSON II

The Plural of Nouns. The 'Possessive' *ezafe*. Possessive Adjectives and Pronouns. Interrogative Pronouns. The Verb 'to be'.

1. The plural of nouns is formed by the addition of ها *-ha* to the singular, e.g.

مداد *medad*, pencil.
مدادها *medadha*, pencils.

2. If a noun denotes a human being the plural can also be formed by adding ان *-an* to the singular, e.g.

زن *zan*, woman.
زنان *zanan*, women.

In Classical Persian the distinction between the plural in ها *-ha* for irrational beings and inaminate objects and the plural in ان *-an* for human beings is usually observed, but in Colloquial Persian there is a tendency to form the plural of all nouns in ها *-ha*.

3. (*a*) If a noun ends in the 'silent' *h* preceded by *e*, unless it represents the Arabic ة (see Part II, Introduction, para. 11), the 'silent' *h* is changed into گ *g* before the plural termination ان *-an*, e.g.

بچه *bacce*, child.
بچگان *baccegan*, children.

(*b*) If a noun ends in ا *a* a ی *y* is inserted between the final ا *a* and the plural termination ان *-an*, e.g.

گدا *gada*, beggar.

گدایان *gadayan*, beggars.

(*c*) If a noun ends in و *u* a ی *y* is inserted between the final و *u* and the plural termination ان *-an*, e.g.

راستگو *rastgu*, (the) truthful person.

راستگویان *rastguyan*, truthful persons.

or there is merely an off-glide from the final و *u* to the plural termination ان *-an*, e.g.

بازو *bazu*, forearm.

بازوان *bazuan*, forearms.[1]

4. The plural terminations ها *-ha* and ان *-an* carry the stress, e.g.

کتابها *ketab'ha*, books.

زنان *za'nan*, women.

5. Possession is shown in Persian by the addition of *e*, known as the *ezafe*, to the thing possessed, which precedes the possessor. The *ezafe* was originally the Old Persian relative pronoun and was an independent word. In New Persian it is an enclitic. It is not represented in writing unless the word to which it is added ends in ا *a* or و *u* (see para. 7 below), e.g.

کتاب آن مرد *ketabe an mard*, that man's book.

باغ منزل *baye manzel*, the garden of the house.

If the direct object of a verb is definite and formed by two or more words connected by the 'possessive' *ezafe*, را *-ra* is added after the final word in the group, e.g.

پسر آن مردرا دید *pesare an mardra did*, He saw that man's son.

6. If the noun to which the *ezafe* is added ends in the 'silent' *h* or in ی *i* the semi-vowel *y* is inserted in pronunciation between the final *e* or *i* and the *e* of the *ezafe* but is not represented in writing. A *hamze* is sometimes written over the 'silent' *h* or the ی *i* to represent the *ezafe*, but is usually omitted, e.g.

بچه این زن *bacceye in zan*, this woman's child.

صندلی آن مرد *sandaliye an mard*, that man's chair.

[1] See Lesson XII, para. 5.

7. If the noun to which the *ezafe* is added ends in ا *a* or و *u*, the *ezafe* is written as ی and in pronunciation the semi-vowel *y* is inserted between the final *a* or *u* of the word and the *e* of the *ezafe*, e.g.

کتابهای آن مرد *ketabhaye an mard*, the books of that man.

بازوی این زن *bazuye in zan*, this woman's forearm.

8. The *ezafe* never carries the stress, e.g.

باغ منزل *'baɣe man'zel*, the garden of the house.

9. The English Possessive Adjectives can be translated by placing the Personal Pronoun after the noun qualified by the English Possessive Adjective and adding the *ezafe* to the noun, e.g.

کتاب من *ketabe man*, my book (lit. the book of me).

اسب شما *asbe ʃoma*, your horse.

10. The English Possessive Pronoun is translated by the Personal Pronoun preceded by the word مال *mal*,[1] to which the *ezafe* is added, e.g.

این کتاب مال من است *in ketab male man ast*, This book is mine.

But این کتاب من است *in ketabe man ast*, This is my book.

11. مال *mal* is also used to express the possessive case of nouns but only when this case is used pronominally, e.g.

این اسب مال آن مرد است *in asb male an mard ast*, This horse is that man's (belongs to that man).

باغ مال پسر اوست *baɣ male pesare ust*, The garden is his son's (belongs to his son).

12. که *ke* and کی *ki* are Interrogative Pronouns meaning 'who'. کی *ki* forms a plural کیها *kiha*. Both که *ke* and کی *ki* take را *-ra*; که *ke* followed by را *-ra* contracts into کرا *kera*, e.g.

کرا دید *kera did*, Whom did he see?

While کی *ki* is more frequently used in Colloquial Persian than که *ke*, the latter is more frequently written.

13. Before describing the Verb and the formation of tenses it will be convenient to introduce here certain tenses of the verb بودن *budan* 'to

[1] مال *mal* means 'possessions, wealth'. It is also used to mean 'horse', 'mule' or 'donkey'. از آن *az an* (lit. 'from those of', with an implication of plurality), with the *ezafe*, can be substituted for مال *mal* in the cases covered by paras. 10 and 11.

be' (Present Stem باش *baʃ*), which is used to conjugate the verb (for stress on verb forms see below Lesson III, para. 9 and Lesson IV, para. 8):

PRETERITE

1st pers. sing.	بودم	*budam*	I was, etc.
2nd pers. sing.	بودی	*budi*	
3rd pers. sing.	بود	*bud*	
1st pers. pl.	بودیم	*budim*	We were, etc.
2nd pers. pl.	بودید	*budid*	
3rd pers. pl.	بودند	*budand*	

PAST PARTICIPLE

بوده *bude*, been.

PRESENT

1st pers. sing.	میباشم	*mibaʃam*	I am, etc.
2nd pers. sing.	میباشی	*mibaʃi*	
3rd pers. sing.	میباشد	*mibaʃad*	
1st pers. pl.	میباشیم	*mibaʃim*	We are, etc.
2nd pers. pl.	میباشید	*mibaʃid*	
3rd pers. pl.	میباشند	*mibaʃand*	

SUBJUNCTIVE PRESENT

1st pers. sing.	باشم	*baʃam*	I may be, etc.[1]
2nd pers. sing.	باشی	*baʃi*	
3rd pers. sing.	باشد	*baʃad*	
1st pers. pl.	باشیم	*baʃim*	We may be, etc.
2nd pers. pl.	باشید	*baʃid*	
3rd pers. pl.	باشند	*baʃand*	

For the formation of the other tenses of بودن *budan* see Lessons III and IV.

[1] There is an alternative form:

1st pers. sing.	بوم	*bovam.*	1st pers. pl.	بویم	*bovim.*
2nd pers. sing.	بوی	*bovi.*	2nd pers. pl.	بوید	*bovid.*
3rd pers. sing.	بود	*bovad.*	3rd pers. pl.	بوند	*bovand.*

This is not used in Colloquial Persian. See also Lesson IV, 1 (*d*).

14. The Negative is formed by adding the prefix ن *na-* to the positive, e.g.

نبودم *nabudam*, I was not.
نمیباشم *namibaʃam*, I am not.
نباشم *nabaʃam*, I may not be.

15. The Present of the verb 'to be' can also be formed:

(*a*) By the addition of the following personal endings to the preceding word, except in the 3rd pers. sing., for which است *ast* 'is' is used:

1st pers. sing.	(ا)م	*-am*, I am, etc.	1st pers. pl.	(ا)یم	*-im.*
2nd pers. sing.	(ا)ی	*-i.*	2nd pers. pl.	(ا)ید	*-id.*
[3rd pers. sing.	(ا)ست	*ast.*]	3rd pers. pl.	(ا)ند	*-and.*

If the personal endings are added to a word ending in the 'silent' *h*, the *alef* is written, e.g. بچه‌ام *bacce am*, I am a child.

In all other cases the *alef* of the personal ending is omitted, e.g.

مرد ید *mard id*, You are a man.

The 2nd pers. sing. personal ending added to a word ending in the 'silent' *h* can also be represented by a *hamze* over the 'silent' *h*, e.g.

بچهٔ *bacce i*, Thou art a child.

If the personal endings other than the 1st pers. sing. and the 3rd pers. pl. are added to a word ending in ا *a* or و *u* a *hamze* over a bearer is inserted between the final ا *a* or و *u* and the personal ending, e.g.

شمائید *ʃoma id*, it is you (lit. 'you are').

(*b*) By the following form which stands alone:

1st pers. sing.	هستم	*hastam.*	1st pers. pl.	هستیم	*hastim.*
2nd pers. sing.	هستی	*hasti.*	2nd pers. pl.	هستید	*hastid.*
3rd pers. sing.	هست	*hast.*	3rd pers. pl.	هستند	*hastand.*

16. The Negative of the forms in para. 15 above is formed as follows[1]:

(*a*)

1st pers. sing.	نیم	*nayam*	I am not, etc.
2nd pers. sing.	نهٔ	*nai*	
3rd pers. sing.	نیست	*nist*	
1st pers. pl.	نئیم	*naim*	We are not, etc.
2nd pers. pl.	نئید	*naid*	
3rd pers. pl.	نیند	*nayand*	

[1] They are not enclitic.

(*b*)

1st pers. sing.	نیستم	*nistam*	I am not, etc.
2nd pers. sing.	نیستی	*nisti*	
3rd pers. sing.	نیست	*nist*	
1st pers. pl.	نیستیم	*nistim*	We are not, etc.
2nd pers. pl.	نیستید	*nistid*	
3rd pers. pl.	نیستند	*nistand*	

The forms in (*a*), with the exception of the 3rd pers. sing., are rare.

17. If که *ke* or کی *ki* 'who' is followed by the Present of the verb 'to be' given in para. 15 (*b*) above the following contractions may take place:

1st pers. sing.	کیستم	*kistam*	Who am I? etc.
2nd pers. sing.	کیستی	*kisti*	
3rd pers. sing.	کیست	*kist*	
1st pers. pl.	کیستیم	*kistim*	Who are we? etc.
2nd pers. pl.	کیستید	*kistid*	
3rd pers. pl.	کیستند	*kistand*	

18. The various forms of the Present of the verb 'to be' are, broadly speaking, interchangeable. هست *hast*, can be emphatic, and is used to mean 'there is' as well as 'he, she or it is'.

After a word ending in ی *-i* the forms هستی *hasti*, هستیم *hastim* and هستید *hastid* are used in preference to ی *-i*, ایم *-im* and اید *-id*, e.g.

ایرانی هستید *irani hastid*, You are a Persian.

19. A plural subject, if it denotes rational beings, takes a plural verb. A plural subject denoting irrational beings or inanimate objects takes a singular verb, e.g.

پدر و مادر من اینجا هستند *pedar va madare man inja hastand*, My father and mother are here.

برادران شما آنجا بودند *baradarane ʃoma anja budand*, Your brothers were there.

مداد و قلم کجاست *medad va qalam kojast*, Where are the pencil and pen?

کتابها آنجاست *ketabha anjast*, The books are there.

This distinction, however, is less carefully observed in Modern than in Classical Persian.

20. The word منزل *manzel* when used to mean 'home' or 'at home' does not usually take a preposition, e.g.

منزل بودم *manzel budam*, I was at home.

Vocabulary

مرد *mard*, man.
زن *zan*, woman.
پسر *pesar*, boy; son.
دختر *doxtar*, girl; daughter.
پدر *pedar*, father.
مادر *madar*, mother.
برادر *baradar*, brother.
خواهر *xahar*, sister.
بچه *bacce*, *bace*, child.
کار *kar*, work.
اطاق *otaq*, room.
منزل *manzel*, house; home.
باغ *baγ*, garden.
گدا *gada*, beggar.
شهر *ʃahr*, city, town.
بازو *bazu*, forearm.
راستگو *rastgu*, truthful; a truthful person.
ایرانی *irani*, Persian (adj.); a Persian.
اسب *asb*, horse.
سگ *sag*, dog.
گربه *gorbe*, cat.
گاو *gav*, ox.[1]
بیرون *birun*, out, outside; when used as a preposition it takes the *ezafe*.
در *dar*, in (prep.); door.
تو *tu*, in; inner; inside; when used as a preposition it normally takes the *ezafe*, thus becoming توی *tuye*.
رو *ru*, on; outer; when used as a preposition meaning 'on' it precedes the noun it governs and takes the *ezafe*, thus becoming روی *ruye*.
که *ke*, کی *ki*, who (interrog.).
کدام *kodam*, which (of two or more; interrog.).
ولی *vali*, but.
دارد *darad*, he, she or it has.
آمد *amad*, he, she or it came.
رفت *raft*, he, she or it went.

[1] گاو *gav* is also used for cow, though strictly speaking a cow is ماده گاو *made gav*.

Exercise 3

این منزل ماست — آن باغ مال کیست — آن باغ مال من است — پدر
این بچه کجاست — این اطاق پنجره دارد — کتاب شما روی میز است — مردی
بمنزل ما آمد — پسر او بیرون است — دختر من گربه دارد — آنهارا در باغ
دید — این زن کتابی بمن داد — کجا رفت — بشهر رفت — کتاب و مداد روی
میز است — مادر شما بمنزل ما آمد — اسب او توی باغ است — این منزل
مال ماست

Exercise 4

1. The room has a door and a window. 2. Whose is this garden? 3. The garden is his. 4. He has a horse. 5. A woman came into our room. 6. The horse and the cow are in the garden. 7. The child is in your room. 8. The pen and the pencil are on the table. 9. He came to your house. 10. Your brother went to the town. 11. He saw the child in the garden. 12. He gave your book to me. 13. This is their house.

LESSON III

The Infinitive. Tenses formed from the Past Stem. Adjectives.

1. The Infinitive of the verb ends in تن *tan*, دن *dan* or یدن *idan*, e.g.

کشتن *koʃtan*, to kill.
آوردن *avardan* (*avordan*), to bring.
خریدن *xaridan*, to buy.

2. The Short Infinitive is the Infinitive from which the ending ن *-an* has fallen away, e.g.

کشت *koʃt*. آورد *avard* (*avord*). خرید *xarid*.

The Past Stem is identical with the Short Infinitive and also with the 3rd pers. sing. of the Preterite.

3. The Present Stem of Regular Verbs is found by cutting off the final تن *tan*, دن *dan* or یدن *idan* of the Infinitive, e.g.

کش *koʃ*. آور *avar* (*avor*). خر *xar*.

Irregular Verbs undergo certain other changes in the formation of the Present Stem. Their irregularity is confined to the changes made in the Present Stem.[1]

4. The following are formed from the Past Stem:

(*a*) The Past Participle by the addition of the 'silent' *h*, preceded by *e*, e.g.

خریده *xaride*, bought.

(*b*) The Preterite by the addition of the personal endings, except in the 3rd pers. sing., which is identical with the Past Stem, e.g.

1st pers. sing.	خریدم	*xaridam*	I bought, etc.
2nd pers. sing.	خریدی	*xaridi*	
3rd pers. sing.	خرید	*xarid*	
1st pers. pl.	خریدیم	*xaridim*	We bought, etc.
2nd pers. pl.	خریدید	*xaridid*	
3rd pers. pl.	خریدند	*xaridand*	

(*c*) The Imperfect by the addition of the personal endings as in the Preterite and the prefix می *mi-*, e.g.

1st pers. sing.	میخریدم	*mixaridam*	I was buying, used to buy, etc.
2nd pers. sing.	میخریدی	*mixaridi*	
3rd pers. sing.	میخرید	*mixarid*	
1st pers. pl.	میخریدیم	*mixaridim*	We were buying, used to buy, etc.
2nd pers. pl.	میخریدید	*mixaridid*	
3rd pers. pl.	میخریدند	*mixaridand*	

If the verb has an initial *alef* with a short vowel, the initial *alef* drops out after the prefix می *mi-*, e.g.

میفتادم *mioftadam*, I was falling (from افتادن *oftadan* 'to fall'),

or the می may be written separately, in which case the initial *alef* does not drop out, e.g.

می‌افتادم *mioftadam*, I was falling.

[1] A list of irregular verbs will be found in Appendix I. In the vocabularies to the lessons the present stem of irregular verbs is given in brackets, but the present stem of irregular compound verbs will not be given if the verbal part of the compound has already been given as a simple verb.

If the verb has an initial آ *a*, the *madde* of the *alef* drops out after مى *mi-*, e.g.

ميامدم *miamadam*, I was coming (from آمدن *amadan* 'to come').

If the verb has an initial اى *i*, the مى *mi-* must be written separately, e.g.

مى ايستادم *miistadam*, I was standing (from ايستادن *istadan* 'to stand').

(*d*) The Perfect by the Past Participle followed by the Present of the verb 'to be' (see Lesson II, para. 15 (*a*) above), e.g.

1st pers. sing.	خريده‌ام	*xaride am*	I have bought, etc.
2nd pers. sing.	خريدهٔ	*xaride i*	
3rd pers. sing.	خريده‌است	*xaride ast*	
1st pers. pl.	خريده‌ايم	*xaride im*	We have bought, etc.
2nd pers. pl.	خريده‌ايد	*xaride id*	
3rd pers. pl.	خريده‌اند	*xaride and*	

The *hamze* in the 2nd pers. sing. is often omitted in writing.

(*e*) The Pluperfect by the Past Participle followed by the Preterite of the verb 'to be' (see Lesson II, para. 13), e.g.

1st pers. sing.	خريده بودم	*xaride budam*	I had bought, etc.
2nd pers. sing.	خريده بودى	*xaride budi*	
3rd pers. sing.	خريده بود	*xaride bud*	
1st pers. pl.	خريده بوديم	*xaride budim*	We had bought, etc.
2nd pers. pl.	خريده بوديد	*xaride budid*	
3rd pers. pl.	خريده بودند	*xaride budand*	

(*f*) The Subjunctive Past by the Past Participle followed by the Subjunctive Present of the verb 'to be' (see Lesson II, para. 13), e.g.

1st pers. sing.	خريده باشم	*xaride baʃam*	I may have bought, etc.
2nd pers. sing.	خريده باشى	*xaride baʃi*	
3rd pers. sing.	خريده باشد	*xaride baʃad*	
1st pers. pl.	حريده باشيم	*xaride baʃim*	We may have bought, etc.
2nd pers. pl.	خريده باشيد	*xaride baʃid*	
3rd pers. pl.	خريده باشند	*xaride baʃand*	

(*g*) The Future by the Indicative Present[1] of خواستن *xastan* 'to desire' (Present Stem خواه *xah*) without the می *mi-*, followed by the Short Infinitive, e.g.

1st pers. sing.	خواهم خريد	*xaham xarid*	I shall buy, etc.
2nd pers. sing.	خواهی خريد	*xahi xarid*	
3rd pers. sing.	خواهد خريد	*xahad xarid*	
1st pers. pl.	خواهيم خريد	*xahim xarid*	We shall buy, etc.
2nd pers. pl.	خواهيد خريد	*xahid xarid*	
3rd pers. pl.	خواهند خريد	*xahand xarid*	

5. The Negative of the verbal forms in para. 4 above is formed by adding the prefix ن *na-* to the main verb, except in the Future, when it is prefixed to the auxiliary verb, e.g.

نخريدم *naxaridam*, I did not buy.
نميخريدم *namixaridam*, I was not buying.
نخريده‌ام *naxaride am*, I have not bought.
نخريده بودم *naxaride budam*, I had not bought.
نخريده باشم *naxaride bašam*, I may not have bought.
نخواهم خريد *naxaham xarid*, I shall not buy.

6. If the verb has an initial آ *a*, a ى (ﻴ) *y* is inserted between the negative prefix and the آ *a* of the verb, which loses its *madde*, e.g.

نيامد *nayamad*, He did not come (from آمدن *amadan* 'to come').

If the verb has an initial *alef* followed by ى *i*, the *alef* is retained after the negative prefix, e.g.

نايستاد *naistad*, He did not stand (from ايستادن *istadan* 'to stand').

If the verb has an initial *alef* with a short vowel a ى (ﻴ) *y* is inserted after the negative prefix and the initial *alef* drops out, e.g.

نيفتاد *nayoftad*, He did not fall (from افتادن *oftadan* 'to fall').

7. The verb داشتن *daštan* 'to have, possess' forms its Imperfect without the prefix می *mi-*. Its Imperfect is thus identical with its Preterite, e.g.

داشتم *daštam*, I had, or I was having.

[1] See Lesson IV, para. 1 (*c*).

Certain Compound Verbs formed with داشتن *daʃtan* (see Lesson IX) form their Imperfect in the usual way.

8. The verb بودن *budan* 'to be' also forms its Imperfect without the prefix می *mi-*. The Subjunctive Past of بودن *budan* is seldom used.

9. (*a*) Stress in the affirmative verbal forms in para. 4 above is carried on the final syllable of the main verb where there is no prefix, except in the Future, when the stress falls on the final syllable of the auxiliary verb. Where there is a prefixed می *mi-* this carries the stress. E.g.

خریدم *xari'dam*, I bought.
میخریدم *'mixaridam*, I was buying.
خریده‌ام *xari'de am*, I have bought.
خریده بودم *xari'de budam*, I had bought.
خریده باشم *xari'de baʃam*, I may have bought.
خواهم خرید *xa'ham xarid*, I shall buy.

(*b*) Stress in the negative verbal forms is carried on the negative prefix, e.g.

نخریدم *'naxaridam*, I did not buy.
نمیخریدم *'namixaridam*, I was not buying.
نخریده ام *'naxaride am*, I have not bought.
نخریده بودم *'naxaride budam*, I had not bought.
نخریده باشم *'naxaride baʃam*, I may not have bought.
نخواهم خرید *'naxaham xarid*, I shall not buy.

10. Adjectives normally follow the noun they qualify, an *ezafe* being added to the noun, e.g.

کتاب بزرگ *ketabe bozorg*, the big book.

Adjectives do not take the plural ending,[1] e.g.

مردان خوب *mardane xub*, good men.

[1] Thus آن *an* 'that' and این *in* 'this' when used as demonstrative adjectives do not take the plural ending. When used as demonstrative pronouns they take the plural endings ها *-ha* or ان *-an*, e.g.

اینها *inha*, these.
آنها *anha* those.

11. The 'qualifying' *ezafe* follows the same rules as those given in Lesson II, paras. 6 and 7 for the 'possessive' *ezafe* if the word to which it is added ends in the 'silent' *h*, ی *i*, ا *a* or و *u*, e.g.

کتابهای بزرگ *ketabhaye bozorg*, big books.
صندلی نو *sandaliye nou*, the new chair.
بچه کوچك *bacceye kucek*, the small child.
پاروی نو *paruye nou*, the new spade.

12. If more than one adjective qualifies a noun, the 'qualifying' *ezafe* is added to each adjective except the final one, e.g.

کتاب بزرگ نو *ketabe bozorge nou*, the big new book.

13. The noun and its attributes are regarded as a syntactical whole and, therefore, if the noun is indefinite, the Indefinite ی *-i* is added to the final adjective only. Similarly if the noun is definite and the direct object of the verb, the را *-ra* is added to the final adjective, e.g.

کتاب بزرگی *ketabe bozorgi*, a big book.
کتاب بزرگ نوئی *ketabe bozorge noui*, a big new book.
کتاب بزرگرا آورد *ketabe bozorgra avard*, He brought the big book.
کتاب بزرگ نورا آورد *ketabe bozorge noura avard*, He brought the big new book.

14. The comparative and superlative degrees are formed by the addition of تر *-tar* and ترین *-tarin* respectively to the positive, e.g.

بزرگ *bozorg*, big.
بزرگتر *bozorgtar*, bigger.
بزرگترین *bozorgtarin*, biggest.

Exceptions are:

خوب *xub*, good.
بهتر *behtar*, better.
بهترین *behtarin*, best.[1]

به *beh* is also used to mean 'better' when it stands alone as the predicate of the verb 'to be'.

[1] خوبتر *xubtar* and خوبترین *xubtarin* are also occasionally used.

In the comparative degree of بد *bad* 'bad' the د *d* is sometimes assimilated to the ت *t* of the comparative ending, thus:

بتر *battar.*

The words کهتر *kehtar* 'smaller, younger' and مهتر *mehtar* 'greater, elder' are seldom used in the positive degree. The Superlative of these forms, کهین *kehin* and مهین *mehin* respectively, is rare also.

15. The comparative follows the noun it qualifies, the *ezafe* being added to the noun, e.g.

کتاب بزرگتر *ketabe bozorgtar*, the bigger book.

کتابهای بزرگتر *ketabhaye bozorgtar*, the bigger books.

16. The superlative precedes the noun it qualifies. It does not take the *ezafe*, e.g.

بهترین کتاب *behtarin ketab*, the best book.

17. Comparison is expressed by the word از *az* preceding the person or object used as a standard of comparison, e.g.

آن پسر از این دختر بزرگتر است *an pesar az in doxtar bozorgtar ast*, That boy is bigger than this girl.

من از شما زودتر آمدم *man az ʃoma zudtar amadam*, I came earlier than you.

Comparison can also be expressed by the word تا *ta* preceding the person or object used as a standard of comparison. This form is used if the person or object used as a standard of comparison is governed by a preposition, e.g.

کتابهای بهتر بمن داد تا باو *ketabhaye behtar be man dad ta be u*, he gave better books to me than to him.

18. بیشتر *biʃtar* and بیش *biʃ* both mean 'more'. The former is used as a noun, adverb or adjective, e.g.

بیشتر باو دادید *biʃtar be u dadid*, You gave him more.

اورا بیشتر دوست داشتند *ura biʃtar dust daʃtand*, They liked him better (more).

مردها بیشتر بودند تا زنها *mardha biʃtar budand ta zanha*, There were more men than women.

When بیشتر *bistar* qualifies a noun it precedes the noun, which is put in the singular, e.g.

بیشتر کتاب داشتید تا او *bistar ketab dastid ta u*, You had more books than he.

بیش *bis* is used as a noun, e.g.

بیش از او خوردید *bis az u xordid*, You ate more than he.

It can also be used predicatively as an adjective, e.g.

کتابهای او بیش از کتابهای من است *ketabhaye u bis az ketabhaye man ast*, His books are more than mine.

بیش از پیش *bis az pis* means 'more than before', e.g.

اورا بیش از پیش دوست دارد *ura bis az pis dust darad*, He likes him better (more) than formerly.

بیشتر *bistar* is also used as a noun meaning 'most', in which case it precedes the noun it qualifies and takes the *ezafe*, e.g.

بیشتر مردها رفته بودند *bistare mardha rafte budand*, Most of the men had gone.

بیشتر آنها جوان بودند *bistare anha javan budand*, Most of them were young.

'Most of all' is rendered by بیشتر از همه *bistar az hame* or از همه بیشتر *az hame bistar*, e.g.

اورا از همه بیشتر دوست داشتیم *ura az hame bistar dust dastim*, We liked him best (most) of all.

19. Adjectives are also used as adverbs, e.g.

آنرا گران خرید *anra geran xarid*, He bought it at a high price (expensively).

20. Adjectives can be strengthened by خیلی *xeili* or بسیار *besyar* 'very'. These words precede the adjective they qualify, e.g.

این میز خیلی بزرگ است *in miz xeili bozorg ast*, This table is very big.

باغ بسیار بزرگی دارد *baγe besyar bozorgi darad*, He has a very large garden.

The comparative degree can be similarly strengthened, e.g.

این خیلی بهتر است *in xeili behtar ast*, This is much better.

21. زیاد *ziad* is used as an adjective, noun or adverb meaning 'much, many, too', or 'too much'. With a negative verb it means 'not very', e.g.

کتابهای زیاد داشت *ketabhaye ziad daſt*, He had many books.

بمن زیاد دادید *be man ziad dadid*, You gave me too much.

این کتاب زیاد گران است *in ketab ziad geran ast*, This book is too expensive.

این کتاب زیاد خوب نیست *in ketab ziad xub nist*, This book is not very good.

زیاد *ziad* may precede the noun it qualifies, in which case the latter is put in the singular, e.g.

زیاد کتاب دارد *ziad ketab darad*, He has many books.

22. Adjectives, like nouns, carry the stress on the final syllable, e.g.

بزرگ *bo'zorg*, big.

بزرگتر *bozorg'tar*, bigger.

بزرگترین *bozorgta'rin*, biggest.

Vocabulary

راه *rah*, road, way.

نامه *name*, letter.

بزرگ *bozorg*, big.

کوچك *kucek*, small.

جوان *javan*, young.

پیر *pir*, an old person; old (of persons); پیر مرد *pire mard*, an old man; پیر زن *pire zan*, an old woman.[1]

مسن *mosenn*, old, aged.

کهنه *kohne*, old, worn-out.

مریض *mariz*, sick, ill.

گران *geran*, expensive, dear.

ارزان *arzan*, cheap.

خوب *xub*, good.

بد *bad*, bad.

نو *nou*, new.

زود *zud*, early; quick, quickly.

دیر *dir*, late (of time).

یواش *yavaſ*, slow.

زیاد *ziad*, much, many; too, too much; (with negative verb) not very.

بسیار *besyar*, very.

خیلی *xeili* very.

چند *cand*, some; for how much? how many?

چرا *cera*, why?

از *az*, from; than.

[1] مرد *mard* and زن *zan* are used in these expressions to define the sex.

همه *hame*, all.

روز *ruz*, day.

امروز *emruz*, to-day.

دیروز *diruz*, yesterday.

پریروز *pariruz*, the day before yesterday.

افتادن (افت) *oftadan* (*oft*), to fall; راه افتادن *rah oftadan*, to set out.[1]

رفتن (رو) *raftan* (*rav-*, *ro͡u*), to go; راه رفتن *rah raftan*, to walk along, about.

آمدن (آ) *amadan* (*a*), to come; زود آمدن *zud amadan*, to be (come) early.

کردن (کن) *kardan* (*kon*), to do; دیر کردن *dir kardan*, to be (come) late.

گفتن (گو) *goftan* (*gu*), to say.

خریدن *xaridan*, to buy.

داشتن (دار) *daʃtan* (*dar*), to have, possess; دوست داشتن *dust daʃtan*, to like.

فروختن (فروش) *foruxtan* (*foruʃ*), to sell.

رسیدن *rasidan*, to arrive; (with the preposition به *be*) reach.

کشتن *koʃtan*, to kill.

نوشتن (نویس) *neveʃtan* (*nevis*), to write.

دیدن (بین) *didan* (*bin*), to see.

دادن (ده) *dadan* (*deh*), to give.

ایستادن (ایست) *istadan* (*ist*), to stand (intrans.).

آوردن *avardan*, to bring.

Exercise 5

کجا رفتید — بمنزل شما رفتیم — این کتابرا چند خریدید — آنرا ارزان خریدم — این مرد باغرا بآن زن فروخت — نامهٔ باو نوشتم — کرا دیدید — پسر و دختر شمارا دیدم — بشهر رسیدیم — این گاورا چند فروختید — اینرا گران فروختم — یواش راه میرفتند — کتابرا باو داد — بمنزل ما آمدند — اسبرا در باغ دید — اینجا آمدند و مرا دیدند — دختر شما از همه کوچکتر است — دیروز بیشتر کار کردیم تا امروز — پریروز بشهر رفتیم — منزل شما کجاست — منزل ما در شهر است — دیروز منزل بودیم

Exercise 6

1. He gave a big book to me. 2. He went to the town. 3. I saw him the day before yesterday. 4. They bought the house and the garden. 5. She came slowly. 6. How much did you buy this for? 7. I bought it cheaply. 8. We saw the man, the woman and the children

[1] See Lesson IX for Compound Verbs.

yesterday. 9. He was writing a letter to me. 10. We were walking in the garden. 11. Where were you yesterday? 12. I was at home. 13. The woman is older than the man. 14. You had more horses than he. 15. He came early. 16. We were late.

LESSON IV

Tenses formed from the Present Stem. The Pronominal Suffixes. خود *xod*, خویش *xiʃ* and خویشتن *xiʃtan*. همین *hamin* and همان *haman*. چون *cun*. چنین *conin* and چنان *conan*. چندین *candin* and چندان *candan*. کسی *kasi* and شخصی *ʃaxsi*. هیچ *hic*. طور *tōur*.

1. The following forms are derived from the Present Stem of the verb:

(*a*) The Present Participle by the addition of ان *-an*, e.g.

خواهان *xahan*, desiring (from خواستن *xastan* 'to desire, wish', Present Stem خواه *xah*).

This form is not found in all verbs.

(*b*) The Noun of the Agent by adding نده *-ande*, e.g.

فروشنده *foruʃande*, seller (from فروختن *foruxtan* 'to sell', Present Stem فروش *foruʃ*).

This form is not found in all verbs.

(*c*) The Present by the addition of the personal endings and the prefix می *mi-*, e.g.

1st pers. sing.	میخرم	*mixaram*	I am buying, etc.
2nd pers. sing.	میخری	*mixari*	
3rd pers. sing.	میخرد	*mixarad*	
1st pers. pl.	میخریم	*mixarim*	We are buying, etc.
2nd pers. pl.	میخرید	*mixarid*	
3rd pers. pl.	میخرند	*mixarand*	

A General Present is formed by the addition of the personal endings, but without the prefix می *mi-*, and is used in Classical Persian for general statements which contain no element of doubt. In Modern Persian the General Present has been confused with the Subjunctive Present (see (*d*) below). The latter, properly speaking, has a prefixed ب *be-*. Modern writers often omit the ب *be-* of the Subjunctive, especially in the case of Compound Verbs, and at times even prefix ب *be-* to what is properly speaking a General Present. No attempt will be made in the following pages to distinguish between the two tenses; indeed, they have become so confused in modern usage that it would be difficult to do so in all cases.

(*d*) The Subjunctive Present by the addition of the personal endings with or without the prefix ب *be-* (see above), e.g.

1st pers. sing.	بخرم	*bexaram*	I may buy, etc.
2nd pers. sing.	بخری	*bexari*	
3rd pers. sing.	بخرد	*bexarad*	
1st pers. pl.	بخریم	*bexarim*	We may buy, etc.
2nd pers. pl.	بخرید	*bexarid*	
3rd pers. pl.	بخرند	*bexarand*	

The verb بودن *budan* 'to be' does not take ب *be-*.

The 1st and 3rd pers. sing. and plural of the Subjunctive Present may be used as a Jussive, e.g.

بخرد *bexarad*, Let him buy.

(*e*) The Imperative Singular is formed by the addition of the prefix ب *be-* to the Present Stem. The plural takes the personal ending ید *-id*, e.g.

بخر *bexar*, Buy (sing.).

بخرید *bexarid*, Buy (pl.).

In compound verbs the prefix ب *be-* is often omitted, in which case the Imperative Singular is identical with the Present Stem.

The verb بودن *budan* 'to be' does not take ب *be-*.

2. If the verb has an initial آ *a*, *alef* followed by ی *i*, or *alef* with a short vowel, it follows in the Present the rules given in Lesson III, para. 4 (*c*) concerning the prefixed می *mi-* of the Imperfect, e.g.

میاورم *miavaram*, I am bringing (from آوردن *avardan* 'to bring').

می ایستم *miistam*, I am standing (from ایستادن *istadan* 'to stand', Present Stem ایست *ist*).

میفتم *mioftam*, I am falling (from افتادن *oftadan* 'to fall', Present Stem افت *oft*).

If the verb has an initial آ *a*, a ی *y* is inserted after the prefix ب *be-* and the *alef* loses its *madde*, e.g.

بیا *beya*, Come (from آمدن *amadan* 'to come', Present Stem آ *a*).

If the verb has an initial *alef* with a short vowel, a ی *y* is inserted after the prefix بـ *be-* and the initial *alef* is dropped, e.g.

بیفتم *beyoftam*, I may fall.

If the verb has an initial *alef* followed by ی *i*, the initial *alef* is retained after the prefix بـ *be-*, e.g.

بایستم *beistam*, I may stand.

3. If the Present Stem ends in ا *a* or و *u*, a ی *y* is inserted after the final vowel of the Present Stem before the endings of the Present Participle and Noun of the Agent and the personal endings of the 1st pers. sing. and the 3rd pers. sing. and pl. A *hamze* is inserted before the personal ending in the 2nd pers. sing. and pl. and the 1st pers. pl. and marks the transition from the final long vowel of the stem to the long vowel of the personal ending. It will not be represented in the transcription. E.g.

شایان *ʃayan*, brilliant, fitting, proper (from the defective verb شایستن *ʃayestan* 'to be fitting').

گوینده *guyande*, speaker (from گفتن *goftan* 'to say').

1st pers. sing.	میگویم	*miguyam*	I am saying, etc.
2nd pers. sing.	میگوئی	*migui*	
3rd pers. sing.	میگوید	*miguyad*	

1st pers. pl.	میگوئیم	*miguim*	We are saying, etc.
2nd pers. pl.	میگوئید	*miguid*	
3rd pers. pl.	میگویند	*miguyand*	

1st pers. sing.	میایم	*miayam*	I am coming, etc.
2nd pers. sing.	میائی	*miai*	
3rd pers. sing.	میاید	*miayad*	

1st pers. pl.	میائیم	*miaim*	We are coming, etc.
2nd pers. pl.	میائید	*miaid*	
3rd pers. pl.	میایند	*miayand*	

4. If the Present Stem ends in و (*av*), this becomes *o͡u* in the Imperative Singular, e.g.

بشنو *beʃeno͡u*, hear (from شنیدن *ʃenidan* 'to hear', Present Stem شنو *ʃenav*).

5. If the Imperative Singular ends in و *ou͡* its prefix in some cases becomes *bo*, e.g.

برو *borou͡*, Go (from رفتن *raftan*).

بدو *bodou͡*, Run (from دویدن *davidan*).

But

بشنو *beʃenou͡*, Hear (from شنیدن *ʃenidan*).

بشو *beʃou͡*, Become (from شدن *ʃodan*).

Note also

بگو *bogu* or *begu*, Say (from گفتن *goftan*).

بگذار *bogozar* or *begozar*, Place, put (from گذاشتن *gozaʃtan*).

6. The negative of the forms in para. 1 (*c*), (*d*) and (*e*) above is formed by the addition of the prefix ن *na-*. The prefix ب *be-* drops out if the verb is negative, e.g.

نمیخرم *namixaram*, I am not buying.

نخرم *naxaram*, I may not buy.

نخر *naxar*, Do not buy.

The negative of the Imperative can also be formed by the prefix م *ma-*, e.g.

مخر *maxar*, Do not buy.

This form is literary.

If the verb has an initial آ *a*, *alef* followed by ی *i*, or *alef* with a short vowel, it follows the same rules when the negative prefix is added as those set out in Lesson III, para. 6.

7. The verb داشتن *daʃtan* 'to have, possess' forms its Present without the prefix می *mi-*. In Colloquial Persian داشته باش *daʃte baʃ* and داشته باشید *daʃte baʃid* are used in place of the Imperative دار *dar* and دارید *darid*.

Certain compounds of داشتن *daʃtan* form their Present and Imperative in the usual way.

8. Stress in the verbal forms given above is carried:

(*a*) On the final syllable in the affirmative except where there is a prefixed می *mi-* or ب *be-*. These prefixes always carry the stress, e.g.

خواهان *xa'han*, desiring.

فروشنده *foruʃan'de*, seller.

میخرم *'mixaram*, I am buying.

بخرم *'bexaram*
خرم *xa'ram* } I may buy.

بخر *'bexar*, Buy.

(*b*) On the negative prefix in the negative, e.g.

نمیخرم *'namixaram*, I am not buying.

نخرم *'naxaram*, I may not buy.

نخر *'naxar*
مخر *'maxar* } Do not buy.

9. The Possessive Adjectives can be translated by Pronominal Suffixes as well as by the method described in Lesson II, para. 9:

-م *-am*, my.

-ت *-at*, thy.

-ش *-aʃ*, *-eʃ*, his, her, its.

-مان *-eman*, our.

-تان *-etan*, your.

-شان *-eʃan*, their.

These may be added to Nouns and Adjectives, e.g.

کتابم *ketabam*, my book.

اسبتان *asbetan*, your horse.

If a Pronominal Suffix is added to a word which is the direct object of the verb را *-ra* is added after the Pronominal Suffix, e.g.

کتابتانرا بمن بدهید *ketabetanra be man bedehid*, Give your book to me.

If the Noun qualified by a possessive adjective is also qualified by an adjective or adjectives, the Pronominal Suffix is added to the final adjective, e.g.

دختر کوچکتان *doxtare kuceketan*, your small (younger) daughter.

If the Pronominal Suffix refers to more than one noun and these are joined by a conjunction, the Suffix is added to the final noun only, e.g.

پدر و مادرتان *pedar va madaretan*, your father and mother.

10. The Pronominal Suffixes are also added to the simple tenses of the verb and prepositions to denote the personal pronouns in the oblique cases,[1] e.g. زدمش *zadamaʃ*, I hit him.

من همراهش رفتم *man hamraheʃ raftam*, I went with him.

کجا دیدیدش *koja dideʃ*, Where did you see him.

The Pronominal Suffixes are never emphatic, whereas the Personal Pronouns may be.

11. If the word to which a Pronominal Suffix is added ends in ا *a* (except in the case of با *ba* 'with') or و *u*, a ی *y* is inserted between the final vowel and the Pronominal Suffix, e.g.

کتابهایم *ketabhayam*, my books.

زانویتان *zanuyetan*, your knee.

In Colloquial Persian this ی *y* is frequently omitted, especially before ش *-aʃ*, *-eʃ*, in which case the vowel of the Pronominal Suffix is elided, e.g.

زانوت *zanut*, thy knee.

کتابهاشان *ketabhaʃan*, their books.

If the word to which a Pronominal Suffix is added ends in ه *e*, an *alef* is written between the final ه *e* and the singular Pronominal Suffixes, e.g.

بچه‌اش *bacceaʃ*, his child.

When a plural Pronominal Suffix is added to a word ending in ه *e*, the *e* of the Pronominal Suffix is elided, e.g.

بچه‌تان *baccetan*, your child.

12. The Pronominal Suffixes never carry the stress.

13. If the possessive adjective or personal pronoun refers to the subject of the sentence, the word خود *xod*, خویش *xiʃ*[2] or خویشتن *xiʃtan* must be used in the 3rd pers. sing. in place of او *u*[3]; these can also be used in place of من *man*, and تو *to*. E.g.

کتاب خودرا بمن داد *ketabe xodra be man dad*, He gave his book to me.

[1] If the 3rd pers. sing. Pronominal Suffix is added to the preposition به *be* 'to', the ه of به is written and the word is pronounced *beʃ* or more vulgarly *beheʃ*.

[2] خویش *xiʃ* also means 'relation, relative'.

[3] This rule is not always observed in Colloquial Persian.

('His' refers to the subject of the sentence, 'he', and therefore خود *xod* must be used and not او *u*: کتاب اورا بمن داد *ketabe ura be man dad* would mean 'he gave somebody else's book to me'.)

کتاب خودرا باو دادم *ketabe xodra be u dadam*, I gave my book to him.

خود *xod* and خویش *xiʃ* are interchangeable when used in place of the Possessive Adjectives, but خیش *xiʃ* is seldom used in Colloquial Persian.
خویشتن *xiʃtan* can only refer to rational beings. (See also Lesson VIII, para. 16.)

14. خود *xod* is also used as an emphatic particle meaning 'self'. It precedes the word it emphasizes and takes the *ezafe*, e.g.

خود او بود *xode u bud*, It was he himself.

خود آن *xode an* and خود این *xode in* mean 'that very' and 'this very' respectively, e.g.

خود آن مرد بود *xode an mard bud*, It was that very man.

خود *xod* can also follow the word it emphasizes standing in apposition to it without the *ezafe*, if this word is the subject of the sentence, e.g.

من خود گفتم *man xod goftam*, I myself said (so).

This latter construction is less common than the former.
The Pronominal Suffixes can be added to خود *xod* when it is used as an emphatic particle, e.g.

خودت برو *xodat boro͡u*, Go thyself.
خودشان آمدند *xodeʃan amadand*, They came themselves.
خودم کردم *xodam kardam*, I did (it) myself.

15. خود *xod* is also used with the Pronominal Suffixes and را *-ra* to form a kind of reflexive, e.g.

خودتانرا گول زدید *xodetanra gul zadid*, You deceived yourselves.

In the 3rd. pers. sing. the Pronominal Suffix can be omitted, e.g.

خودرا گول زد *xodra gul zad*, He deceived himself.

16. خود *xod*, خویش *xiʃ* and خویشتن *xiʃtan* carry the stress; it falls on the final syllable of خویشتن *xiʃtan*.

17. The Demonstrative این *in* 'this' and آن *an* 'that' can be strengthened by هم *ham*,[1] e.g.

همین هفته *hamin hafte*, this very week.

همان روز *haman ruz*, that very day.

Note also the use of همین in the following:

همین یکی ماند *hamin yaki mand*, Only this one remained.

18. چون *cun* 'like' can be contracted and prefixed to the demonstratives این *in* 'this' and آن *an* 'that', e.g.

چنین *conin* }
چنان *conan* } such, such a one.

چنین *conin* and چنان *conan* are also used to mean 'thus', 'in such a manner', e.g.

چنین گفت *conin goft*, He spoke thus.

چنین *conin* and چنان *conan* can be strengthened by the addition of هم *ham*, e.g.

همچنین آمد و گفت *hamconin amad va goft*, He came in this way and spoke (thus).

19. چند *cand* can also be prefixed to the demonstratives این *in* 'this' and آن *an* 'that', e.g.

چندین *candin*, several; so much, so many.

چندان *candan*, so much, so many.

چندین *candin* is used adjectivally and adverbially; when it is used as an adjective the noun follows and is put in the singular, e.g.

چندین کتاب بمن داد *candin ketab beman dad*, He gave several books to me.

چندان *candan* if used with a negative verb means 'not very', 'not much', e.g.

چندان خوب نبود *candan xub nabud*, It was not very good.

20. In those of the forms in paras. 17–19 above of which هم *ham* is one of the component parts, stress can be carried on هم *ham* or on the final syllable, e.g.

همان *'haman* or *ha'man*, that very.

همچنین *'hamconin* or *hamco'nin*, just such as this, just like this.

[1] هم *ham* can also stand alone as an emphatic particle. As an adverb it means 'also'.

The other forms in paras. 18 and 19 above carry the stress on the final syllable, e.g.

چندان *can'dan*, so much, so many.

چنین *co'nin*, such, such a one.

21. کسی *kasi*, formed from کس *kas* 'person'[1] by the addition of the Indefinite ی *-i*, and شخصی *ʃaxsi*, formed in the same way from شخص *ʃaxs* 'person'[2], are used to mean 'someone, somebody'. With a negative verb they mean 'no one, nobody'. E.g.

کسی هست *kasi hast*, Is any one there?

کسی نیست *kasi nist*, No one is there.

22. هیچ *hic* is an adjective meaning 'any'. It precedes the Noun it qualifies. With a negative verb it means 'none, not any'. E.g.

هیچ نان دارید *hic nan darid*, Have you any bread?

هیچ نان ندارم *hic nan nadaram*, I have no bread.

In Colloquial Persian هیچ *hic* 'any' tends to be omitted in the affirmative unless it is emphatic, thus نان دارید *nan darid* 'have you any bread', whereas هیچ نان دارید *hic nan darid* would rather mean 'have you any bread whatsoever?'

A noun qualified by هیچ *hic* 'not any' with a negative verb is always put in the singular, e.g.

هیچ بچه ندارد *hic bacce nadarad*, He has no children.

هیچ کس *hic kas* means 'anyone'. With a negative verb or in answer to a question it means 'no one'. E.g.

هیچ کس آمد *hic kas amad*, Has any one come?[3]

هیچ کس *hic kas*, No one.

هیچ کس آنجا نبود *hic kas anja nabud*, No one was there.

[1] The phrase کس و کار *kas o kar* is also used to mean 'household, retainers', e.g.

از کس و کار او بودند *az kas o kare u budand*, They were some of his retainers (household).

Note also یکی از کسان او *yaki az kasane u*, one of his people.

[2] شخص *ʃaxs* is also used as an emphatic particle. It precedes the word it emphasizes and takes the *ezafe*, e.g.

شخص او بود *ʃaxse u bud*, It was he himself.

[3] For the use of the Preterite where the Perfect is used in English, see Lesson XIII, para. 5 (*h*).

هیچ یك *hic yak* means 'any' referring to more than one. With a negative verb it means 'none'. It is usually followed by از *az*, e.g.

هیچ یك از این کتابهارا ندارم *hic yak az in ketabhara nadaram*, I have none of these books.

هیچ کدام *hic kodam* is an interrogative pronoun meaning 'any' referring to more than one. With a negative verb it means 'none'. It is usually followed by از *az*, or takes the *ezafe*, e.g.

هیچ کدام از آنهارا دیدید *hic kodam az anhara didid*, Did you see any of them?

هیچ کدام آنها نرفته اند *hic kodame anha narafte and*, Have none of them gone?

In Colloquial Persian هیچ کدام *hic kodam* is also used as a pronoun (not as an Interrogative), e.g.

هیچ کدام از این اسبها مال او نیست *hic kodam az in asbha male u nist*, None of these horses are his.

هیچ *hic* is also used as a noun meaning 'anything'. With a negative verb or in answer to a question it means 'nothing'. E.g.

از او هیچ گرفتید *az u hic gereftid*, Did you take anything from him?

هیچ نگرفتم *hic nagereftam*, I took nothing.

هیچ *hic* is sometimes used with an affirmative verb to mean 'nothing', e.g.

این همه هیچ است *in hame hic ast*, All this is nothing.

هیچ *hic* is also used as an adverb to mean 'ever, at all'. With a negative verb it means 'never', e.g.

آنجا هیچ رفته‌اید *anja hic rafte id*, Have you ever gone there?

هیچ نرفته‌ام *hic narafte am*, I have never gone there.

هیچ وقت *hic vaqt* means 'ever'. With a negative verb or in answer to a question it means 'never', e.g.

هیچ وقت اورا دیده‌اید *hic vaqt ura dide id*, Have you ever seen him?

هیچ وقت اورا ندیده‌ام *hic vaqt ura nadide am*, I have never seen him.

هیچ *hic* 'anything' and with a negative verb 'nothing' can be strengthened colloquially by the addition of the Indefinite ی *-i*, e.g.

هیچی نخورد *hici naxord*, He ate (absolutely) nothing.

23. کسی *kasi*, شخصی *ʃaxsi* and هیچی *hici* carry the stress on the first syllable, since the Indefinite ی *-i* never carries the stress.

In compounds formed with هیچ *hic*, the stress falls on هیچ *hic*, e.g.

هیچ کس *'hic kas*, no one.

24. The word طور *tour* meaning 'way, manner' is used in the following compounds:

چطور *ce tour*, how (interrog.).
اینطور *in tour*, in this way, thus.
آنطور *an tour*, in that way, thus.
همینطور *hamin tour*, in this very way.
همانطور *haman tour*, in that very way.

Stress is carried on the first part of the compound, e.g.

چطور *'ce tour*, how.
اینطور *'in tour*, in this way.

طور *tour* takes the Indefinite ی *-i* in the following expressions:

طوری نمیشود *touri namiʃavad*, It will not matter.
طوری نیست *touri nist*, It does not matter.

Vocabulary

کلید *kelid*, key.	دهن *dahan*, mouth.
قهوه *qahve*, coffee.	بینی *bini*, nose.
چای *cai*, tea.	لب *lab*, lip.
گوشت *guʃt*, meat.	دندان *dandan*, tooth.
بازار *bazar*, bazaar.	زبان *zaban*, tongue; language.
آب *ab*, water.	انگشت *angoʃt*, finger.
درخت *daraxt*, tree.	تن *tan*, body; person.
شاخ *ʃax*, branch; horn (of animal).	خاك *xak*, dust, earth.
برگ *barg*, leaf.	فارسی *farsi*, Persian (the language).
گل *gol*, flower.	ایران *iran*, Persia.
صورت *surat*, face.	رنگ *rang*, colour.
دست *dast*, hand.	سیاه *siah* } black.
سر *sar*, head.	مشکی *meʃki* } black.
چشم *caʃm*, eye.	سفید *sefid*, white.

قرمز *qermez*, red.
زرد *zard*, yellow.
سبز *sabz*, green.
آبی *abi*, blue.
صورتی *surati*, pink.
خاکی *xaki*, khaki.
سرد *sard*, cold.
گرم *garm*, warm.
داغ *daɣ*, hot.
جوش *juʃ*, boiling.
برای *baraye*, for.
با *ba*, with.
همراه *hamrah*, together, together with; if used as a preposition it takes the *ezafe*, e.g. همراه او *hamrahe u*, together with him.
گرفتن (گیر) *gereftan* (*gir*), to take.
گذاشتن (گذار) *gozaʃtan* (*gozar*), to place, put.
شنیدن (شنو) *ʃenidan* (*ʃenav-*, *ʃenou*), to hear, listen.
بر داشتن (بر دار) *bar daʃtan* (*bar dar*), to take up, away.
ورداشتن (وردار) *var daʃtan* (*var dar*), to take up, away.
زدن (زن) *zadan* (*zan*), to strike.
گول زدن *gul zadan*, to deceive.
آوردن *avardan*[1], to bring; the Present Stem is formed regularly آور *avar* or irregularly آر *ar*.
بردن (بر) *bordan* (*bar*), to carry, take, take away.
خوردن *xordan*, to eat.
شدن (شو) *ʃodan* (*ʃav-*, *ʃou*), to become.
دویدن *davidan* (*dav-*, *dou*), to run.

Exercise 7

این آب سرد است — آب گرم برای من بیاورید — کجا میروید — کلید در باغرا بمن بدهید — همراه پسر و دختر خویش بشهر رفت — کتابرا روی میز بگذار — بچه‌هارا همراه خود ببر — آن پسر آب میخورد و دختر چای — آن کتاب سیاهرا از روی میز بر دارید و باو بدهید — منزل و باغ خودرا فروخت — چای و قهوه و گوشت در شهر خرید — خود آن مردرا دیروز در شهر دیدم — خودشان رفتند — کسی در باغ نبود — اورا چندان زیاد دوست ندارم — هیچی بمن نگفت — هیچ وقت در ایران نبوده‌ام — همین امروز خواهد آمد

[1] Also pronounced *avordan*.

Exercise 8

1. He saw the child in the garden. 2. He is writing a letter with my pen. 3. He sold his horse yesterday. 4. They are drinking (eating) tea in my room. 5. I shall go to the town tomorrow. 6. Take this book and give it to that man. 7. The children were running in the garden. 8. He has many horses. 9. This book was expensive. 10. He will sell this to me. 11. The pink flower is bigger than the yellow. 12. The leaves of the tree are green. 13. It was not a very good book. 14. He has no children. 15. I did not see anyone. 16. Have you ever been there? 17. He never told me that.

LESSON V

Numerals. خیلی *xeĭli*. بسیار *besyar*. یك *yak*. یکی *yaki*. دیگر *digar*. دیگری *digari*. چند *cand*. چندی *candi*. How to express time. How to express age.

1. The numerals are given in the following table. The ordinals are formed from the cardinals by the addition of م *-om*.[1] Figures are read from left to right.

CARDINAL	ORDINAL		
یك *yak, yek*[2]	یکم *yakom, yekom*[2]	١	1
دو *do*	دوم *dovvom*; دویم *doyyom*[2]	٢	2
سه *se*	سوم *sevvom*; سیم *seyyom*[2]	٣	3
چهار *cahar*	چهارم *caharom*	٤ (۴)	4
پنج *panj*	پنجم *panjom*	٥	5
شش *ſeſ*	ششم *ſeſom*	٦	6
هفت *haft*	هفتم *haftom*	٧	7
هشت *haſt*	هشتم *haſtom*	٨	8
نه *noh*	نهم *nohom*	٩	9
ده *dah*	دهم *dahom*	١٠	10
یازده *yazdah*	یازدهم *yazdahom*	١١	11

[1] The ending م *-om* is also added to چند *cand* 'how many', e.g.

چندم ماه است *candome mah ast*, What day of the month is it?

[2] See below, para. 2.

CARDINAL		ORDINAL			
دوازده	*davazdah*	دوازدهم	*davazdahom*	١٢	12
سیزده	*sizdah*	سیزدهم	*sizdahom*	١٣	13
چهارده	*cahardah*	چهاردهم	*cahardahom*	١٤	14
پانزده	*panzdah*[1]	پانزدهم	*panzdahom*[1]	١٥	15
شانزده	*ʃanzdah*[1]	شانزدهم	*ʃanzdahom*[1]	١٦	16
هفده	*hevdah*	هفدهم	*hevdahom*	١٧	17
هیجده	*hijdah*[1]	هیجدهم	*hijdahom*[1]	١٨	18
نوزده	*nuzdah*	نوزدهم	*nuzdahom*	١٩	19
بیست	*bist*	بیستم	*bistom*	٢٠	20
بیست و یك	*bist o yak*[2]	بیست و یکم	*bist o yakom*	٢١	21
بیست و دو	*bist o do*	بیست و دوم	*bist o dovvom*	٢٢	22
بیست و سه	*bist o se*	بیست و سوم	*bist o sevvom*	٢٣	23
بیست و چهار	*bist o cahar*	بیست و چهارم	*bist o caharom*	٢٤	24
بیست و پنج	*bist o panj*	بیست و پنجم	*bist o panjom*	٢٥	25
بیست و شش	*bist o ʃeʃ*	بیست و ششم	*bist o ʃeʃom*	٢٦	26
بیست و هفت	*bist o haft*	بیست و هفتم	*bist o haftom*	٢٧	27
بیست و هشت	*bist o haʃt*	بیست و هشتم	*bist o haʃtom*	٢٨	28
بیست و نه	*bist o noh*	بیست و نهم	*bist o nohom*	٢٩	29
سی	*si*	سی‌ام	*siom*	٣٠	30
چهل	*cehel*	چهلم	*cehelom*	٤٠	40
پنجاه	*panjah*	پنجاهم	*panjahom*	٥٠	50
شصت	*ʃast*	شصتم	*ʃastom*	٦٠	60
هفتاد	*haftad*	هفتادم	*haftadom*	٧٠	70
هشتاد	*haʃtad*	هشتادم	*haʃtadom*	٨٠	80
نود	*navad*	نودم	*navadom*	٩٠	90
صد	*sad*	صدم	*sadom*	١٠٠	100
صد و یك	*sad o yak*	صد و یکم	*sad o yakom*	١٠١	101
صد و بیست و یك	*sad o bist* *o yak*	صد و بیست و یکم	*sad o bist* *o yakom*	١٢١	121
دویست	*devist*	دویستم	*devistom*	٢٠٠	200

[1] See below, para. 2.

[2] This و *o* 'and' is a survival from the Middle Persian *uδ* and is not the Arabic و *va* 'and'. It survives in certain other positions, notably in compounds (see Lesson x). In pronunciation it approximates to *o* (see Introduction, para. 2); in articulation time it approximates to the group *e*, *a*, *o* rather than to the group *i*, *a*, *u* (see Introduction, para. 2).

CARDINAL		ORDINAL			
سیصد	*si sad*	سیصدم	*si sadom*	۳۰۰	300
چهار صد	*cahar sad*	چهار صدم	*cahar sadom*	٤۰۰	400
پانصد	*pansad*[1]	پانصدم	*pansadom*[1]	٥۰۰	500
شش صد	*ʃeʃ sad*	شش صدم	*ʃeʃ sadom*	٦۰۰	600
هفت صد	*haft sad*	هفت صدم	*haft sadom*	۷۰۰	700
هشت صد	*haʃt sad*	هشت صدم	*haʃt sadom*	۸۰۰	800
نه صد	*noh sad*	نه صدم	*noh sadom*	۹۰۰	900
هزار	*hazar*	هزارم	*hazarom*	۱۰۰۰	1,000
هزار و یك	*hazar o yak*	هزار و یکم	*hazar o yakom*	۱۰۰۱	1,001
هزار و بیست	*hazar o bist*	هزار و بیست و	*hazar o bist o*	۱۰۲۱	1,021
و یك	*o yak*	یکم	*yakom*		
هزار و صد	*hazar o sad*	هزار و صد و	*hazar o sad o*	۱۱۲۱	1,121
و بیست و یك	*o bist o yak*	بیست و یکم	*bist o yakom*		
دو هزار	*do hazar*	دو هزارم	*do hazarom*	۲۰۰۰	2,000
ملیون	*meliun*				1,000,000
صفر	*sefr*			۰	0

2. The Arabic word اول *avval* is usually substituted for the Persian ordinal یکم *yakom*, when this stands alone, e.g.

شب اول *ʃabe avval*, the first night.

دو *do* 'two' and سه *se* 'three' form their ordinals irregularly, as follows: دوم *dovvom* and سوم *sevvom* respectively. دویم *doyyom* and سیم *seyyom* are alternative forms.

For the pronunciation of دو *do* 'two' and شش *ʃeʃ* 'six' see Introduction, alphabetical table and para. 2 (*b*).

yek and *yekom* tend to be used rather than *yak* and *yakom*, and *yeki* rather than *yaki* (see below, paras. 6, 19 and 20).

چهار *cahar*, both standing alone and in compounds, is often contracted into *car*.

The first vowel of پانزده 'fifteen' and شانزده 'sixteen' and پانصد 'five hundred' is pronounced *u* or as a nasalized vowel intermediate between *a* and *o*.

هیجده *hijdah* 'eighteen' is usually pronounced *hejdah* or *heʒdah*.

The *f* of هفده is assimilated to the following *d* and becomes *v*, thus *hevdah*; it is also pronounced *hivdah*.

[1] See below, para. 2.

3. 'Once', 'twice', etc., are translated by the cardinal numbers followed by بار *bar*, دفعه *daf'e* or مرتبه *martabe*, 'time', e.g.

يك دفعه *yak daf'e*, once.

صد بار *sad bar*, a hundred times.

دو مرتبه *do martabe*, twice.

'Twice as much', 'twice as many', etc., are translated by the cardinal number followed by برابر *barabar* 'equal', e.g.

دو برابر *do barabar*, twice as much.

عده ما چهار برابر شد *eddeye ma cahar barabar ʃod*, Our number became four times as many.

4. Multiplicatives are formed by the addition of گانه *-gane* to the cardinal, e.g.

دوگانه *dogane*, double. سه گانه *segane*, triple.

5. لا *la* is used to express '-fold', e.g.

دو لا *do la*, double (=two-fold).

سه لا *se la*, triple (=three-fold).

6. Distributives are formed by repeating the cardinal with or without به *be* in between, e.g.

سه بسه *se be se*, three by three.

يك *yak* 'one' takes the Indefinite ی *-i* when used as a distributive, e.g.

یکی یکی *yaki yaki*, one by one.

The forms یکايك *yakayak* and يگان يگان *yagan yagan* 'one by one' are obsolete.

7. Recurring numerals are expressed as follows:

يك روز در ميان *yak ruz dar mian*, (on) alternate days.

شش روز بشش روز *ʃeʃ ruz be ʃeʃ ruz*, every six days.

هفت روز يك بار *haft ruz yak bar*, once in seven days.

8. Approximate numbers are expressed as follows:

دو سه *do se*, two or three.

چهار پنج *cahar panj*, four or five.

هفت هشت *haft haʃt* seven or eight.

ده دوازده *dah davazdah*, ten or twelve.

9. The Arabic forms are often used to express fractions (see Part II, Lesson XXI, para. 7). Fractions are also expressed by the cardinal numbers in apposition, the denominator preceding the numerator, e.g.

سه يك *se yak*, $\frac{1}{3}$; چهار يك *cahar yak*, $\frac{1}{4}$;

پنج يك *panj yak*, $\frac{1}{5}$;

or by the cardinal of the numerator preceding the ordinal of the denominator, e.g.

سه پنجم *se panjom*, $\frac{3}{5}$.

نيم *nim* means 'half'. In combinations such as 'one and a half', etc., نيم *nim* 'half' follows the noun qualified by the numeral, e.g.

يك ساعت و نيم *yak sa'at o nim*, one hour and a half.

شش صفحه و نيم *ʃeʃ safhe o nim*, six pages and a half.

ربع *rob'* 'quarter' takes a similar construction, e.g.

پنج صفحه و ربع *panj safhe o rob'*, five pages and a quarter.

10. Percentage is expressed as follows:

صدى ده *sadi dah*, 10%.

ده در صد *dah dar sad*, 10 %.

11. اند *and* is used to express 'odd' with numbers above nineteen, e.g.

بيست و اند *bist o and*, twenty odd.

12. Arithmetical operations are performed as follows:

Multiplication:

دو دو تا ميشود چهار تا *do do ta miʃavad cahar ta*, $2\times2=4$

Division:

دوازده تقسيم بر سه ميشود چهار *davazdah taqsim bar se miʃavad cahar*, $12\div3=4$.

Addition:

شش باضافه شش مساوى است با دوازده *ʃeʃ be ezafeye ʃeʃ mosavist ba davazdah*, $6+6=12$.

Subtraction:

نه منهاى پنج مساوى است با چهار *noh menhaye*[1] *panj mosavist ba cahar*, $9-5=4$.

[1] منها *menha* is compounded of the Arabic preposition من *men* 'from' and the 3rd pers. fem. sing. Pronominal Suffix ها *-ha*. For its pronunciation see Introduction, Part II, para. 12.

13. The cardinal numbers precede the noun they qualify, which is put in the singular, e.g.

دو رأس اسب *do ra'S*[1] *asb*, two horses.

صد نفر *sad nafar*, a hundred persons.

A Noun qualified by a cardinal does not take را *-ra* when it is the direct object of the verb, unless it is qualified by some such word as این *in* 'this' or آن *an* 'that', e.g.

دو جلد کتاب خرید *do jeld*[1] *ketab xarid*, He bought two books.

آن دو کتابرا خرید *an do ketabra xarid*, He bought those two books.

14. The ordinals are used as adjectives and follow the noun they qualify, e.g.

کتاب سومرا بمن بدهید *ketabe sevvomra be man bedehid*, Give me the third book.

نخست *naxost* and نخستین *naxostin* are also used as the ordinal of 'one', but cannot be used to form the ordinals of compound numerals. They precede the noun they qualify, e.g.

نخستین بار *naxostin bar*, the first time.

An adjectival form of the ordinal ending in ین *-in*, which also precedes the noun it qualifies without the *ezafe*, is sometimes found, e.g.

یك صد و هشتمین روز *yak sad o haštomin ruz*, the hundred and eighth day.

15. صد *sad* 'hundred' and هزار *hazar* 'thousand' when used indefinitely can take the plural ending ها *ha-*. They precede the noun they qualify, which is put in the singular, e.g.

صدها کتاب *sadha ketab*, hundreds of books.

هزارها گل *hazarha gol*, thousands of flowers.

هزاران *hazaran* is also used referring to rational beings. هزاران هزار *hazaran hazar* means 'thousands upon thousands' (referring to rational beings).

[1] See para. 16 below.

Similar constructions are:

سالهای سال *salhaye sal*, many long years.

قرنهای قرن *qarnhaye qarn*, many long centuries.

16. Certain words are used with cardinals as classifiers, except when referring to units of time. These words are placed between the cardinal and the word qualified by the cardinal. Among them are:

(*a*) نفر *nafar* (=person) used for persons,[1] e.g.

سه نفر زن آمدند *se nafar zan amadand*, Three women came.

یك نفر *yak nafar* means 'a certain person, someone'.

(*b*) رأس *ra's* (=head in Arabic) for horses and cattle, e.g.

صد رأس گاو دارد *sad ra's gav darad*, He has a hundred head of oxen.

(*c*) عدد *adad* (=number) for small articles, e.g.

پنج عدد مداد بمن داد *panj adad medad be man dad*, He gave me five pencils.

(*d*) جلد *jeld* (=volume) for books, e.g.

چهار جلد کتاب خرید *cahar jeld ketab xarid*, He bought four books.

(*e*) دست *dast* (=hand) for clothes, furniture, etc., e.g.

یك دست لباس خرید *yak dast lebas xarid*, He bought a suit of clothes.

(*f*) باب *bab* (=door in Arabic) for houses, e.g.

دو باب خانه دارد *do bab xane darad*, He has two houses.

(*g*) دانه *dane* (=grain) for eggs and small articles, e.g.

ده دانه تخم مرغ آورد *dah dane toxme morγ avard*, He brought ten (hen's) eggs.

(*h*) تا *ta* is used in Colloquial Persian for almost anything but is seldom written (although it has the sanction of early classical usage).

[1] نفر *nafar* is also used for camels.

(*i*) The following are also used:

دستگاه *dastgah* for clocks, furniture and machinery, etc.
قبضه *qabze* for swords and rifles, etc.
عراده *arrade* for guns, cannons, etc.
فروند *farvand* and قطعه *qat'e* for ships.
زنجیر *zanjir* for elephants.
قطار *qetar* and مهار *mehar* for camels.
پارچه *parce* for villages.
تن *tan* for persons.

In certain cases where some sort of classifier is contained in the phrase qualified by a numeral an additional classifying word is not added after یك *yak* 'one' and is optional after other numerals,[1] e.g.

یك فنجان چای *yak fenjan cai*, a (one) cup of tea.
یك لیوان آب *yak livan ab*, a (one) glass of water.

17. Real estate is divided into six units known as دانگ *dang*[2], e.g.

شش دانگ خانه مال اوست *ʃeʃ dange xane male ust*, Six *dangs* of the house belong to him (i.e. he is the sole owner of the house).

دو دانگ ده مال اوست *do dange deh male ust*, Two *dangs* of the village belong to him (i.e. one-third of the village is his).

18. خیلی *xeili* and بسیار *besyar* mean 'very' (see Lesson III, para. 20) and also 'many'. They precede the noun they qualify, which is put in the singular, e.g.

خیلی اسب دارد *xeili asb darad*, He has many horses.

بسیار *besyar* can also follow the noun it qualifies, in which case the latter is put in the plural, e.g.

اسبهای بسیار دارد *asbhaye besyar darad*, He has many horses.

[1] See also Lesson XII, para. 2 (*f*).

[2] دانگ *dang* can be applied to certain other objects as well, e.g. آواز شش دانگ *avaze ʃeʃ dang*, a good (and loud) voice; شش دانگ جهان *ʃeʃ dange jahan*, the whole world. See also Lesson XIV, para. 2 (*b*).

19. یک *yak* 'one' is sometimes used with a noun to which the Indefinite ی *-i* has been added. Its addition does not materially alter the meaning, e.g.

مردی *mardi* or یک مردی *yak mardi*, a man,

but یک مرد *yak mard*, one man.

20. The Indefinite ی *-i* can be added to یک *yak* to mean 'one', e.g.

یکی بمن بدهید *yaki be man bedehid*, Give me one.

'One of' is rendered by یکی از *yaki az*, e.g.

یکی از آن کتابها را بمن بدهید *yaki az an ketabhara be man bedehid*, Give me one of those books.

21. دیگر *digar* 'other' is used as an adjective, e.g.

اسب دیگر *asbe digar*, the other horse.

اسب دیگری *asbe digari*, another horse.

With the Indefinite ی *-i* added to it, it is used as an Indefinite Pronoun meaning 'another', e.g.

دیگری آمد *digari amad*, another came.

یکی دیگر *yaki digar* also means 'another', e.g.

یکی دیگر بمن بدهید *yaki digar be man bedehid*, Give me another.

یک دیگر *yak digar* and هم دیگر *ham digar* both mean 'each other', e.g.

از یک دیگر جدا شدند *az yak digar joda ʃodand*, They separated from each other.

از هم دیگر خدا حافظی کردند *az ham digar xoda hafezi kardand*, They said good-bye to each other.

دیگر *digar* also means 'next',[1] e.g.

دفعه دیگر *daf'eye digar*, next time.

روز دیگر *ruze digar*, the next day.

Used as an adverb دیگر *digar* means 'further, in addition, again', e.g.

دیگر چه میخواهید *digar ce mixahid*, What further do you want, What else do you want?

دیگر نیامد *digar nayamad*, He did not come again.

(See also Lesson XIV, para. 3.)

[1] In Classical Persian دیگر *digar* also means 'second', e.g. بار دیگر *bare digar*, the second time; نماز دیگر *namaze digar* means 'the afternoon prayer'.

22. چند *cand* 'some, several, a few' usually precedes the noun it qualifies, which is put in the singular, e.g.

چند نفر آمدند *cand nafar amadand*, A few persons came.

If it follows the noun, the Indefinite ى *-i* must be added to the Noun, e.g.

سالی چند گذشت *sali cand goẓast*, A few years passed.

چند *cand* is also used as an interrogative meaning 'how much, how many, how long', e.g.

چند نفر بودند *cand nafar budand*, How many people were there?
آنرا چند خریدید *anra cand xaridid*, How much did you buy that for?
تا چند صبر کنم *ta cand sabr konam*, (Until) how long shall I wait?[1]

چند *cand* used as a noun with the Indefinite ى *-i* means 'some time, a little while', e.g.

چندی ماند و رفت *candi mand o raft*, He stayed a little while and (then) went.

چند *cand* and چندی *candi* 'a little while' can be preceded by یك *yak*, e.g.

یك چندی آنجا بودم *yak candi anja budam*, I was there for a little while.

یك چند صبر کنید *yak cand sabr konid*, Wait just a little longer.

23. Time of day is expressed by the cardinal number following the word ساعت *sa'at* 'hour', which takes the *eẓafe*, e.g.

ساعت ده *sa'ate dah*, ten o'clock.

'Half an hour' is نیم ساعت *nim sa'at*.
'Quarter of an hour' is ربع ساعت *rob' sa'at*.
Half hours are expressed as follows:

ده و نیم	*dah o nim*	10.30.
نیم ساعت از ده گذشته	*nim sa'at aẓ dah goẓaste*	
نیم ساعت بیازده مانده	*nim sa'at be yaẓdah mande*	

Quarter hours are expressed as follows:

ده و ربع	*dah o rob'*	10.15.
یك ربع از ده گذشته	*yak rob' aẓ dah goẓaste*	
ده ربع بالا	*dah rob' bala*	

[1] See Lesson XIII, para. 11 (*j*), for this use of the Subjunctive.

یازده ربع کم *yazdah rob‘ kam*
یك ربع بیازده مانده *yak rob‘ be yazdah mande* } 10.45

‘Minute’ is دقیقه *daqiqe*. Minutes are expressed as follows:

پنج دقیقه از ده گذشته *panj daqiqe az dah gozaʃte*
ده و پنج دقیقه *dah o panj daqiqe* } 10.5.

پنج دقیقه بیازده مانده *panj daqiqe be yazdah mande*
یازده پنج دقیقه کم *yazdah panj daqiqe kam* } 10.55.

24. ‘Midday’ and ‘midnight’ are ظهر *zohr* and نصف شب *nesfe ʃab* respectively, and are used in place of دوازده *davazdah* ‘twelve’. The construction with و *o* ‘and’ to express half hours and quarters is not used with ظهر *zohr* or نصف شب *nesfe ʃab*; one of the other forms must be used, e.g.

نیم ساعت از ظهر گذشته *nim sa‘at az zohr gozaʃte*, 12.30 p.m.

یك ربع بظهر مانده *yak rob‘ be zohr mande*, 11.45 a.m.

سه ربع از نصف شب گذشته *se rob‘ az nesfe ʃab gozaʃte*, 12.45 a.m.

نیم ساعت بنصف شب مانده *nim sa‘at be nesfe ʃab mande*, 11.30 p.m.

a.m. is پیش از ظهر *piʃ az zohr*.
p.m. is بعد از ظهر *ba‘d az zohr*.

صبح *sobh* means ‘morning’, عصر *asr* ‘afternoon’ and شب *ʃab* ‘evening’ or ‘night’; سحر *sahar* is the period from midnight to dawn and is used especially for the period just before dawn; آفتاب نزده *aftab nazade* means ‘before sunrise’; سفیده صبح *sefideye sobh* ‘the early dawn’.

25. In country districts time is sometimes reckoned with reference to three points, sunrise, sunset and midday, e.g.

چند از روز بالا آمده *cand az ruz bala amade*, How long (is) it after daybreak?

چند بظهر مانده *cand be zohr mande*, How long remains till midday?

چند بغروب مانده *cand be ɣorub mande*, How long remains till sunset?

دو ساعت از غروب گذشته *do sa‘at az ɣorub gozaʃte*, two hours after sunset.

26. The week is reckoned from Saturday. The days of the week are as follows:

شنبه *ſambe*, Saturday.
یکشنبه *yak ſambe*, Sunday.
دو شنبه *do ſambe*, Monday.
سه شنبه *se ſambe*, Tuesday.
چهار شنبه *cahar ſambe*, Wednesday.
پنج شنبه *panj ſambe*, Thursday.
جمعه *jomʿe*, Friday.

The following forms generally refer to the latter part of the day:

شب یکشنبه *ſabe yak ſambe*, Saturday.
شب دو شنبه *ſabe do ſambe*, Sunday.
شب سه شنبه *ſabe se ſambe*, Monday.
شب چهار شنبه *ſabe cahar ſambe*, Tuesday.
شب پنج شنبه *ſabe panj ſambe*, Wednesday.
شب جمعه *ſabe jomʿe*, Thursday.
شب شنبه *ſabe ſambe*, Friday.

To express the morning, etc., of a certain day, the time of day is put in apposition to the day, e.g.

دو شنبه صبح *do ſambe sobh*, Monday morning.
چهار شنبه شب *cahar ſambe ſab*, Wednesday evening.
جمعه شب *jomʿe ſab*, Friday evening.

صبح *sobh* 'morning' and عصر *asr* 'afternoon' can instead precede the day of the week, in which case they take an *eẓafe*, e.g.

صبح چهار شنبه *sobhe cahar ſambe*, Wednesday morning.
عصر شب جمعه *asre ſabe jomʿe*, Thursday afternoon.

27. Expressions of 'time at' or 'time in' do not require a preposition, e.g.

صبح آمد *sobh amad*, He came in the morning.
ساعت ده رفت *saʿate dah raft*, He went at ten o'clock.
جمعه آمد *jomʿe amad*, He came on Friday.

روزی *ruzi* and یک روزی *yak ruzi* mean 'one day'. عصری *asri* may mean 'in the afternoon' (if a single occurrence) or 'in the afternoons' (habitually); similarly ظهری *zohri* 'at midday' may be used for a single or for a habitual action. صبحی *sobhi*, شبی *ʃabi* and غروبی *ɣorubi* 'in the morning', 'in the evening' and 'at sunset' respectively usually signify habitual actions.

28. سال *sal* 'year' and ماه *mah* 'month' can form plurals سالیان *salian* and ماهیان *mahian* respectively when used indefinitely, e.g.

سالیان دراز *saliane daraz*, (for) long years.

These forms are rare.

29. 'Ago' is expressed by پیش *piʃ* following the noun, which takes the *ezafe*, e.g.

یك هفته پیش بشهر رفت *yak hafteye piʃ be ʃahr raft*, He went to the town a week ago.

Note also

بعد از یك هفته خواهد آمد *ba'd az yak hafte xahad amad*, He will come in a week's time.

تا یك شنبه بر میگردد *ta yak ʃambe bar migardad*, He will return by Sunday.

30. Age is expressed by the verb داشتن *daʃtan* 'to have' together with the number of years or by the verb بودن *budan* 'to be' with سن *senn* 'age' and the number, e.g.

چند سال دارد *cand sal darad* } How old is he?
سن او چقدر است *senne u ce qadr ast* }

بیست سال دارد *bist sal darad* } He is twenty years old.
سن او بیست سال است *senne u bist sal ast* }

The following expressions should also be noted:

سال بیستش تمام شد *sale bisteʃ tamam ʃod*, His twentieth year is completed, i.e. he is twenty years old.

تو بیست میرود *tu*[1] *bist miravad*, He is entering his twentieth year, i.e. he is nineteen years old.

جوان بیست و چند سالهٔ بود *javane bist o cand salei bud*, He was a young man of twenty odd years.

[1] In this phrase تو *tu* is usually used without the *ezafe*.

Vocabulary

هوا *hava*, weather.

آب و هوا *ab o hava*, climate.

بهار *bahar*, spring.

تابستان *tabestan*, summer.

پائیز *paiz*, autumn.

زمستان *zamestan*, winter.

آفتاب *aftab*, sun.

ستاره *setare*, star.

آسمان *asman*, sky.

ماه *mah*, moon, month.

طلوع *tolu'*, rising; طلوع آفتاب *tolu'e aftab*, sunrise; طلوع کردن *tolu' k.*, to rise (the sun, etc.).

غروب *γorub*, sunset; غروب کردن *γorub k.*, to set.

شب *ʃab*, night, evening.

امشب *emʃab*, to-night.

دیشب *diʃab*, last night.

پریشب *pariʃab*, the night before last.

صبح *sobh*, morning.

عصر *asr*, afternoon.

صبحانه *sobhane*, breakfast.

عصرانه *asrane*, afternoon tea.

ناهار *nahar*, *nahar*, lunch.

ناشتائی *naʃtai*, breakfast.

شام *ʃam*, supper.

هفته *hafte*, week.

سال *sal*, year.

امسال *emsal*, this year.

پارسال *parsal*, last year.

پیرارسال *pirarsal*, the year before last.

نصف *nesf*, half; نصف شب *nesfe ʃab*, midnight.

ساعت *sa'at*, hour; timepiece.

دقیقه *daqiqe*, minute.

ربع *rob'*, quarter.

نیم *nim*, half.

عمر *omr*, life.

سن *senn*, age (of persons).

قیمت *qeimat*, value, price.

قدر *qadr*, amount; چقدر *ce qadr*, how much.

زمان *zaman*, time, season.

آینده *ayande*, future, coming; دفعه آینده *daf'eye ayande*, the coming time, i.e. next time.

لیوان *livan*, glass, tumbler.

فنجان *fenjan*, cup.

حاضر *hazer*, present, ready; حاضر کردن *hazer k.*, to make or get ready.

جدا *joda*, separate; جدا شدن *joda ʃ.*, to separate (intrans.); جدا کردن *joda k.*, to separate (trans.).

بالا *bala*, high; up.

بیدار *bidar*, awake; بیدار شدن *bidar ʃ.*, to wake, wake up (intrans.); بیدار کردن *bidar k.*, to wake (trans.).

بلند *boland*, tall; high; بلند شدن *boland ʃ.*, to get up, rise; بلند کردن *boland k.*, to raise.

وقت *vaqt*, time; چند وقت *cand vaqt*, how long.

دراز *daraz*, long.

نان *nan*, bread.

صفحه *safhe*, page (of book, etc.).

پول *pul*, money.

خانه *xane*, house.

تخم *toxm*, egg, seed; تخم مرغ *toxme morɣ*, hen's egg.

خروس *xorus*, cock.

جوجه *juje*, chicken.

یخ *yax*, ice; یخ بستن *yax bastan*, to freeze (intrans.) (بستن *bastan* 'to bind, tie', Present Stem بند *band*).

فردا *farda*, to-morrow.

پسفردا *pasfarda*, the day after to-morrow.

باز *baz*, open; باز کردن *baz k.*, to open (trans.).

دیگر *digar*, other; again; further.

چند *cand*, some, a few; how much, how many, how long.

پس *pas*, then, after (adv.); پس از *pas az*, after (prep.).

بعد *ba'd*, then, after (adv.); بعد از *ba'd az*, after (prep.).

پیش *piʃ*, before (adv.); *piʃ(e)* (prep.), in front of; in the presence of; پیش از *piʃ az* (prep., time), before.

جلو *jelou*, in front, forward; *jelou(e)* (prep.) in front of; fast (of a watch).

عقب *aqab*, behind; when used as a prep. it takes the *ezafe*; slow (of a watch).

تا *ta*, until.

هر *har*, every.

چون *cun*, when; since, like.

فقط *faqat*, only.

آواز *avaz*, voice, sound.

جهان *jahan*, world.

گذشتن (گذر) *gozaʃtan* (*gozar*), to pass (intrans.); گذشته *gozaʃte*, past; دفعه گذشته *daf'eye gozaʃte*, the last, i.e. the preceding, time.

ارزیدن *arzidan*, to be worth.

صبر کردن *sabr k.*, to wait.

دانستن (دان) *danestan* (*dan*), to know (of things).

بر گشتن (بر گرد) *bar gaʃtan* (*bar gard*), to return (intrans.).

خوابیدن *xabidan*, to sleep; to go to bed.

خدا حافظی کردن *xoda hafeʒi k.*, to say good-bye (خدا حافظ *xoda hafeʒ* means [may] God [be your] protector).

پرسیدن *porsidan*, to ask (a question).

شناختن (شناس) *ʃenaxtan* (*ʃenas*), to recognize, know (a person).

بر خاستن (بر خیز) *bar xastan* (*bar xiʒ*), to rise.

ماندن *mandan*, to remain.

Exercise 9

پارسال چند وقت آنجا بودید — پارسال شش ماه ماندم ولی امسال فقط پنج ماه میمانم — روز چهارشنبه گذشته پنج جلد کتاب خرید — پسفردا پیش از ظهر بشهر میرویم — ساعت ده صبح راه افتاد — زمستان پیرارسال خیلی سرد بود — دو دانگ این خانه مال برادر من است و یك دانگش مال هر یکی از خواهرهایم — یکی یکی جلو آمدند — این منزل اطاقهای زیاد دارد — اسب دیگری برای من حاضر کنید — شب جمعه پیش او بودیم — چند نفر آنجا بودند ولی هیچ یکی از آنهارا نمیشناختم — این کتاب هیچی نمی‌ارزد — ساعت شما نیم ساعت عقب است — تا دو بعد از ظهر برای شما صبر کردم — سه روز پیش آمد و بعد از سه روز دیگر خواهد رفت — در شهر از یك دیگر جدا شدند — بعد از چند دقیقه بر گشت — ده دانه تخم مرغ برای من آورد

Exercise 10

1. The woman came back at noon with her two daughters. 2. He went to bed early last night. 3. We started before sunrise. 4. Wait for me until 10 o'clock. 5. His elder son is nine years old and his younger son seven years old. 6. Give me one of those pencils. 7. After an hour and a half we returned home. 8. He bought a suit of clothes the day before yesterday. 9. Your garden is bigger than our garden. 10. My watch is a quarter of an hour fast. 11. Next week the sun will rise at 5.30 and set at 6.45. 12. We got up early yesterday.

LESSON VI

The Passive Voice. توانستن *tavanestan.* خواستن *xastan.* گذاشتن *gozaſtan.* بایستن *bayestan.* شایستن *ſayestan.* Impersonal Verbs. The Use of the Subjunctive after تا *ta* and که *ke.*

1. The Passive Voice is formed with the Auxiliary Verb شدن *ſodan* 'to become' (Present Stem شو *ſav-*, *ſou͡*) and the Past Participle of the main verb:

Infinitive	کشته شدن	*koſte ſodan,* to be killed.
Past Participle	کشته شده	*koſte ſode.*
Preterite	کشته شدم	*koſte ſodam,* etc.
Imperfect	کشته میشدم	*koſte miſodam,* etc.
Perfect	کشته شده‌ام	*koſte ſode am,* etc.
Pluperfect	کشته شده بودم	*koſte ſode budam,* etc.
Future	کشته خواهم شد	*koſte xaham ſod,* etc.
Present	کشته میشوم	*koſte miſavam,* etc.
Imperative	کشته شو	*koſte ſou͡,*[1] etc.
Subjunctive Present	کشته بشوم	*koſte beſavam,*[1] etc.
Subjunctive Past	کشته شده باشم	*koſte ſode baſam,* etc.

2. The negative is formed by adding نـ *na-* to the auxiliary شدن *ſodan* in the usual way, e.g.

کشته نشدم *koſte naſodam,* I was not killed.
کشته نشده ام *koſte naſode am,* I have not been killed.
کشته نخواهم شد *koſte naxaham ſod,* I shall not be killed.

3. Stress in the affirmative is carried on the final syllable of the main verb, e.g.

کشته شدم *koſ'te ſodam,* I was killed.
کشته خواهم شد *koſ'te xaham ſod,* I shall be killed.

In the negative it is carried on the negative prefix, e.g.

کشته نمیشوم *koſte 'namiſavam,* I shall not be killed.
کشته نشدم *koſte 'naſodam,* I was not killed.

[1] There is a tendency to omit the prefix بـ *be-* in the Imperative and the Subjunctive Present of the Passive Voice.

4. The Verbs گشتن *gaʃtan* (Present Stem گرد *gard*)[1] and گردیدن *gardidan*[2] 'to become' can be used in place of شدن *ʃodan* to form the Passive Voice.

5. The Passive Voice is not used in Persian if the Active Voice can be used. Thus 'I was hit by him' must be translated as 'he hit me'.

6. The Passive Voice can in some cases be expressed by the 3rd pers. pl. of the Active Voice. Certain verbs take this construction in preference to the Passive construction with شدن *ʃodan*, e.g.

اورا زدند *ura zadand*, He was hit (they hit him).
گفتند *goftand*, It was said (they said).

7. In addition to the auxiliary verbs بودن *budan* 'to be' and شدن *ʃodan* 'to become', the following auxiliaries are in common use:

توانستن *tavanestan* (Present Stem توان *tavan*) to be able.[3]
خواستن *xastan* (Present Stem خواه *xah*), to want.[4]

Both are normally followed by the Subjunctive Present,[5] e.g.

میتوانم بروم *mitavanam beravam*, I can go.
نتوانستم بروم *natavanestam beravam*, I could not go.
خواهم توانست بروم *xaham tavanest beravam*, I shall be able to go.
میخواهم بروم *mixaham beravam*, I want to go.
میخواستم بروم *mixastam beravam*, I wanted to go.

8. خواستن *xastan* is sometimes used to mean 'to be on the point of doing something', e.g.

میخواست بمیرد *mixast bemirad*, He was about to die.

1 گشتن *gaʃtan* is also used standing alone to mean 'to go for a walk', 'to search (for)', e.g.
توی شهر گشتیم *tuye ʃahr gaʃtim*, We walked about in the town.
عقب او گشتم *aqabe u gaʃtam*, I went to look for him.

2 گردیدن *gardidan* standing alone means 'to go round', 'revolve'.

3 The obsolete verb یارستن *yarastan* 'to be able' was used in Classical Persian in the same way as توانستن *tavanestan*.

4 خواستن *xastan* as a transitive verb means 'to send for, summon, desire'.

5 Note, however, نمیتواند رفته باشد *namitavanad rafte baʃad*, he cannot have gone.

9. گذاشتن *gozaʃtan* (Present Stem گذار *gozar*) meaning 'to allow' is followed by the Subjunctive Present with or without که *ke*, e.g.

نگذاشت که بروم *nagozaʃt ke beravam*, He did not allow me to go.

10. The defective verb بایستن *bayestan* is used as an auxiliary and is followed by the Subjunctive. The only forms in common use are the 3rd pers. sing. باید *bayad* 'ought, must', بایست *bayest* and میبایست *mibayest*, 'ought to have'. A form میباید *mibayad* 'must' is occasionally found in place of باید *bayad*.

1st pers. sing.	باید بروم	*bayad beravam*	I must go, ought to go, etc.
2nd pers. sing.	باید بروی	*bayad beravi*	
3rd pers. sing.	باید برود	*bayad beravad*	
1st pers. pl.	باید برویم	*bayad beravim*	We must go, ought to go, etc.
2nd pers. pl.	باید بروید	*bayad beravid*	
3rd pers. pl.	باید بروند	*bayad beravand*	
1st pers. sing.	بایست رفته باشم	*bayest rafte baʃam*	I must have gone, ought to have gone, etc.
2nd pers. sing.	بایست رفته باشی	*bayest rafte baʃi*	
3rd pers. sing.	بایست رفته باشد	*bayest rafte baʃad*	
1st pers. pl.	بایست رفته باشیم	*bayest rafte baʃim*	We must have gone, ought to have gone, etc.
2nd pers. pl.	بایست رفته باشید	*bayest rafte baʃid*	
3rd pers. pl.	بایست رفته باشند	*bayest rafte baʃand*	

باید *bayad* is also used with the Subjunctive Past and has the same meaning as بایست *bayest* followed by the Subjunctive Past. میبایست *mibayest* is sometimes used in place of بایست *bayest*.[1]

11. The only forms of the defective verb شایستن *ʃayestan* in use are the Participles شایان *ʃayan* 'fitting, splendid, brilliant', شایسته *ʃayeste* 'fitting, proper' and شاید *ʃayad*. The latter means 'perhaps'. When referring to the present it is followed by the Indicative Present, but when referring to the future or past by the Subjunctive:[2]

1st pers. sing.	شاید بروم	*ʃayad beravam*	Perhaps I shall go, etc.
2nd pers. sing.	شاید بروی	*ʃayad beravi*	
3rd pers. sing.	شاید برود	*ʃayad beravad*	

[1] See also Lesson XII, paras. 1 (*b*), and 3, and Lesson XIII, paras. 1 (*e*), 5 (*h*), 11 (*g*), and 12 (*d* and *f*).

[2] See also Lesson VII, para. 5 (*b*), Lesson XII, para. 3, and Lesson XIII, para. 6 (*a*).

1st pers. pl.	شاید برویم	*ʃayad beravim*	Perhaps we shall go, etc.
2nd pers. pl.	شاید بروید	*ʃayad beravid*	
3rd pers. pl.	شاید بروند	*ʃayad beravand*	
1st pers. sing.	شاید رفته باشم	*ʃayad rafte baʃam*	Perhaps I have gone, etc.
2nd pers. sing.	شاید رفته باشی	*ʃayad rafte baʃi*	
3rd pers. sing.	شاید رفته باشد	*ʃayad rafte baʃad*	
1st pers. pl.	شاید رفته باشیم	*ʃayad rafte baʃim*	Perhaps we have gone, etc.
2nd pers. pl.	شاید رفته باشید	*ʃayad rafte baʃid*	
3rd pers. pl.	شاید رفته باشند	*ʃayad rafte baʃand*	

In the case of بودن *budan* 'to be', the Preterite is used after شاید referring to past time, e.g.

شاید آنجا بود *ʃayad anja bud*, perhaps he was there.

12. The 3rd pers. sing. of بایستن *bayestan* and شدن *ʃodan*, and of the Subjunctive and Indicative Present of توانستن *tavanestan* can be used impersonally, in which case they are followed by the Short Infinitive.

If توانستن *tavanestan* is used impersonally the forms بتوان *betavan* and میتوان *mitavan* are used in the Subjunctive Present and the Indicative Present respectively, e.g.

اینرا میتوان کرد *inra mitavan kard*, One can do this.

باید رفت *bayad raft*, One must go.

شدن *ʃodan* used impersonally means 'to be possible', e.g.

میشود رفت *miʃavad raft*, It is possible to go.

13. The 3rd pers. sing. pres. of the obsolete verb مانستن *manestan* 'to resemble' is used in Colloquial Persian to mean 'it seems', e.g.

اینطور میماند *in tour mimanad*, It seems (to be) thus.

14. The negative prefix نَ *na-* is added to the auxiliaries خواستن *xastan*, بایستن *bayestan*, and توانستن *tavanestan* (and not to the main verb) if the proposition is negative, e.g.

نباید بروید *nabayad beravid*, You must not go.

نمیتواند بماند *namitavanad bemanad*, He cannot stay.

نمیخواست بگوید *namixast beguyad*, He did not want to say.

A similar construction is used with توانستن *tavanestan*, بایستن *bayestan* and شدن *ʃodan* when these are used impersonally, e.g.

نباید رفت *nabayad raft*, One must not go.

نمیشود کرد *namiʃavad kard*, It is impossible to do (this).

نمیتوان کرد *namitavan kard*, One cannot do (this).

15. In the case of شاید *ʃayad* the negative prefix is added to the main Verb, e.g.

شاید نروم *ʃayad naravam*, Perhaps I shall not go.

16. In Classical Persian the 2nd pers. sing. is sometimes used impersonally, e.g.

تو گفتی *to gofti* = One would have said.

گوئی *gui* = One would say.

17. The Subjunctive Present is used after certain conjunctions. Among them are:

(*a*) که *ke* and تا *ta* introducing a final clause, e.g.

اینرا باو دادم که بمنزل ببرد *inra be u dadam ke be manzel bebarad*, I gave him this to take to the house.

کتابرا بمن داد تا مرا کمك کند *ketabra be man dad ta mara komak konad*, He gave me the book to help me.

اینرا باو گفتم تا زودتر برود *inra be u goftam ta zudtar beravad*, I told him this in order that he should go earlier.

اورا بشهر فرستادند که نان بخرد *ura be ʃahr ferestadand ke nan bexarad*, They sent him to the town to buy (some) bread.

In the above examples تا *ta* and که *ke* are interchangeable.

تا *ta* is used in Persian to express consequence where 'and' is used in English, e.g.

اینرا بکن تا پولت بدهم *inra bekon ta pulet bedeham*, Do this and I will give you (some) money.

(*b*) تا *ta* 'by the time that' referring to future time, e.g.

تا بشهر برسید خسته میشوید *ta be ʃahr berasid xaste miʃavid*, You will be tired by the time you reach the town.

تا شما بیائید رفته‌ام *ta ʃoma beyaid rafte am*, By the time you come I shall have gone.

(*c*) تا *ta* 'until' referring to future time, usually with نه *na*, e.g.

تا اینرا نخوانم باور نمیکنم *ta inra naxanam bavar namikonam*, I shall not believe this until I read it.

Note however that the نه *na* is by usage omitted in such sentences as the following:

تا شما بیائید صبر میکنم *ta ʃoma beyaid sabr mikonam*, I will wait until you come.

(See also Lesson XIII, paras. 11 and 18.)

Temporal Clauses introduced by تا *ta* usually precede the principal sentence.

18. The Subjunctive is also used in substantive clauses implying intention or determination, with or without که *ke*, e.g.

مصمم شد که ببرادر خود بنویسد *mosammam ʃod ke be baradare xod benevisad*, He determined to write to his brother.

VOCABULARY

دروغ *doruɣ*, lie; دروغ گفتن *doruɣ goftan*, to lie.

خسته *xaste*, tired; خسته شدن *xaste ʃ.*, to be tired.

مصمم *mosammam*, decided, determined upon; مصمم شدن *mosammam ʃ.*, to be determined, decided upon.

خراب *xarab*, destroyed; broken, out of order; bad (of food, etc.).

درست *dorost*, right; in order.

تشنه *teʃne*, thirsty.

تشنگی *teʃnegi*, thirst.

گرسنه *gorosne*, hungry.

گرسنگی *gorosnegi*, hunger.

برف *barf*, snow; برف آمدن (باریدن) *barf amadan* (*baridan*), to snow.

باران *baran*, rain; باران آمدن *baran amadan* to rain.

بارندگی *barandegi*, rain.

باریدن *baridan*, to rain.

رعد *ra'd*, thunder.

برق *barq*, lightning; electricity.

تگرگ *tegarg*, hail.

توفان *tufan*, storm.

باد *bad*, wind.

موسم *mousem*, season (of year, etc.).

شدید *ʃadid*, severe; strict.

قوه *qovve*, power; قوه برق *qovveye barq*, electric power.

تولید *toulid*, production; تولید کردن *toulid k.*, to produce.

سطح *sath*, standard, level (noun).

زندگی *zendegi*, life; سطح زندگی *sathe zendegi*, standard of life.

گندم *gandom*, wheat.

جو *jou*, barley.

پشم *paʃm*, wool.

پنبه *pambe*, cotton.

قماش *qomaʃ*, cotton piece goods.

صادرات *saderat*, exports.

واردات *varedat*, imports.

صادر کردن *sader k.*, to export; to issue.

وارد کردن *vared k.*, to import; وارد شدن *vared ʃ.*, to be imported; to enter, come in.

خشک *xoʃk*, dry; خشک بار *xoʃke bar*, dried fruits.

خشکی *xoʃki*, dryness, dry land; از راه خشکی *az rahe xoʃki*, by land.

تجارت *tejarat*, trade.

تجارت خانه *tejaratxane*, trading house, firm.

تجارتی *tejarati*, commercial.

تاجر *tajer*, merchant.

دکان *dokkan*, shop.

قند *qand*, lump sugar.

ماشین آلات *maʃinalat*, machinery.

مملکت *mamlekat*, country.

دنیا *donya*, world.

عبارت بودن (از) *ebarat b.* (*az*), to consist (of).

صنعت *san'at*, industry.

صنعتی *san'ati*, industrial.

زراعت *zera'at*, agriculture.

زراعتی *zera'ati*, agricultural.

مواد *mavadd*, materials; مواد اولیه *mavadde avvaliye*, raw materials.

جنس *jens*, kind, sort.

اجناس *ajnas* (broken plural of جنس),[1] kinds, sorts; goods.

کارخانه *karxane*, factory.

زیرا (که) *zira* (*ke*), because.

با وجودیکه *ba vojudike*, با اینکه *ba inke*, in spite of the fact that, notwithstanding.

باورکردن *bavar k.*, to believe.

زیاد کردن *ziad k.*, to increase (trans.).

کم کردن *kam k.*, to decrease (trans.).

مردن (میر) *mordan* (*mir*), to die.

تهران *tehran*, Tehran.

تا *ta*, as long as (with Indic.).

خواندن *xandan*, to read.

[1] For Broken Plurals see Part II, Lesson xx. The use of broken plurals, while not obligatory, is customary with many Arabic words.

EXERCISE 11

شاید فردا بیاید — سال آینده میخواهم بتهران بروم — امروز نمیتواند بیاید ولی شاید فردا بتواند بیاید — تا اینرا نبینم باور نمیکنم — میخواست این باغرا بفروشد ولی نشد — صبر میکنیم تا بیائید — فردا آفتاب نزده باید راه بیفتیم — پس از چهار روز دیگر میخواهد برود — پریروز سه نفر مرد در شهر کشته شدند — امسال باران خیلی کم آمده است — روز دو شنبه دو سه ساعت در شهر گشتیم — نمیتوانم صبر کنم تا بیاید — ساعت شما باید خراب باشد زیراکه نیم ساعت عقب است — با اینکه میخواستم اورا ببینم نمیتوانستم صبر کنم تا بیاید — ساعتهای کاررا زیاد کردند تا قوه تولید کارخانه بیشتر شود — صادرات این مملکت بیشتر مواد زراعتی است تا صنعتی — صادرات این مملکت عبارت است از گندم و پشم و خشکبار و وارداتش بیشتر عبارت است از قند و چای و قماش و ماشین آلات

EXERCISE 12*a*

1. As long as the children are here you must stay. 2. In spite of the fact that he wanted to go, he was unable to do so. 3. It is impossible to go. 4. He ought to have gone yesterday. 5. She must go to see her children the day after tomorrow. 6. I shall not come unless you write to me. 7. He was summoned by his father. 8. He could not come earlier than this. 9. He must have gone before us. 10. We ought to have gone the day before yesterday. 11. He wanted to write to his brother. 12. It will be night by the time you arrive home. 13. There was a severe storm yesterday. 14. I gave him my book to read. 15. He wants to see you.

EXERCISE 12*b*

1. The exports of this country consist of agricultural goods. 2. The standard of living of the country must be raised. 3. I must go now because it is late. 4. The production of this factory has decreased. 5. Although we had (ate) breakfast very late, I am hungry. 6. Although he was tired, he remained in the town with his brother until after midnight. 7. It rained a great deal yesterday and there was a severe storm in the early morning. 8. The merchant opened a business in the town; he wants to import industrial goods and to export dried fruits and wool.

9. There was nobody in the room when I came in. 10. I have never seen him but I should like to know him. 11. Perhaps he has gone; he was getting (himself) ready half an hour ago. 12. Last summer I used to go for a walk every day. 13. I shall not allow you to go. 14. It is impossible to read this. 15. Where were you going this morning?

LESSON VII

Adverbs.[1] Conditional Sentences. The Causative.

1. There are no formally distinct adverbs in Persian but certain words correspond in use to the English adverb. These are mainly nouns, or words which were formerly used as nouns, and nouns combined with prepositions. Many adjectives are also used as adverbs.

آری *ari*, yes (this is often pronounced *are*).[2]

نه *na*, no (not normally used alone in polite speech).

نخیر *naxeir*, no.

چرا *cera*, why; yes.

هم *ham*, also (used also as an emphatic particle, see note to Lesson IV, para. 17).

با هم *ba ham*, together.

نیز *niz*, also.

خیلی *xeili* }
بسیار *besyar* } very.[3]

تنها *tanha*, alone.

چند *cand*, how much.

چندین *candin* }
چندان *candan* } so much; (with negative verb) not very.

زیاد *ziad*, much, too; (with negative verb) not very, not much.

اکنون *aknun*, now.

هرگز *hargez*, ever; (with negative verb) never.

[1] See also Part II, Lesson XXI, paras. 16–18.

[2] بله *bale* is more frequently used for 'yes' in polite conversation.

[3] See also Lesson V, para. 18.

همیشه *hamiʃe*
همواره *hamvare* } always.

فرو *foru*
فرود *forud* } down.

بس *bas*, very (used to intensify Adjectives), e.g.

مقامی بس ارجمند دارد *maqami bas arjmand darad*, He has a very exalted position.

و بس *va bas* means 'nothing more, only', e.g.

این کاررا کردم و بس *in karra kardam va bas*, I did this and nothing more.[1]

هنوز *hanuz*, still, yet; (with negative verb) not yet.

چه *ce*, how, e.g.

چه خوش گفت فردوسی *ce xoʃ goft ferdou͡si*, How well spoke Ferdousi.

بارها *barha*, often (from بار *bar* 'time').

اینجا *inja*, here.

آنجا *anja*, there.

کجا *koja*, where (interrog.).

اینطور *in tou͡r*, thus, in this way.

آنطور *an tou͡r*, thus, in that way.

چطور *ce tou͡r*, how.

اینگونه *ingune*, thus, in this way.

آنگونه *angune*, thus, in that way.

چگونه *cegune*, how.

آنگاه *angah*, then.

گاهی *gahi*, sometimes.

گاه گاهی *gah gahi*, sometimes, from time to time.

گاه بگاه *gah be gah*, from time to time.

ناگاه *nagah*, suddenly.

بخودی خود *be xodiye xod*, involuntarily.

[1] بس *bas* used as a noun means 'enough', e.g.

باو بس دادید *be u bas dadid*, You gave him enough.

کمابیش *kamabiʃ*, کم و بیش *kam o biʃ*, more or less.
هر آینه (آئینه) *har ayene (aine)*, in any case; assuredly.
روی هم رفته *ruye ham rafte*, altogether, on the whole.
دست کم *daste kam*, at least.
گویا *guya*,[1] apparently, perhaps, e.g.

گویا این مال شماست *guya in male ʃomast*, It seems this is yours.

بالا *bala*, above.[2]
پائین *pain*, below.[3]
کم *kam*, seldom.
دور *dur*, far.
تند *tond*, quickly.
خوب *xub*, well.
سخت *saxt*, strictly, severely; very (used to intensify an adjective), e.g.

سخت مریض است *saxt mariz̧ ast*, He is very ill.

پر *por*, very (used to intensify an adjective), e.g.

این پر گران است *in por geran ast*, This is very expensive.

پیوسته *peivaste*, continually.[4]

Adjectives formed by the suffixes ه *-e*, ینه *-ine* and انه *-ane* are frequently used as adverbs, e.g.

هر ساله *har sale*, annually (every year).
پنجروزه *panjruz̧e*, in or for five days.
روزینه *ruz̧ine*, daily.[5]
عاقلانه *aqelane*, intelligently, wisely.

[1] This is apparently a verbal adjective, see Lesson x, para. 6 (*a*).

[2] Used as an adjective بالا *bala* means 'upper', e.g.

طبقه بالا *tabaqeye bala*, the upper storey.

[3] Used as an adjective پائین *pain* means 'lower', e.g.

طبقه پائین *tabaqeye pain*, the lower storey.

[4] پیوسته *peivaste* is the past participle of پیوستن *peivastan* 'to join'.

[5] The modern usage is روزانه *ruz̧ane*.

Many abstract nouns (see Lesson X, para. 1) are combined with the preposition به *be* and used as adverbs, e.g.

باسانی *be asani*, easily (from آسانی *asani*, ease).

بخوبی *be xubi*, well (from خوبی *xubi*, goodness).

2. 'As (in the capacity of)' is expressed by بعنوان *be envan* with the *ezafe*, e.g.

بعنوان نماینده دولت آمد *be envane namayandeye dŏulat amad*, He came as the government's representative.

'As...as possible' is rendered by هر چه *har ce* with the comparative adjective, e.g.

هر چه زودتر *har ce zudtar*, as quickly as possible.

هر چه تمامتر *har ce tamamtar*, as completely as possible.

هر چه تمامتر *har ce tamamtar* is also used as follows:

با خوشحالی هر چه تمامتر *ba xoʃhaliye har ce tamamtar*, with the greatest possible happiness.

3. Stress in the forms given in para. 1 above is carried on the final syllable in the majority of cases.

The following carry the stress on the initial syllable:

آره *are*, yes.

چرا *cera*, why?

گاهی *gahi*, sometimes.

هر آینه (آئینه) *har ayene (aine)*, in any case.

In compounds formed with طور *tŏur* and گونه *gune* the stress is carried on the first component, e.g.

چطور *'ce tŏur*, how.

آنگونه *'angune*, thus.

The following carry the stress on the initial or final syllable:

نخیر *naxĕir*, no.

خیلی *xĕili*, very.

کجا *koja*, where?

4. Adverbs or adverbial phrases denoting time normally precede other adverbs or adverbial phrases. Adverbs or adverbial phrases of manner usually precede those of place, e.g.

دیروز ساعت ده با اسب بشهر آمد *diruz̤ sa'ate dah ba asb be ʃahr amad*, Yesterday at ten o'clock he came on horseback to the town.

5. Conditional Sentences are introduced by اگر *agar* 'if'. The protasis normally precedes the apodosis.

(*a*) Possible Conditions. (i) Possible Conditions which refer to the future take the present or future in the apodosis and the Subjunctive Present in the protasis, e.g.

اگر بروید من هم میروم *agar beravid man ham miravam*, If you go, I shall go also.

If the action in the 'if clause' is a single action and precedes the action in the main clause, the preterite can be used in the 'if clause', e.g.

اگر آمد باو بگوئید *agar amad be u beguid*, If he comes tell him.

See also Lesson XIII, paras. 5 (*c*), 5 (*e*) and 9 (*e*).

(ii) Possible conditions which refer to the present in the protasis, i.e. to an action which may be actually taking place, or to a state which may be actually in existence, take the Indicative Present in the protasis and the Indicative Present or Future in the apodosis, e.g.

اگر کتاب خودرا میخواند چیزی باو نخواهم گفت *agar ketabe xodra mixanad ciz̤i be u naxaham goft*, If he is reading his book I shall not say anything to him.

If, however, the verb بودن *budan* is used in the protasis of a conditional sentence of this type, it is usual to use the Subjunctive Present, e.g.

اگر مریض باشد نخواهد آمد *agar mariz̤ baʃad naxahad amad*, If he is ill he will not come.

(iii) Possible Conditions referring to past time in the protasis and present or future in the apodosis take the Subjunctive Past in the protasis and the present or future in the apodosis, e.g.

اگر نرفته باشد باو میگویم *agar narafte baʃad be u miguyam*, If he has not gone I will tell him.

اگر اورا دیده باشید کافی است *agar ura dide bafid kafist*, If you have seen him it is enough.

اگر کتابرا گم کرده باشید یکی دیگر میخرم *agar ketabra gom karde bafid yaki digar mixaram*, If you have lost the book I will buy another.

(*b*) Impossible Conditions, whether relating to the past or present, take the Imperfect in both parts, e.g.

اگر میتوانستم میامدم *agar mitavanestam miamadam*, I would have come if I could; if I could come I would (but I cannot).

اگر زودتر میرفتید میرسیدید *agar zudtar miraftid mirasidid*, If you had gone earlier you would have arrived (in time).

اگر جوان بودم[1] میرفتم *agar javan budam miraftam*, If I had been young I would have gone; I would go if I was young (but I am not).

The Pluperfect can be used in either or both parts instead of the Imperfect in Impossible Conditions relating to the past, e.g.

اگر تفنگ داشت[2] مرا کشته بود *agar tofang daft mara kofte bud*, If he had had a gun he would have killed me.

اگر ارزان بود[1] خریده بودم *agar arzan bud xaride budam*, If it had been cheap I would have bought it.

اگر پائیز میامدید هنوز نرفته بودیم *agar paiz miamadid hanuz narafte budim*, If you had come in the autumn we would still have been there (we should not yet have gone).

If شاید *fayad* 'perhaps' is introduced into the main sentence, the tense is not affected, e.g.

اگر آنجا میرفتید شاید اورا میدیدید *agar anja miraftid fayad ura mididid*, If you had gone there, perhaps you would have seen him.

See also Lesson XIII, para. 27.

[1] بودن *budan* does not take می *mi-* in the Imperfect, see Lesson III, para. 8.

[2] داشتن *daftan* does not take می *mi-* in the Imperfect, see Lesson III, para. 7.

6. 'But if not', 'or else', 'otherwise' are rendered by و اگر نه *va agar na* or و الا *va ella*, e.g.

اگر ممکن باشد میروم و اگر نه اینجا میمانم

agar momken bašad miravam va agar na inja mimanam,
If it is possible I shall go, but if not I shall stay here.

باید اینرا بخورید و الا گرسنه میمانید

bayad inra bexorid va ella gorosne mimanid,
You must eat this or else you will be (remain) hungry.

7. چنانچه *conance* is also used as a conditional conjunction, e.g.

چنانچه مایل باشید میتوانید بیائید *conance mayel bašid mitavanid beyaid*, If you care (to come) you can come.

چنانچه جویای حال ما باشید بد نیستیم *conance juyaye hale ma bašid bad nistim*, If you want to know how we are (are inquiring of our state), we are well.

چنانچه کاری ندارید با ما بیائید *conance kari nadarid ba ma beyaid*, If you have no work, come with us.

هرگاه *hargah* 'whenever' is also used as a conditional conjunction = 'if', e.g.

هرگاه اورا دیدید سلام مرا برسانید *hargah ura didid salame mara berasanid*, If (whenever) you see him remember me (to him).

هرگاه مسافرت کنید یادی از ما بکنید *hargah mosaferat konid yadi az ma bekonid*, If (whenever) you go on a journey, think of us.

که *ke* is also used occasionally to mean 'if' when referring to the future and is followed by the Indicative Present, e.g.

این پولرا که باو میدهیم از دستمان میرود *in pulra ke be u midehim az dasteman miravad*, If we give him this money it will be lost to us.

8. The infinitive of the Causative is formed by the addition of انیدن *-anidan* or اندن *-andan* to the present stem of the verb, e.g.

رسانیدن *rasanidan*, رساندن *rasandan*, to cause to arrive, transmit (from رسیدن *rasidan* 'to arrive').

جوشانیدن *juſanidan*, جوشاندن *juſandan* to boil (trans.) (from جوشیدن *juſidan* to boil (intrans.)).

In Colloquial Persian the causative in اندن *-andan* tends to be used rather than the form in انیدن *-anidan*. نشستن *neſastan* 'to sit down' forms its causative irregularly thus: نشاندن *neſandan* 'to cause to sit down, to seat'.

Verbs the Present Stem of which ends in ان *an*, such as ماندن *mandan* 'to remain', cannot form a Causative.

9. Possibility is expressed by such expressions as ممکن است *momken ast* 'it is possible', or احتمال دارد *ehtemal darad* 'it is probable'. 'May' is normally translated by ممکن است *momken ast* followed by the Subjunctive Present with or without که *ke*.

Vocabulary

فکر *fekr*, thinking, thought; فکر کردن *fekr k.*, to think.

سر وقت *sare vaqt*, on time, punctually.

وقتیکه *vaqtike*, when.

درس *dars*, lesson; درس خواندن *dars xandan*, to take a lesson, have lessons, study.

حال *hal*, state, condition.

مسافرت *mosaferat*, journey.

کشتی *kaſti*, ship; با کشتی *ba kaſti*, by ship.

اقامت *eqamat*, residence, sojourn.

پایتخت *pâitaxt*, capital city.

طبقه *tabaqe*, class (of people, etc.); storey (of building).

مقام *maqam*, place; rank, position.

کوه *kuh*, mountain.

رودخانه *rudxane*, river.

دریا *darya*, sea.

قصبه *qasabe*, small town.

ممکن *momken*, possible.

قدری *qadri*, a little.

ارجمند *arjmand*, exalted, high.

طولانی *tulani*, long, lengthy.

مختصر *moxtasar*, brief.

مدید *madid*, lengthy (of time).

قشنگ *qaſang*, beautiful.

خوش *xoʃ*, happy.
خوشی *xoʃi*, happiness.
آسان *asan*, easy.
آسانی *asani*, ease.
تفنگ *tofang*, gun, rifle.
تمام *tamam*, whole, complete; تمام کردن *tamam k.*, to complete, finish.
لازم *lazem*, necessary; لازم داشتن *lazem daʃtan*, to need.
مدرسه *madrase*, school.
قد *qadd*, stature.
بلند قد *boland qadd*, tall (of person).
کوتاه قد *kutah qadd*, short (of person).
مؤدب *mo'addab*, polite.
روان *ravan*, flowing, fluent.
تنبل *tambal*, lazy.
تنبلی *tambali*, laziness; تنبلی کردن *tambali k.*, to be lazy.
حالا *hala*, now.
هرگاه *hargah*, whenever.
هرجا *harja*, wherever, everywhere.
هم *ham*, also.
اگرچه *agarce*, although.
نشستن (نشین) *neʃastan (neʃin)*, to sit.
نشان *neʃan*, sign, badge; نشان دادن *neʃan dadan*, to show.
گم *gom*, lost; گم کردن *gom k.*, to lose.
سعی *saʿi*, effort; سعی کردن *saʿi k.*, to try, strive.[1]
سلام *salam*, greeting.
یاد *yad*, memory, mind.
حرف زدن *harf zadan*, to speak.

Exercise 13

پایتخت این مملکت شهر بزرگی است — اگر خواهر مرا دیدید این نامه‌را باو بدهید — اگر زودتر میامدید شمارا آنجا میبردم — وقتیکه همراه خواهر و برادر خود بشهر میرفت مارا دید — ایران کوههای زیاد دارد — با سعی هرچه تمامتر درس میخواند — اگر زودتر راه افتاده بودیم این قدر دیر نمیرسیدیم — امسال باران هنوز نیامده است — شاید رفته باشد — اینرا باید از خواهر خودتان بپرسید — اگر منزل باشد از او میپرسم — باید آمده باشد — اگر فردا هوا خوب باشد بشهر میرویم — اگر این کتابرا خوانده باشید دیگر لازم ندارید — این پسر پیوسته درس میخواند همیشه زود در مدرسه حاضر میشود بسیار خوب درس میخواند و هرگز تنبلی نمیکند بیشتر کار میکند و کمتر حرف میزند با همه مؤدب است و همواره سعی میکند درس خودرا خوب روان کند

[1] See Introduction, Alphabetical Table, under ع.

EXERCISE 14*a*

1. If you go into the town buy me a little tea and coffee. 2. If your brother goes home he will take you with him. 3. It would have been better if you had gone last week. 4. They went to Persia by sea but they returned by land. 5. If I go tomorrow will you come with me? 6. There are many small towns and villages in this country. 7. If it is cold tonight it may freeze. 8. If it snows heavily the road may be closed. 9. This is worth at least twenty *rials*. 10. We go every year to the capital. 11. When I saw him he was walking quickly in the garden. 12. If you had come a fortnight ago the summer would not yet have been over.

EXERCISE 14*b*

1. He did not allow us to go together. 2. I said this to him and nothing more. 3. Altogether it was not a bad book. 4. He suddenly got up and went out of the room. 5. He is given a certain amount of money every week. 6. We used to go to the town every year and stay there two months. 7. Persia consists chiefly of mountain and desert. 8. There are two hundred and fifty children in the school and all of them are under fifteen years of age. 9. I will come with you so that you do not get lost. 10. Let us sit down here because I am tired. 11. If you want to arrive punctually you had better go now (it is better that you go now). 12. You must go or you will be late.

LESSON VIII

Conjunctions.[1] Relative Clauses. هر *har*. چنانکه *conanke* and چنینکه *coninke*. چنانچه *conance* and چنینچه *conince*. Indefinite Nouns and Pronouns.

1. Conjunctions can be divided into two main classes: co-ordinating conjunctions and subordinating conjunctions.

(*a*) Co-ordinating Conjunctions, e.g.

آیا . . . یا *aya . . . ya*, whether . . . or (interrog.).

چه . . . چه *ce . . . ce* } whether . . . or.
خواه . . . خواه *xah . . . xah* }

[1] See also Part II, Lesson XXI, paras. 19–21.

هم...(و)هم *ham...(va) ham*, both...and.

نه...(و)نه *na...(va) na*, neither...nor.

مگر[1] *magar*, but (used with a negative question expecting the answer 'yes' or with an affirmative question expecting the answer 'no'), e.g.

مگر اینطور نیست *magar in tour nist*, But is it not so?

مگر نرفتید *magar naraftid*, But did you not go?

مگر آنجا بودید *magar anja budid*, But were you there?

(*b*) Subordinating Conjunctions. These can be subdivided into

(i) Adversative, e.g.

مبادا (که) *mabada (ke)*, lest.

(ii) Conditional, e.g.

اگر *agar*, if.

هرگاه *hargah*, if.

که *ke*, if.

چنانچه *conance*, if.

مگر (اینکه) *magar (inke)*, unless.

بدون اینکه *bedune inke*, unless (without this that)

تا *ta*, unless.

(iii) Concessive, e.g.

با اینکه (آنکه) *ba inke (anke)*, in spite of the fact that, notwithstanding that.

هرچند (که) *har cand (ke)*, even if, however much, although.

چنانچه *conance*, as, lest.

چندانکه *candanke*, notwithstanding that.

اگرچه *agarce*, although, even if.

If a concessive clause is introduced by اگرچه *agarce* the main clause is sometimes introduced by some such word as ولی *vali* 'but' or باز *baz* 'still', or with a negative verb by هنوز *hanuz*, e.g.

[1] In Classical Persian مگر *magar* is also used in story-telling = 'now, now it happened that'.

اگرچه مدتی با او زندگی کرده‌ام هنوز اورا نمیشناسم
agarce moddati ba u ȥendegi karde am hanuȥ ura namiʃenasam,
Although I lived with him for a (long) time, I do not know him.

اگرچه دیر وقت بود باز بمنزل برگشتیم
agarce dir vaqt bud baȥ be manȥel bar gaʃtim,
Although it was late we returned home.

(iv) Causal, e.g.

چون (که)	*cun (ke)*	because.
چه	*ce*	
زیرا (که)	*ȥira (ke)*	
از اینکه	*aȥ inke*	
که	*ke*	

(v) Final, e.g.

که *ke*, that, in order that.

تا	*ta*	in order that.
تا اینکه	*ta inke*	

(vi) Consecutive, e.g.

آنقدر...که	*an qadr...ke*	so...that, e.g.
چنان...که	*conan...ke*	

اوقاتش چنان تلخ شد که نتوانست حرف بزند
ōuqateʃ conan talx ʃod ke natavanest harf beȥanad,
He was so angry he could not speak.

از بس که *aȥ bas ke*, so long, so much...that, e.g.

از بس که گفتم خسته شدم *aȥ bas ke goftam xaste ʃodam*, I have said (it) so much that I am tired.

از بس که نشستم خوابم میبرد *aȥ bas ke neʃastam xabam mibarad*, I have sat so long I am sleepy.

(vii) Temporal, e.g.

تا *ta*, as long as, until, by the time that, since, as soon as.

تا اینکه (آنکه) *ta inke (anke)*, as long as, by the time that; until.

چون *cun*, when.

از موقعیکه *aȥ mōuqe'ike*, since (from the time that).

پس از آنکه (اینکه) *pas az anke* (*inke*), after.
پیش از آنکه (اینکه) *pif az anke* (*inke*), before.
هرگاه *hargah*, whenever.
همینکه *haminke*, as soon as.
که *ke*, when.
وقتیکه *vaqtike*, when.
موقعیکه *mõuqe'ike*, when, as.

The subject of the temporal clause precedes که *ke* 'when', e.g.

زمستان که میشود میرویم *zamestan ke mifavad miravim*, When it is winter we will go.

(viii) Comparative, e.g.

که *ke*, than, e.g.

بقدریکه *be qadrike*, as much as, e.g.

بقدریکه شما خوانده‌اید من نخوانده‌ام *be qadrike foma xande id man naxande am*, I have not read as much as you.

اینقدر (آنقدر)... که *in qadr* (*an qadr*)...*ke*, as much...as, e.g.

هیچ وقت اینقدر حرف نمیزد که امشب حرف زد

hic vaqt in qadr harf namizad ke emfab harf zad,

He never used to speak as much as he spoke to-night.

2. Final Conjunctions take the Subjunctive Present (see Lesson VI, para. 17 (*a*). تا *ta* 'by the time that' and تا *ta* 'until' referring to future time also take the Subjunctive Present (see Lesson VI, para. 17 (*b*) and (*c*)).

مبادا (که) *mabada* (*ke*) 'lest' takes the subjunctive, e.g.

ترسیدم مبادا فراموش کرده باشید *tarsidam mabada faramuf karde bafid*, I feared (lest) you had forgotten.

میترسم مبادا فراموش بکند *mitarsam mabada faramuf bekonad*, I fear (lest) he may forget.

مگر اینکه *magar inke* 'unless' and بدون اینکه *bedune inke* 'unless' also take the Subjunctive except in impossible conditions when they are followed by the Imperfect or Pluperfect.

نمیایم مگر اینکه بمن بنویسید *namiayam magar inke be man benevisid*, I shall not come unless you write to me.

پیش از آنکه (اینکه) *piʃ az anke (inke)* 'before' takes the Subjunctive Present even when referring to time past, e.g.

پیش از آنکه اورا ببینم کاغذرا نوشتم *piʃ az anke ura bebinam kaɣazra neveʃtam*, I wrote the letter before I saw him.

بجای اینکه *bejaye inke* 'instead of (this that)', its synonym درعوض اینکه *dar avaze inke*, and جز اینکه *joz inke* and غیر از اینکه *ɣeır az inke* 'except' are also followed by Present Subjunctive.

Other conjunctions, except Conditional Conjunctions,[1] are followed by the Indicative or Subjunctive according to whether the statement is one of fact or contains an element of doubt. Thus خواه...خواه *xah... xah* 'whether...or' referring to the future takes the Subjunctive, e.g.

خواه بیاید خواه نیاید میروم *xah beyayad xah nayayad miravam*, Whether he comes or not I shall go.

Clauses introduced by Conditional, Concessive, Consecutive or Temporal Conjunctions normally precede the principal sentence. Clauses introduced by Adversative, Causal (except از اینکه *az inke*) and Final Conjunctions follow the principal sentence.

3. Stress falls on the initial syllable of the following conjunctions:

مگر *magar*, but, unless.
هرچند (که) *har cand (ke)*, even if.
مبادا (که) *mabada (ke)*, lest.
هرگاه *hargah*, whenever.
اگرچه *agarce*, although.
چون (که) *cun (ke)* } because.
زیرا (که) *zira (ke)* } because.
چرا (که) *cera (ke)* } because.
همینکه *haminke*, as soon as.
چندانکه *candanke*, not withstanding that.

In the case of اگر *agar* 'if' it falls on the initial or final syllable.
In the following it falls on the initial syllable or on این *in* or آن *an*:

با اینکه (آنکه) *ba inke (anke)*, notwithstanding.
تا اینکه (آنکه) *ta inke (anke)*, until, etc.

[1] See Lesson VII, paras. 5–7 above.

پیش از آنکه (اینکه) *piʃ az anke (inke)*, before.

پس از آنکه (اینکه) *pas az anke (inke)*, after.

In از بس که *az bas ke* 'so long' stress falls on بس *bas*.

4. تا *ta* is also used to mean 'let us see, behold, beware, namely' and is usually followed by the Subjunctive Present. This use of تا *ta* is common in Classical Persian especially in poetry, e.g.

ببین تا چه بازی کند روزگار

bebin ta ce bazi konad ruzgar,

See (let us see) what tricks time will play.

عمر گرانمایه در این صرف شد * تا چه خورم صیف و چه پوشم شتا

omre geranmaye dar in sarf ʃod ta ce xoram sei͡f o ce puʃam ʃeta,

(My) precious life was spent in this, namely (in thinking) what shall I eat in summer and what shall I wear in winter.

ای که شخص منت حقیر نمود * تا درشتی هنر نپنداری

e͡i ke ʃaxse manat haqir namud ta doroʃti honar napandari,

O thou to whom my person appeared contemptible, beware lest thou consider size (largeness) virtue.

5. Relative Clauses are introduced by the Relative Pronoun که *ke* 'who, which'. ی *-i* is added to the antecedent if definite unless this is a proper noun, a personal pronoun, a singular demonstrative pronoun,[1] a word doing duty for a pronoun,[2] a word to which a pronominal suffix has been added, a plural which is not particularized, or a noun used generically (see para. 12 below), e.g.

مردیکه آنجا بود کتابرا بمن داد *mardi ke anja bud ketabra beman dad*, The man who was there gave me the book.

If the antecedent is qualified by an adjective or adjectives these with the antecedent are regarded as a syntactical whole and the Relative ی *-i* is added to the final qualifying word, e.g.

دختر کوچکیکه پیش شما بود کی بود *doxtare kuceki ke piʃe ʃoma bud ki bud*, Who was the small girl who was with you?

[1] See below, para. 13.

[2] E.g. بنده *bande* 'slave', which is used for the Personal Pronoun 1st pers. sing. (see Lesson XIV, para. 1 (*a*) below).

If the word to which the Relative ی *-i* is added ends in ا *a*, و *u*, or ه *e* it follows the same rules when the Relative ی *-i* is added as when the Indefinite ی *-i* is added, see Lesson I, para. 2.

6. If the antecedent is definite and the direct object of the verb of the principal sentence, and the relative pronoun is the subject of the relative clause, the use of را *-ra* is optional. The Demonstrative Pronoun آن *an* frequently qualifies the antecedent, e.g.

آن زنیرا که دیروز آمد دیدم *an zanira ke diruz amad didam*, I saw the woman who came yesterday,

or آن زنیکه دیروز آمد دیدم *an zani ke diruz amad didam.*

7. If the antecedent is definite and the subject of the principal sentence and the relative pronoun is the direct object in the relative clause, the antecedent can take را *-ra*; this, again, is optional, e.g.

زنیرا که دیدید اینجاست *zanira ke didid injast*, The woman whom you saw is here,

or زنی که دیدید اینجاست *zani ke didid injast.*

کتابیرا که بمن دادید گم شده است *ketabira ke be man dadid gom ʃode ast*, The book which you gave me is lost,

or کتابی که بمن دادید گم شده است *ketabi ke be man dadid gom ʃode ast.*

8. If the relative pronoun is the indirect object of the relative clause or governed by a preposition, a pronoun or pronominal suffix must be used in the relative clause in addition to the Relative که *ke*, e.g.

مردهائیکه کتابهارا بآنها داده بودید رفتند *mardhai ke ketabhara be anha dade budid raftand*, The men to whom you gave the books went.

این همان مردیست که اسبی از او خریدم *in haman mardist ke asbi az u xaridam*, This is the (same) man from whom I bought a horse.

این همان شخصی‌است که دیروز برادر شما با او بود *in haman ʃaxsist ke diruz baradare ʃoma ba u bud*, This is the same person with whom your brother was yesterday.

9. If the antecedent is the predicate of the principal sentence, the verb of the principal sentence precedes the Relative که *ke* (see the last two examples in para. 8 above).

10. Since ی *-i* is added to the antecedent where this is definite, it follows that there will be a confusion between a definite antecedent followed by the Relative که *ke* and an indefinite antecedent to which the Indefinite ی *-i* has been already added, and that therefore پسریکه *pesari ke*...may mean 'the boy who' or 'a boy who'.

11. A distinction is made between 'descriptive' and 'restrictive' relative clauses. The latter type is closely linked to the antecedent in thought, whereas the former, while in a formal sense a dependent clause, does not limit the application of the antecedent, so that it is logically an independent proposition. In a 'descriptive' relative clause the relative pronoun که *ke* only is used, e.g.

مؤلف که نویسنده خوبی‌است این سبکرا اختیار کرده‌است

mo'allef ke nevisandeye xubist in sabkra exteyar karde ast,

The author, who is a good writer, has chosen this style.

12. If the antecedent is a plural which refers to a class or group as a whole, the Relative ی *-i* is not added to the antecedent, e.g.

باعتماد حسن ظن سیاستمداران جهان که در حل اینگونه مسائل تجربه زیاد دارند موضوعرا مطرح میکنیم

be e'temade hosne zanne siasatmadarane jahan ke dar halle ingune masa'el tajrebeye ziad darand mouzu'ra matrah mikonim.

Trusting in the good-will of the statesmen of the world, who have (had) much experience in solving such problems, we are bringing up the matter.

If the Relative ی *-i* were added to the antecedent in the above example, the meaning would be '...to those of the statesmen of the world who have...'.

Similarly if the antecedent is an abstract noun used generically, it does not take the Relative ی *-i*, e.g.

عقل که انسان بدان بر حیوان برتری دارد نعمت بزرگیست

aql ke ensan bedan bar heivan bartari darad ne'mate bozorgist.

Reason, by which man has superiority over animals, is a great gift.

When not used generically abstract nouns take the Relative ی *-i* unless they end in ی *-i*, in which case the Relative ی *-i* is not added, e.g.

عقلیکه دارید ناقص است *aqli ke darid naqes ast*, Your reason (the reason which you have) is defective.

مهربانیرا[1] که بمن نشان دادید فراموش نمیکنم *mehrabanira ke be man neʃan dadid faramuʃ namikonam*, I shall not forget the kindness which you showed me.

13. The Relative ی *-i* is sometimes added to the Demonstrative Pronouns آنها *anha* 'those' and اینها *inha* 'these', e.g.

آنهائیکه آنجا بودند رفتند *anhai ke anja budand raftand*, Those who were there went.

Other Pronouns do not take the Relative ی *-i*, e.g.

شما که آنجا بودید بما بگوئید چه دیدید *ʃoma ke anja budid be ma beguid ce didid*, You, who were there, tell us what you saw.

In Colloquial Persian the Relative ی *-i* can be added to the personal pronouns; thus in the preceding example it would be possible to say شمائی که *ʃomai ke*... instead of شما که *ʃoma ke*.

In Colloquial Persian, also, the plural termination ها *-ha* can be added to the 1st and 2nd pers. pl. of the personal pronouns with the Relative ی *-i* to single out a group, e.g.

شماهائی که آنجا بودید چه دیدید *ʃomahai ke anja budid ce didid*, Those of you who were there, what did you see?

14. After آن *an* 'that' and این *in* 'this' چه *ce* is used as a Relative Pronoun, e.g.

از آنچه گفته شد معلوم میشود *az ance gofte ʃod maʿlum miʃavad*, It is (will be) evident from what has been said.

15. The Relative ی *-i* and the Relative Pronouns که *ke* and چه *ce* do not carry the stress.

[1] مهربانی *mehrabani*, kindness.

16. خود *xod*, خویش *xiʃ* and خویشتن *xiʃtan* used in a relative clause refer to the subject of that clause and not to the subject of the principal sentence, e.g.

حسین نامه‌ای بمن داد که علی بپدر خود نوشته بود

hosein namei be man dad ke ali be pedare xod neveʃte bud.

Hosein gave me a letter which Ali had written to his (Ali's) father.

حسین نامه‌ای بمن داد که علی بپدرش نوشته بود

hosein namei be man dad ke ali be pedaraʃ neveʃte bud.

Hosein gave me a letter which Ali had written to his (Hosein's) father.

17. هر *har* 'every' is a distributive adjective which precedes the noun it qualifies. Prefixed to چه *ce*, که *ke* and کدام *kodam*, it means 'whatever', 'whoever' and 'whichever' respectively, e.g.

هرکه میخواهد بیاید زود بیاید *har ke mixahad beyayad zud beyayad*, Whoever wants to come must be quick (let him be quick).

هرکدام از شما حاضر است برود *har kodam az ʃoma hazer ast beravad*, Whichever of you is ready can go (let him go).

هرچه کرد نتوانست دررا باز کند *har ce kard natavanest darra baz konad*, Whatever he did he could not open the door.

هرچه *har ce* also means 'however much', e.g.

هرچه گشتم اورا پیدا نکردم *har ce gaʃtam ura peida nakardam*, However much I looked I did not find him.

هرکس *har kas* means 'anyone', e.g.

هر کسی که بیاید اورا بنشانید *har kasi ke beyayad ura beneʃanid*, Make whoever comes sit down.

هرکسیکه اینرا میداند بگوید *har kasi ke inra midanad beguyad*, Let anyone who knows this speak.

هر دو *har do* means 'both', e.g.

هر دوشان رفتند *har doeʃan raftand*, They both went.

هرسه *har se*, هر چهار *har cahar*, etc., mean 'all three', 'all four', etc.

18. The Relative Pronoun که *ke* is suffixed to the Demonstratives چنان *conan* and چنین *conin* to mean 'just as, in the same way that, in this way that'.

19. چه *ce* is suffixed to چنان *conan* to mean 'just as, in the same way that, in case'.

20. There are a number of indefinite nouns, pronouns and adjectives in use. Among them are the following:

(*a*) همه *hame* 'all', e.g.

همه رفتند *hame raftand*, All went.

همه شما بیائید *hameye ʃoma beyaid*, All of you come.

همه‌کس *hame kas* means 'everyone'.

If the Pronominal Suffix for the 3rd pers. sing. is added to همه *hame* the *e* of *hame* is elided, e.g.

باغ همه‌اش سبز بود *baɣ hamaʃ sabz bud*, The whole garden was green (the garden, the whole of it, was green).

(*b*) تمام *tamam* 'the whole, whole, complete', e.g.

تمام روز در شهر بود *tamame ruz dar ʃahr bud*, He was the whole day in the town.

آنرا تمام خورد *anra tamam xord*, He ate it all (wholly).

با خوشی تمام بیرون رفت *ba xoʃiye tamam birun raft*, He went out completely happy (with complete happiness).

(*c*) سائر *sa'er* (also written سایر and pronounced *sayer*) 'the rest', e.g.

سائر کتابهارا فروخت *sa'ere ketabhara foruxt*, He sold the rest of the books.

(*d*) فلان *folan* means 'such a one, such and such, so-and-so' and is used as a noun or adjective, e.g.

فلان کس آمد *folan kas amad*, Such and such a person came.

The Indefinite ی *-i* can be added to فلان *folan* when it is used as a noun, e.g.

فلانی آمد *folani amad*, So-and-so came.

(*e*) بعضی *ba'zi* means 'some'. It precedes the noun it qualifies, which is put in the plural, and does not take the *ezafe*, e.g.

بعضی کتابها *ba'zi ketabha*, some books.

در بعضی جاها *dar ba'zi jaha*, in some places.

It is also used as a noun, e.g.

بعضی رفتند بعضی ماندند *ba'zi raftand ba'zi mandand*, Some went (and) some remained.

When used as a noun بعضی *ba'zi* takes از *az* rather than the *ezafe*, e.g.

بعضی از شما *ba'zi az ʃoma*, some of you.

بعضی از آنها *ba'zi az anha*, some of them.

بعضی از برادران او *ba'zi az baradarane u*, some of his brothers.

In Colloquial Persian the plural termination ها *-ha* is often added to بعضی *ba'zi* when it is used as a noun, e.g.

بعضیها آنجا هستند *ba'ziha anja hastand*, Some are there.

(*f*) برخی *barxi* 'some' is used in the same way as بعضی *ba'zi* above, but it does not take the plural termination ها *-ha*.

(*g*) اندك *andak* means 'a little, few'. It usually precedes the word it qualifies, e.g.

اندك فرصت بمن بدهید *andak forsat be man bedehid*, Give me a little (short) respite.

It can be strengthened by the addition of the Indefinite ی *-i*, e.g.

اندکی فکر کرد *andaki fekr kard*, He thought a little.

(*h*) بس *bas* means 'many a'. It precedes the noun it qualifies, which is put in the singular, e.g.

بس جان بلب آمد *bas jan be lab amad*, Many a soul has passed away.

The Indefinite ی *-i* is added to بس *bas* to mean 'many a'. The following noun is put in the plural, e.g.

بسی مردم *basi mardom* }
بسی اشخاص *basi aʃxas* } many people.

بسی *basi* is also used to mean 'a long while'.

(*i*) The Indefinite ی *-i* is added to بسیار *besyar* to mean 'many'. It is used as a noun and followed by از *az*, e.g.

بسیاری از مردم میگویند *besyari az mardom miguyand*, Many people say.

(*j*) يك خرده *yak xorde* means 'a little', e.g.

يك خرده آب بمن بدهید *yak xorde ab be man bedehid*, Give me a little water.

(*k*) جزئی *joz'i* (from جزء *joz'* 'part, portion') also means 'a little', e.g.

جزئی کسالت دارد *joz'i kesalat darad*, He is slightly indisposed.

Vocabulary

شمال *ʃemal*, *ʃamal*, north (subs.).
جنوب *jonub*, south (subs.).
مغرب *maɣreb*, west (subs.).
مشرق *maʃreq*, east (subs.)
عید *id*, festival, feast-day; عید گرفتن *id gereftan*, to celebrate a festival.
علم *elm*, knowledge.
عیب *eib*, fault.
هنر *honar*, skill; knowledge.
فائده *fa'ede*, benefit.
اندیشه *andiʃe*, thought.
فرق *farq*, difference; فرق کردن *farq k.*, to make a difference.
نوروز *nouruz*, New Year's day (1st Farvardin, which coincides with 20th, 21st or 22nd March).
ییلاق *yeilaq*, summer quarters, hill station.
قشلاق *qeʃlaq*, winter quarters (of a tribe).
مدت *moddat*, period (length of time).
جان *jan*, soul.
جنگ *jang*, war.
صلح *solh*, peace.
ریال *rial*, a unit of currency.
شماره *ʃomare*, number.
مردم *mardom*, people.
روزنامه *ruzname*, newspaper.
مبلغ *mablaɣ*, sum (of money).
حساب *hesab*, account, bill.
بانك *bank*, bank.
نشانی *neʃani*, address.
دفتر *daftar*, office; exercise book.
درد *dard*, pain; بدرد خوردن *be dard xordan*, to be useful; بدرد من نمیخورد *be darde man namixorad*, it is no use to me.
ملایم *molayem*, soft.
معتدل *mo'tadel*, moderate.
تاریك *tarik*, dark.
تاریکی *tariki*, darkness.
روشن *rouʃan*, light, clear.
روشنائی *rouʃanai*, light, clearness.
ملی *melli*, national, popular.
منتشر *montaʃer*, published; منتشر کردن *montaʃer k.*, to publish.
دریافت *daryaft*, receipt (of something).
مرتب *morattab*, orderly, regular.
تحویل *tahvil*, handing over, transfer; تحویل کردن *tahvil k.*, to hand over.
کامل *kamel*, complete, full, perfect.
اتفاق *ettefaq*, happening; اتفاق افتادن *ettefaq oftadan*, to happen, take place.

وزیدن *vazidan* to blow (wind, etc.).
مهربان *mehraban*, kind.
مهربانی *mehrabani*, kindness.
فراموش کردن *faramuʃ kardan*, to forget.
معلوم *ma'lum*, evident, known.
ناقص *naqes*, defective.
پشیمان *paʃiman*, regretful.
آخر *axer*, end; last; finally.
اختیار *exteyar*, freedom of choice.
حرف *harf*, word, speech.
عمل *amal*, action, practice.
مایل بودن *mayel budan*, to desire, be inclined (to).
فرستادن (فرست) *ferestadan* (*ferest*), to send.
اعتماد *e'temad*, confidence; reliance (on).
انسان *ensan*, mankind, man (used generically).
تجربه *tajrebe*, experience.
حسن *hosn*, beauty, goodness; حسن ظن *hosne zann*, good-will.
حل *hall*, solving, solution.
مسئله *mas'ale*, problem (pl. مسائل *masa'el*).
حیوان *heivan*, animal (pl. حیوانات *heivanat*).[1]

سیاست *siasat*, policy; politics; diplomacy.
سیاستمدار *siasatmadar*, statesman.
سبك *sabk*, style.
زیان *zian*, loss, injury; زیان دیدن *zian didan*, to suffer loss.
نصیحت *nasihat*, اندرز *andarz*, advice.
خیر *xeir*, good (noun); خیر خواه *xeirxah*, well-wisher.
وصول *vosul*, arrival, arriving.
عقل *aql*, reason, intelligence.
مطرح کردن *matrah kardan*, to bring up, discuss, debate.
موضوع *mouzu'*, subject, matter.
بر حذر بودن *bar hazar b.*, to be beware.
مراجعت *moraje'at*, return; مراجعت کردن *moraje'at k.*, to return.
آموختن (آموز) *amuxtan* (*amuz*), to learn; teach.
پذیرفتن (پذیر) *paziroftan* (*pazir*), to accept; to entertain.
عاید گردیدن *ayed gardidan*, to accrue.
کسالت *kesalat*, indisposition.

[1] This is an Arabic sound feminine plural (see Part II, Lesson XIX).

Exercise 15

آن کتابیراکه دیروز خریدید بمن نشان بدهید — پسریکه بمنزل ما آمد برادر
آن دختر است — هرکسی که میخواهد بیاید باید زود بیاید — بچه‌هائیکه
همراه او بودند کوچك بودند — آنچه‌را که گفته شد شنید[1] — عید نوروز که در
اول بهار اتفاق می‌افتد بزرگترین عید ملی ایران است — بعضی روزها در تابستان
هوا بسیار گرم میشود — بهار که میشود بیشتر مردم بییلاق میروند — کسانیکه
مایل بدریافت مرتب روزنامه باشند[2] میتوانند مبلغ یك صد و هشتاد ریال برای
مدت یك سال و یك صد ریال برای شش ماه بحساب روزنامه ببانك ملی تحویل
کنند و نشانی کامل خودرا بدفتر روزنامه بنویسند تا هر روزه یك شماره مرتب
فرستاده شود — هرکه عیب دیگران با تو گوید از او بر حذر باش که عیب ترا
نیز بدیگران گوید — تا توانید علم و هنر آموزید که فائده آن بشما عاید گردد —
بسیار فرق باشد از حرف تا عمل — تا مراجعت کنید درسمرا حاضر خواهم کرد —
چه بگوید چه نگوید این کاررا خواهم کرد — چه کردید که اینگونه پشیمان
شدید — اندرز خیرخواهان‌را بپذیرید چه هرکه نصیحت نشنود زیان بیند

Exercise 16

1. This is the man who was here yesterday. 2. He waited for the man whom I had seen in the garden. 3. Perhaps the boy who was in the garden opened the door so that his sister might go in. 4. Last night it was dark when I returned home. 5. He could not come because he was ill. 6. The boy cannot come until his father returns. 7. Notwithstanding the fact that we went early it was dark by the time that we arrived at the town. 8. He thought for a little and then answered. 9. When we arrived everyone (all) had gone. 10. You are so late I feared you had forgotten. 11. Write the letter before you go. 12. I did not stay long (much) after you went home. 13. There is no point in your coming unless you want to come (it has no benefit that you should come unless...). 14. Whenever I go there I want to stay (there).

[1] آنچه *ance* cannot be divided by را *ra*. If را *ra* is used که *ke* must usually be added.

[2] See Lesson XIII, para. 10 for the use of the General Present.

Exercise 17

1. I saw him yesterday after I had seen you. 2. As soon as it rained we returned. 3. I wanted to buy the rest of the books. 4. At (the time of the) New Year, which is the biggest festival of the year in Persia, the people go to see each other and celebrate the holiday for at least five days. 5. If you wish to receive the newspaper regularly you must send 250 rials to the office of the newspaper. 6. If you rely upon their good-will you will be disappointed. 7. If you are unable to come it does not matter. 8. If I knew the solution of this problem I would tell you. 9. He feared that his mother was ill. 10. If you go to Tehran write a letter to me. 11. If he has not gone I will tell him. 12. He forgot to tell you. 13. I should like to come with you to Persia, because I have never been there. 14. In my opinion, it would be better if we discussed the matter now. 15. Whether you go or not makes no difference. 16. This book will be useful to you.

LESSON IX

Compound Verbs

1. Compound verbs are formed by a simple verb combined with a noun, adjective, adverb or prepositional phrase. The following simple verbs are commonly used to form compounds: (کن) کردن *kardan* (*kon*) 'to do, make', (نما) نمودن *namudan* (*nama*) 'to show', (دار) داشتن *daʃtan* (*dar*) 'to have, possess', (ده) دادن *dadan* (*deh*) 'to give', (زن) زدن *zadan* (*zan*) 'to strike', (شو) شدن *ʃodan* (*ʃav-*, *ʃou*) 'to become', (گرد) گشتن *gaʃtan* (*gard*) 'to become', خوردن *xordan* 'to eat', (آ) آمدن *amadan* (*a*) 'to come', کشیدن *kaʃidan* 'to pull, draw', (افت) افتادن *oftadan* (*oft*) 'to fall', (گیر) گرفتن *gereftan* (*gir*) 'to take', (یاب) یافتن *yaftan* (*yab*) 'to find' and (بر) بردن *bordan* (*bar*) 'to take, carry'.

شدن *ʃodan* and گشتن *gaʃtan*, while interchangeable when used to form the Passive Voice (see Lesson VI, para. 4), are not in all cases interchangeable when used to form compound verbs. نمودن *namudan* can usually be substituted for کردن *kardan*.

(*a*) Compound verbs formed by a simple verb[1] and a noun, e.g. (دادن) گوش کردن *guʃ kardan* (*dadan*), to listen.

[1] For the Present Stems of Irregular Verbs see Appendix I.

گردش کردن	*gardeʃ kardan*, to go for a walk.
دست دادن	*dast dadan*, to shake hands.
چانه زدن	*cane zadan*, to bargain (over a price, etc.).
آتش زدن	*ateʃ zadan*, to set fire to.
آتش گرفتن	*ateʃ gereftan*, to catch fire.
آتش کردن	*ateʃ kardan*, to start (an engine, trans.).
کشتی گرفتن	*koʃti gereftan*, to wrestle.
پاس دادن	*pas dadan*, to keep watch (sentry-go).
سپری شدن	*separi ʃodan*, to disappear, come to an end.
سوگند خوردن	*so͡ugand xordan*, to swear, take an oath.
زمین خوردن	*zamin xordan*, to fall down (usually of persons).
سر آمدن	*sar amadan*, to overflow, boil over; fall due.
بار آمدن	*bar amadan*, to be trained, brought up.
رنج کشیدن (بردن)	*ranj kaʃidan* (*bordan*), to suffer, take trouble.
سر کشیدن	*sar kaʃidan*, to drink to the dregs; to revolt, turn aside; to oversee.
راه افتادن	*rah oftadan*, to set out, start (on a journey).
رخت بستن	*raxt bastan*, to set off on a journey, pack; to die.
یخ بستن	*yax bastan*, to freeze (intrans.).
نام گذاشتن	*nam gozaʃtan*, to give a name to (someone).
نماز گذاشتن	*namaz gozaʃtan*, to perform one's prayers, to pray.

Many verbs are formed with a Verbal Noun and a simple verb such as کردن *kardan*. The tendency in Modern Persian is to use such compounds rather than the simple verb, e.g.

وادار کردن	*vadar k.* 'to persuade, oblige' rather than وا داشتن *va daʃtan*.
کوشش کردن	*kuʃeʃ kardan*, 'to try, strive' rather than کوشیدن *kuʃidan*.

(*b*) Compound verbs formed by a simple verb and an adjective, e.g.

باز کردن	*baz kardan*, to open.
پیدا کردن	*pe͡ida kardan*, to find.

جوش آمدن *juʃ amadan*, to boil (intrans.).

پسند آمدن *pasand amadan*, to be agreeable.

دور افتادن *dur oftadan*, to be separated.

بلند کردن *boland kardan*, to raise, lift; to steal (colloq.).

(*c*) Compound verbs formed by a simple verb and a preposition or adverb equivalent:

باز *baz*, again, back, e.g.

باز آمدن *baz amadan*, to come again.

باز داشتن *baz daʃtan*, to restrain, intern, detain.

وا *va* (used only in compounds), back, again, e.g.

وا داشتن *va daʃtan*, to restrain; persuade, oblige (someone to do something).

وا زدن *va zadan*, to reject, refuse.

واگذاشتن *va gozaʃtan*, to leave, abandon; cede, make over.

بر *bar*, on, up, off, e.g.

بر آمدن *bar amadan*, to be accomplished; to rise, swell.

بر آوردن *bar avardan*, to fulfil, accomplish, estimate.

بر آشفتن *bar aʃoftan*, to disturb, agitate.

بر افراشتن *bar afraʃtan*, to raise up.

بر انداختن *bar andaxtan*, to overthrow.

بر انگیختن *bar angixtan*, to stir up, excite.

بر خاستن *bar xastan*, to rise, get up.

برخوردن (به) *bar xordan* (*be*), to meet (fortuitously); to offend.

بر داشتن *bar daʃtan*, to take up, off, remove; کلاه بر داشتن *kolah bar daʃtan*, to swindle; محصول بر داشتن *mahsul bar daʃtan*, to collect the crops, harvest.

بر کندن *bar kandan*, to take off (clothes); to uproot.

بر گزیدن *bar gozidan*, to choose, select.

بر گشتن *bar gaʃtan*, to return.

ور *var*, away, off, up (used only in compounds), e.g.

ور آمدن *var amadan*, to rise (bread, etc.).

ور رفتن *var raftan*, to fiddle, fidget.

پیش *piʃ*, before, forward, e.g.

پیش آمدن *piʃ amadan*, to occur, happen.

پیش افتادن *piʃ oftadan*, to come to the fore, take the lead.

پیش کشیدن *piʃ kaʃidan*, to bring forward.

پیش بردن *piʃ bordan*, to win, gain the upper hand.

در *dar*, in; also conveys a sense of completion. E.g.

در آمدن *dar amadan*, to come out (in Modern Persian); to go in, to come out (in Classical Persian).

در آموختن *dar amuxtan*, to learn thoroughly.

در آوردن *dar avardan*, to bring in, out, take out; to learn.

در رسیدن *dar rasidan*, to overtake, come upon.

در رفتن *dar raftan*, to flee, slip away; to go off (a gun, etc.).

در گذشتن *dar gozaʃtan*, to die; to pass over, forgive.

در گرفتن *dar gereftan*, to catch (a fire, etc.); to 'catch on'.

در ماندن *dar mandan*, to become helpless, distressed, destitute; to be tired out.

در کردن *dar kardan*, to let off (a gun, etc.).

فرا *fara*, behind, back, again; the addition of فرا *fara* makes the verb emphatic.[1] E.g.

فرا آمدن *fara amadan*, to come.

فرا رفتن *fara raftan*, to go.

فرا افکندن *fara afkandan*, to throw.

فرا گرفتن *fara gereftan*, to learn (well).

فرو *foru*, فرود *forud* down; فرو *foru* is also used to make the verb emphatic. E.g.

فرود آمدن *forud amadan*, to alight, come down.

فرو بردن *foru bordan*, to swallow; to immerse.

[1] فرا *fara* is used to form compound verbs in Classical rather than Modern Persian. فراز *faraz*, up, again, under, back, is similarly used in Classical Persian to emphasize the verb, e.g.

فراز آمدن *faraz amadan*, to approach, enter.

فراز دادن *faraz dadan*, to give back.

فراز آوردن *faraz avardan*, to obtain.

فرو رفتن	*foru raftan*	to sink, go under.
فرو شدن	*foru ʃodan*	

فرو نشستن *foru neʃastan*, to subside (a rebellion, etc.); to sit down.

فرو ایستادن *foru istadan*, to stop (rain, etc.).

(*d*) Compound verbs formed by a simple verb and a prepositional phrase, e.g.

بجا آوردن *be ja avardan*, to perform, accomplish.

در صدد بر آمدن *dar sadad bar amadan*, to intend (to do something).

بکار بردن *be kar bordan*, to make use of.

بسر بردن *be sar bordan*, to spend, pass (time).

بسر آمدن *be sar amadan*, to fall due.

از دست دادن *az dast dadan*, to give up, lose.

از بین رفتن *az bein raftan*, to disappear, be lost.

سر بسر گذاشتن *sar be sar gozaʃtan*, to tease.

بشمار رفتن *be ʃomar raftan*, to be considered, reckoned as.

در بر گرفتن *dar bar gereftan*, to embrace.

در میان نهادن *dar mian nehadan*, to lay before (someone, something), discuss.

(*e*) Compound verbs formed by a simple verb and the present stem or some part of another verb, e.g.

گیر کردن *gir kardan*, to get stuck.

گیر آوردن *gir avardan*, to get, obtain (possession of something).

نیست و نابود کردن *nist o nabud kardan*, to destroy utterly.

2. Compound verbs are also formed by a simple verb combined with an Arabic participle, noun or adjective:[1]

(*a*) With an Arabic Noun, e.g.

فکر کردن *fekr kardan*, to think.

حرکت کردن *harakat kardan*, to set out, start.

صبر کردن *sabr kardan*, to wait, have patience.

[1] For Arabic forms see Part II.

قناعت کردن *qana'at kardan*, to be contented, satisfied (with), make do (with).
تعلیم کردن *ta'lim kardan*, to teach.
مطالعه کردن *motale'e kardan*, to study, read.
غارت کردن *γarat kardan*, to plunder.
تعجب کردن *ta'ajjob kardan*, to be surprised.
التفات کردن *eltefat kardan*, to pay attention.
دوام کردن *davam kardan*, to be durable.
نقش بستن *naqʃ bastan*, to stamp (cloth, etc.).
فائده بردن (از) *fa'ede bordan* (*az*), to benefit (from).
حمله بردن (به) *hamle bordan* (*be*), to attack.
اتفاق افتادن *ettefaq oftadan*, to happen, occur.
ارسال داشتن *ersal daʃtan*, to send.
امکان داشتن *emkan daʃtan*, to be possible.
جرأت داشتن *jor'at daʃtan*, to dare.
شهرت داشتن *ʃohrat daʃtan*, to be famous.
حرف زدن *harf zadan*, to talk.
قدم زدن *qadam zadan*, to walk (up and down).
صدا زدن *sada zadan*, to call.
طعنه زدن *ta'ne zadan*, to make insulting insinuations.
شعله زدن *ʃo'le zadan*, to be in flames.
نسبت دادن (به) *nesbat dadan* (*be*), to attribute (to).
خبر کردن (دادن) *xabar kardan* (*dadan*), to inform, notify.
عذر خواستن *ozr xastan*, to ask pardon.
مصلحت دیدن *maslahat didan*, to consider expedient.
طول کشیدن *tul kaʃidan*, to last (of time).
انس گرفتن *ons gereftan*, to become fond of.
قرار گرفتن *qarar gereftan*, to become established, settled; to be calmed, consoled.
تصمیم گرفتن *tasmim gereftan*, to decide.
عیب گرفتن *eib gereftan*, to find fault.
تغافل ورزیدن *taγafol varzidan*, to show neglect.
وفات یافتن *vafat yaftan*, to die.

تأسف خوردن *ta'assof xordan*, to regret.

سفره انداختن *sofre andaxtan*, to lay the table.

ادامه پیدا کردن *edame peīda kardan*, to continue (intrans.).

(*b*) With an Arabic Participle, e.g.

منکوب کردن *mankub kardan*, to conquer.

مغلوب کردن *maɣlub kardan*, to defeat.

منصرف کردن *monsaref kardan*, to dissuade.

متحیر کردن *motahaīyer kardan*, to surprise, astonish.

غالب آمدن (بر) *ɣaleb amadan* (*bar*), to conquer.

(*c*) With an Arabic Adjective, e.g.

اسیر گرفتن (کردن) *asir gereftan* (*kardan*), to take prisoner.

مریض شدن *mariz ʃodan*, to be, become ill.

سوار کردن *savar kardan*, to take on board, to put on a horse, etc.

(*d*) With an Arabic Noun combined with a preposition, e.g.

باتمام رساندن *be etmam rasandan*, to finish, bring to an end.

بوجود آوردن *be vojud avardan*, to bring into existence.

بخاطر آوردن *be xater avardan*, to bring to mind, recall.

بغارت بردن *be ɣarat bordan*, to carry off as plunder.

بهدر رفتن *be hadar raftan*, to be wasted, go to waste.

3. Compound verbs, with certain exceptions, form their passive in the usual way with شدن *ʃodan*, e.g.

بر انداخته شدن *bar andaxte ʃodan*, to be overthrown.

بر گزیده شدن *bar gozide ʃodan*, to be chosen.

(*a*) If a compound verb formed with کردن *kardan* is transitive شدن *ʃodan* replaces کردن in the Passive Voice, e.g.

اعلام کردن *e'lam kardan*, to announce.

اعلام شدن *e'lam ʃodan*, to be announced.

راضی کردن *razi kardan*, to satisfy, secure the agreement of (someone).

راضی شدن *razi ʃodan*, to be satisfied.

اسیر کردن *asir kardan*, to take prisoner.

اسیر شدن *asir ʃodan*, to be taken prisoner.

(*b*) Some compound verbs formed with زدن *zadan* change this into خوردن *xordan* in the Passive Voice, e.g.

گول زدن *gul zadan*, to deceive.

گول خوردن *gul xordan*, to be deceived.

بهم زدن *be ham zadan*, to disturb, break up, dissolve (a meeting, etc.).

بهم خوردن *be ham xordan*, to be broken up, dissolved.

مجلس بهم خورد *majles be ham xord*, The meeting (assembly) broke up.

Note also the colloquial phrase (used only of persons)

میانشان بهم خورد *mianeʃan be ham xord*, Relations between them were broken off, they quarrelled.

(*c*) Some compound verbs formed with دادن *dadan* also change this into خوردن *xordan* in the Passive Voice, e.g.

شکست دادن *ʃekast dadan*, to defeat.

شکست خوردن *ʃekast xordan*, to be defeated.

(*d*) Some compound verbs formed with دادن *dadan* change this into یافتن *yaftan* in the Passive Voice, e.g.

پرورش دادن *parvareʃ dadan*, to educate, bring up.

پرورش یافتن *parvareʃ yaftan*, to be educated.

انجام دادن *anjam dadan*, to accomplish.

انجام یافتن *anjam yaftan*, to be accomplished.

(*e*) ارسال داشتن *ersal daʃtan* 'to send' becomes ارسال شدن *ersal ʃodan* in the Passive Voice.

4. The verbal prefixes are affixed in the normal way to the verbal part of a compound, e.g.

بر میگردم *bar migardam*, I will return.

فکر نمیکنم *fekr namikonam*, I do not think.

Compound verbs formed with بر *bar*, باز *baz*, وا *va*, ور *var* or در *dar* and a simple verb omit the verbal prefix ب *be*, e.g.

بر گرد *bar gard*, Return.

5. The Pronominal Suffixes are added to the non-verbal part of the verb, e.g.

بیرونش کردم	*birune∫ kardam*, I turned him out.
بهمش زد	*be hame∫ zad*, He broke it up.
خبرشان کرد	*xabare∫an kard*, He informed them.
برش گرداندم	*bare∫ gardandam*, I caused him to return, turned him back.

Not only are the Pronominal Suffixes interposed between the verbal and the non-verbal parts of the compound, but, if the compound is formed by a simple verb and a noun or participle, other words and phrases can be so interposed with the *ezafe*, e.g.

جرأت این کاررا نداشت	*jor'ate in karra nada∫t*, He did not dare do this (work).
سوار کشتی شد	*savare ka∫ti ∫od*, He went on board the ship.

6. Stress in compound verbs falls:

(*a*) In the affirmative on the final syllable of the non-verbal part of the compound, e.g.

پرورش یافت	*parva're∫ yaft*, He was educated.
پیدا میکند	*pei'da mikonad*, He will find.
بر میگردیم	*'bar migardim*, We shall return.
بکار خواهد برد	*be 'kar xahad bord*, He will use (it).
حرکت کرده است	*hara'kat karde ast*, He has set out.
راضی شد	*ra'zi ∫od*, He was satisfied.
بوجود آورد	*be vo'jud avard*, He created.

(*b*) In the negative on the negative prefix. A secondary stress may also be carried on the final syllable of the non-verbal part of the compound, e.g.

بر نمیگردیم	*bar 'namigardim* or *'bar 'namigardim*, We shall not return.
حرکت نکرده است	*harakat 'nakarde ast* or *hara'kat 'nakarde ast*, He has not set out.

7. Secondary verbs are in some cases formed from the Present Stem of irregular verbs, e.g.

کوبیدن	*kubidan* 'to pound' from کوفتن *kuftan* (کوب *kub*).
تابیدن	*tabidan* 'to twist, shine' from تافتن *taftan* (تاب *tab*).

Vocabulary

استیلا *estila*, conquest.
مغول *moɣul*, *moɣol*, Mongol.
دوره *do͡ure*, period.
تاریخ *tarix*, history; تاریخی *tarixi*, historical.
امیر تیمور گورکان *amir te͡imur gurakan*, Tamerlane.
واقعه *vaqe'e*, event, happening (pl. وقایع *vaqaye'*).
قبل از *qabl aȥ*, before.
صفویه *safaviye*, the Safavid Dynasty (which ruled in Persia A.D. 1502–1736).
صفوی *safavi*, Safavid.
نوبه *no͡ube*, turn.
باعث *ba'es*, cause.
قتل *qatl*, murder, killing.
غارت *ɣarat*, plunder.
خونریزی *xunriȥi*, bloodshed.
خرابی *xarabi*, ruin, devastation.
بیشمار *biʃomar*, innumerable.
کشور *keʃvar*, country.
اسلامی *eslami*, Islamic.
عموماً[1] *omuman*, in general.
خصوصاً[1] *xosusan*, in particular.
حمله *hamle*, attack (pl. حملات *hamalat*).
صدمه *sadame*, injury, blow; صدمه دیدن *sadame didan*, to suffer injury.
پرتگاه *partgah*, precipice.
انحطاط *enhetat*, decay, decline.
عجیب *ajib*, strange, wonderful.
قوس *qo͡us*, arc.
نزولی *noȥuli*, descending.
پیمودن (پیما) *pe͡imudan* (*pe͡ima*), to measure, tread.
تنزل *tanaȥȥol*, decline.
کمك *komak*, help; کمك کردن *komak k.*, to help.
ترقی *taraqqi*, progress.
بر رو(ی) *bar ru(ye)*, on.
گذشته از *goȥaʃte aȥ*, apart from.
خرافات *xorafat*, superstition(s).
وهم *vahm*, vanity, fancy (pl. اوهام *o͡uham*).
ترك *tork*, Turk; Turkish (adj.).
نتیجه *natije*, result.
تعصب *ta'assob*, fanaticism.
جاهلانه *jahelane*, ignorant.
مرکز *markaȥ*, centre.
تمدن *tamaddon*, civilization.
اروپا *orupa*, Europe.
غربی *ɣarbi*, western.
امریکا *amrika*, America.
مانع *mane'*, impediment, obstacle (pl. موانع *mavane'*).
داخل *daxel*, inner, inside; داخل شدن *daxel ʃ.*, to enter.
داخلی *daxeli*, internal, interior.

[1] See Part II, Lesson XXI, for the formation of Arabic Adverbs.

رابطه *rabete*, connexion, relation (pl. روابط *ravabet*).

خارج *xarej*, abroad, outside.

خارجه *xareje*, abroad, a foreign country.

سهولت *sohulat*, ease; بسهولت *be sohulat*, easily, with ease.

اخذ کردن *axz kardan*, to take.

مانند *manand*, like; it is followed by the noun it governs and takes the *ezafe*.

ممالك *mamalek*, pl. of مملکت *mamlekat*, country.

قدم *qadam*, step; قدم بر داشتن *qadam bar daštan*, to advance, progress.

استیلای مغول در ایران[1]

دوره دویست ساله تاریخی مغول و استیلای امیر تیمور گورکان و وقایع دیگریکه قبل از صفویه در ایران اتفاق افتاد هریك بنوبه خود باعث قتل و غارت و خونریزی و خرابیهای بیشمار در کشورهای اسلامی عموماً و کشور ایران خصوصاً گردید ایران از همه بیشتر در این حملات صدمه دید و در پرتگاه انحطاط عجیب افتاده[1] قوس نزولیرا میپیمود و چیز دیگری که بانحطاط و تنزل ایران کمك میکرد و روز بروز درهای ترقیرا بر روی آن میبست گذشته از خرافات و اوهامیکه از استیلای مغول و ترکان نتیجه شده بود تعصب جاهلانه مردم و قرار گرفتن مرکز[2] تمدن در اروپای غربی و امریکا بود و ایران با موانع داخلی که برای روابط با خارج داشت دیگر نمیتوانست از اروپا بسهولت اخذ تمدن کند یا مانند آن ممالك در راه ترقی قدم بر دارد

[1] اقتباس از تاریخ ایران از مغول تا افشاریه تألیف رضا پازوکی

Exercise 18

1. In winter when it is cold it freezes. 2. Yesterday morning we went for a walk outside the town. 3. What we said offended them. 4. Before you return you must listen to what I have (want) to say. 5. He has not yet come out of his room. 6. It is a long time since he died. 7. This book is attributed to him. 8. He determined to go to Persia. 9. He died twenty years ago. 10. I was reading a book when he came in. 11. He was defeated. 12. The village was plundered. 13. We considered it expedient to go because it was late and we wanted

[1] For this use of the Past Participle see Lesson XIII, para. 2 (*c*).

[2] For this use of the Infinitive see Lesson XIII, para. 1 (*a*).

to reach home before it got dark. 14. The Mongol invasion, which took place in the thirteenth century, caused much damage to Persia and it was many years before the country recovered from the devastation caused by the Mongols; many centres of learning and civilization were destroyed and thousands of people were killed.

LESSON X

Word Formation. Abstract Nouns. Verbal Nouns. Nominal Suffixes. Diminutives. Adjectival Suffixes. Compound Nouns. Compound Adjectives.

1. Abstract Nouns are formed by the suffix ی *-i*, e.g.

خوبی *xubi*, goodness (from خوب *xub* 'good').

مردی *mardi*, manliness, generosity (from مرد *mard* 'man').

درشتی *doroſti*, thickness (from درشت *doroſt* 'thick').

If the Abstract ی *-i* is added to a word ending in ا *a* or و *u*, a *hamze* over a bearer is prefixed to it. This marks the transition from one vowel to another and is not represented in the transcription, e.g.

دانائی *danai*, wisdom (from دانا *dana* 'wise').

خوشروئی *xoſrui*, beauty (from خوشرو *xoſru* 'beautiful').

If the Abstract ی *-i* is added to a word ending in ه *-e*, the latter is changed into گ *g*, e.g.

خستگی *xastegi*, fatigue (from خسته *xaste* 'tired').

شایستگی *ſayestegi*, fitness, worthiness (from شایسته *ſayeste* 'worthy fitting').

زندگی *zendegi*, life (from زنده *zende* 'alive').

بچگی *baccegi*, childhood (from بچه *bacce* 'child').

2. The Abstract ی *-i* carries the stress, which distinguishes it from the Indefinite ی *-i* and the Relative ی *-i*.

3. Verbal Nouns are formed by the addition of ش *-eſ*,[1] اك *-ak*, or ه *-e* to the Present Stem, e.g.

فرمایش *farmayeſ*, command (from فرمودن *farmudan* 'to command').

سوزش *suzeſ*, burning (from سوختن *suxtan* 'to burn').

[1] If the present Stem of the verb to which ش *-eſ* is added ends in ا *a* or و *u* a ی *y* is inserted between the final vowel and the suffix ش *-eſ*.

گردش *gardeʃ*, a walk, turn, excursion (from گشتن *gaʃtan* 'to go for a walk').

کوشش *kuʃeʃ*, effort (from کوشیدن *kuʃidan* 'to strive').

پوشاك *puʃak*, clothing (from پوشیدن *puʃidan* 'to wear').

خوراك *xorak*, food (from خوردن *xordan* 'to eat').

شماره *ʃomare*, number (from شمردن *ʃomordan* 'to count').

خنده *xande*, laugh (from خندیدن *xandidan* 'to laugh').

شپره *ʃappare*, bat (=شب پره *ʃab pare* from شب *ʃab* 'night' and پریدن *paridan* 'to fly, jump, flit').

ناله *nale*, whine, wail, complaint (from نالیدن *nalidan* 'to whine', etc.).

A Verbal Noun is also formed, but less commonly, in ن *-n*, e.g.

فرمان *farman*, order (from فرمودن *farmudan* 'to order').

پیمان *peiman*, measure (from پیمودن *peimudan* 'to measure').

A form in ار *-ar* which originally expressed 'the agent', is used as a Verbal Noun, e.g.

رفتار *raftar*, conduct (from رفتن *raftan* 'to go').

گفتار *goftar*, speech, talk (from گفتن *goftan* 'to say').

گرفتار *gereftar* (used as an adj.), being overtaken by, suffering from (from گرفتن *gereftan* 'to take').

کردار *kerdar*, action (from کردن *kardan* 'to do' with modification of the stem vowel).

خریدار *xaridar*, purchaser, buyer (from خریدن *xaridan* 'to buy').

In the last example the original force of the suffix has been retained.

Some verbs do not form verbal nouns.

4. The following suffixes are used to form nouns:

(*a*) ا *-a* and نا *-na* added to adjectives, e.g.

گرما *garma*, warmth (from گرم *garm* 'warm').

پهنا *pahna*, width, breadth (from پهن *pahn* 'wide').

تنگنا *tangna*, ravine (from تنگ *tang* 'narrow').

(*b*) ه *-e* added to nouns and numerals, e.g.

نیمه *nime*, half (from نیم *nim* 'half').

کینه *kine*, vengeance (from کین *kin* 'vengeance').

چشمه *caʃme*, spring, river-source (from چشم *caʃm* 'eye').

پنجه *panje*, claw (from پنج *panj* 'five').

دسته *daste*, handle (from دست *dast* 'hand').

دهکده *dehkade*, small village (from ده *deh* 'village' and کد *kad* 'house, household', the latter used only in compounds).

آتشکده *ateʃkade*, fire-temple (from آتش *ateʃ* 'fire' and کد *kad*, see above).

(*c*) بان *-ban*, وان *-van* 'keeper', e.g.

باغبان *baɣban*, gardener (from باغ *baɣ* 'garden').

دربان *darban*, gate-keeper, door-keeper (from در *dar* 'door').

پاسبان *pasban*, policeman, watchman (from پاس *pas* 'watch').

شتربان (شتروان) *ʃotorban* (*ʃotorvan*), camel-driver (from شتر *ʃotor* 'camel').

وان *-van* is seldom used in Colloquial Persian.

(*d*) بد *-bod* 'lord, master', e.g.

سپهبد *sepahbod*, lieutenant-general (from سپه *sepah* 'army').

(*e*) کار *-kar*, گار *-gar*, گر *-gar* 'agent' or 'worker in', e.g.

گناهکار *gonahkar*, sinner (from گناه *gonah* 'sin').

خدمتکار *xedmatkar*, servant (from خدمت *xedmat* 'service').

آفریدگار *afaridegar*, the Creator (from آفریدن *afaridan* 'to create').

یادگار *yadgar*, memorial (from یاد *yad* 'memory').

روزگار *ruzgar*, time (from روز *ruz* 'day').

آموزگار *amuzgar*, teacher (from آموختن *amuxtan* 'to teach').

زرگر *zargar*, goldsmith (from زر *zar* 'gold').

آهنگر *ahangar*, ironsmith (from آهن *ahan* 'iron').

توانگر *tavangar*, a powerful person (from توانستن *tavanestan* 'to be able').

دادگر *dadgar*, a just person (from داد *dad* 'justice').

(*f*) دان *-dan* 'receptacle', e.g.

قلمدان *qalamdan*, pencase (from قلم *qalam* 'pen').

قنددان *qanddan*, sugar-bowl (from قند *qand* 'lump sugar').

(*g*) ستان *-estan*, *-stan* 'place of', e.g.

هندوستان *hendustan*, India (from هندو *hendu* 'Hindu').

گلستان *golestan*, rose-garden (from گل *gol* 'rose, flower').

(*h*) لاخ *-lax*, سار *-sar*, زار *-zar*, بار *-bar*, شن *-ʃan* 'place abounding in', e.g.

سنگلاخ *sanglax*
سنگسار *sangsar* } stony place (from سنگ *sang* 'stone').

گلزار *golzar*
گلشن *golʃan* } flower-bed (from گل *gol* 'flower, rose').

رودبار *rudbar*, place abounding in rivers or streams (from رود *rud* 'river, stream').

کارزار *karzar*, battle, battlefield (from کار *kar* in its obsolete meaning of 'army' or 'group of people moving about').

مرغزار *maryzar*, water-meadow (from مرغ *mary* 'a kind of grass').

چمنزار *camanzar*, meadow (from چمن *caman* 'turf').

(*i*) ان *-an*[1]

(1) names of places, e.g.

توران *turan*, Turania (from تور Tur).

بیابان *biaban*, desert (from بی آب *bi ab* 'without water').

(2) patronymics, e.g.

بابکان *babakan*, son of Babak.

(*j*) گان *-gan* 'origin, relation, similarity', e.g.

گروگان *gerougan*, hostage (from گرو *gerou* 'pledge').

(*k*) چی *-ci*, جی *-ji* 'agent', e.g.

درشکه‌چی *doroʃkeci*, cabman (from درشکه *doroʃke* 'cab').

This suffix is derived from Turkish.

(*l*) اباد *-abad* 'place of abode', used in place-names, e.g.

خرم‌اباد *xorramabad*, Khorramabad (from خرم *xorram* 'happiness, gladness').

اسداباد *asadabad*, Asadabad (from اسد *asad* 'lion').

[1] If the word to which ان *-an* is added ends in ا *a* or و *u* a ی *y* is inserted between the final vowel and the suffix.

5. Diminutives are formed by the addition of one of the following suffixes: ك -*ak*, ه -*e*, كه -*eke*, چه -*ce*, یچه -*ice* or و -*u*.

The diminutive suffixes when applied to rational beings denote also affection or contempt, e.g.

دخترك *doxtarak* } little girl.
دختره *doxtare* }

مردكه *mardeke*, little man, manikin.

پسرو *pesaru*, little boy.

يارو *yaru*, fellow (used in a derogatory sense from يار *yar* 'helper, friend').

باغچه *baɣce*, little garden.

دریچه *darice*, little door.

Less commonly used are the diminutive suffixes یجه -*ije*, یزه -*ize*, and یژه -*iʒe*.

6. There are a variety of adjectival suffixes. Among them are:

(*a*) ا -*a*, added to the Present Stem of verbs, used to form verbal adjectives, e.g.

دانا *dana*, wise (from دانستن *danestan* 'to know').

توانا *tavana*, powerful (from توانستن *tavanestan* 'to be able').

زيبا *ziba*, comely (from the obsolete verb زيبيدن *zibidan* 'to be comely').

(*b*) مند -*mand*, 'possessed of', e.g.

خردمند *xeradmand*, wise (from خرد *xerad* 'wisdom').

ثروتمند *servatmand*, rich (from ثروت *servat* 'wealth').

گله‌مند *gelemand*, complaining (from گله *gele* 'complaint').

(*c*) ور -*var*, اور -*avar* 'characterized by', e.g.

شعله‌ور *ʃo'levar*, blazing, flaming (from شعله *ʃo'le* 'flame').

نامور *namvar*, famous, illustrious (from نام *nam* 'name').

دلاور *delavar*, courageous (from دل *del* 'heart, stomach').

The form جانور *janevar*, originally adjectival meaning 'having a soul' (جان *jan*), is now used as a noun meaning 'animal'.

(*d*) وار *-var*, 'fit for, characterized by', e.g.

شاهوار *ʃahvar*, fit for a king (from شاه *ʃah* 'king').

دیوانه‌وار *divanevar*, like a madman (from دیوانه *divane* 'mad').

بزرگوار *bozorgvar*, great, worthy of a great man (from بزرگ *bozorg* 'great').

(*e*) وش *-vaʃ*, مان *-man*, سا *-sa*, اسا *-asa*, سار *-sar*, سان *-san* 'like', e.g.

ماهوش *mahvaʃ*, like the moon (from ماه *mah* 'moon').

پریوش *parivaʃ*, like a fairy (from پری *pari* 'fairy').

شادمان *ʃadman*, happy (from شاد *ʃad* 'happy').

فیلسا *filsa* / فیل‌آسا *filasa* } like an elephant (from فیل *fil* 'elephant').

شرمسار *ʃarmsar*, ashamed (from شرم *ʃarm* 'shame').

گرگسان *gorgsan*, like a wolf (from گرگ *gorg* 'wolf').

یکسان *yaksan*, equal, like (from یك *yak* 'one').

(*f*) ین *-in*, ینه *-ine*, added to a 'material' to express the meaning 'made of' the substance, e.g.

زرین *zarrin*,[1] made of gold (from زر *zar* 'gold').

پشمینه[2] *paʃmine*, woollen (from پشم *paʃm* 'wool').

دیرینه *dirine*, ancient (from دیر *dir* 'late').

(*g*) ین *-in*, added to certain numerals and prepositions to form adjectives denoting time or place, e.g.

برین *barin*, upper (from بر *bar* 'on').

پسین *pasin*, posterior (of time; from پس *pas* 'after').

اولین *avvalin*, first (from اول *avval* 'first').

نخستین *naxostin*, first (from نخست *naxost* 'first').

آخرین *axerin*, last (from آخر *axer* 'last').

(*h*) گین *-gin*, ناك *-nak* 'full of', e.g.

غمگین *ɣamgin*, sorrowful (from غم *ɣam* 'grief').

سهمگین *sahmgin*, dreadful (from سهم *sahm* 'terror, dread').

دردناك *dardnak*, painful (from درد *dard* 'pain').

[1] The doubling of the *r* would appear to be irregular.

[2] پشمی *paʃmi* is more commonly used to mean 'woollen'.

(*i*) یار *-yar*, e.g.

هوشیار *huʃyar*, intelligent (from هوش *huʃ* 'intelligence').

بختیار *baxtyar*, fortunate (from بخت *baxt* 'fortune, luck').

(*j*) ی *-i* 'belonging to', e.g.

دهاتی *dehati*, belonging to the country, a countryman (from دهات *dehat* 'country').

شهری *ʃahri*, belonging to the town, townsman (from شهر *ʃahr* 'town').

شیرازی *ʃirazi*, belonging to Shiraz, a native of Shiraz.

If this ی *-i* is added to certain Persian words ending in the 'silent' *h*, the latter is changed into گ, e.g.

خانگی *xanegi*, belonging to the house (from خانه *xane* 'house').

But

سرمهٔ *sormei*, dark blue (from سرمه *sorme* 'collyrium').

The adjectival ی *-i* carries the stress like the Abstract ی *-i* (see para. 2 above) and is thereby distinguished from the Indefinite ی *-i* and the Relative ی *-i*.

The Arabic termination ـِيٌّ *-iyon*, which forms Relative Adjectives (see Part II, Lesson XVI, para. 18), becomes ی *-i* in Persian, e.g.

مصری *mesri*, Egyptian, an Egyptian (from مصر *mesr* 'Egypt').

(*k*) ه *-e*, added to compounds, e.g.

چکاره *ce kare*, belonging to what profession.

7. Compound nouns are formed in a variety of ways, e.g.

(*a*) By a qualifying noun with a noun, e.g.

مهمانخانه *mehmanxane*, hotel (مهمان *mehman* 'guest'; خانه *xane* 'house').

سربازخانه *sarbazxane*, barracks (سرباز *sarbaz* 'soldier'; خانه *xane* 'house').

پالایشگاه *palayeʃgah*, refinery (پالایش *palayeʃ* 'refining'; گاه *gah* 'place').

(*b*) By two nouns placed in apposition, e.g.

پدر زن *pedarzan*, father-in-law (of the husband) (پدر *pedar* 'father'; زن *zan* 'woman, wife').

دختر عمو *doxtaramu*, cousin (daughter of a paternal uncle) (دختر *doxtar*, 'girl, daughter'; عمو *amu* 'paternal uncle').

صاحب خانه *sahebxane*, landlord, owner or master of the house (صاحب *saheb* 'master, owner'; خانه *xane* 'house').

میراب *mirab*, an official in charge of the distribution of water (میر *mir* a title; آب *ab* 'water').

(*c*) By two nouns with the *eẓafe*, e.g.

تخت خواب *taxte xab*, bed (تخت *taxt* 'wooden platform or seat' خواب *xab*, 'sleep').

(*d*) By two nouns joined by و *o* 'and',[1] e.g.

آب و هوا *ab o hava*, climate (آب *ab* 'water'; هوا *hava* 'air').

(*e*) By a noun and an adjective, e.g.

نوروز *nou͡ruẓ*, New Year (نو *nou͡* new; روز *ruẓ* 'day').

(*f*) By a noun and the Present Stem of a verb, e.g.

سرباز *sarbaẓ* soldier (سر *sar* 'head'; باختن *baxtan* 'to lose').

پیغامبر *pei͡γambar*, messenger (پیغام *pei͡γam* 'message'; بردن *bordan* 'to carry').

(*g*) By the Short Infinitive of two verbs united by و *o* 'and',[1] e.g.

آمد و شد *amad o ʃod*, traffic, coming and going (آمدن *amadan* 'to come'; شدن *ʃodan* in its obsolete meaning 'to go').

(*h*) By the Present Stem and Short Infinitive of a verb with or without و *o* 'and', e.g.

گفتگو *goftogu*, *goftegu*, or گفت‌وگو *goftogu*, conversation, discussion (from گفتن *goftan* 'to say').

جستجو *jostoju*, *josteju*, or جست‌وجو *jostoju*, search, seeking (from *jostan* 'to seek').

(*i*) By the Present Stem of two verbs united by و *o* 'and', e.g.

گیرودار *girodar*, struggle (گرفتن *gereftan* 'to take'; داشتن *daʃtan* 'to have, hold').

[1] See above, p. 38, footnote 2, for this و *o*.

(*j*) By a noun and a Past Participle, e.g.

شاهزاده *ʃahzade*, prince (شاه *ʃah* 'king'; زائيدن *zaidan* 'to give birth to'; زاده being a contracted form of زائيده).

(*k*) By a word used as an adverb and the Present Stem of a verb, e.g.

پيشكش *piʃkaʃ*, present (from an inferior to a superior) (پيش *piʃ* 'forward'; كشيدن *kaʃidan* 'to pull, draw').

پس انداز *pasandaz*, savings (پس *pas* 'behind'; انداختن *andaxtan* 'to throw').

(*l*) By an adjective and the Present Stem of a verb, e.g.

نو آموز *nouamuz*, beginner (نو *nou* 'new'; آموختن *amuxtan* 'to learn, teach').

(*m*) By two nouns united by a preposition, e.g.

اعتماد بنفس *e'temad be nafs*, self-reliance (اعتماد *e'temad* 'reliance'; نفس *nafs* 'self').

The plural of compound nouns is formed by adding the plural termination to the last part of the compound, e.g.

مهمانخانه ها *mehmanxaneha*, hotels.

8. Compound adjectives are formed by

(*a*) Two nouns in juxtaposition, e.g.

سنگدل *sangdel*, stony-hearted (سنگ *sang* 'stone'; دل *del*, 'heart, stomach').

(*b*) An adjective and a noun, e.g.

خوش اخلاق *xoʃaxlaq*, good-natured (خوش *xoʃ* 'pleasant, happy'; اخلاق *axlaq* 'morals, ethics, character').

بزرگمنش *bozorgmaneʃ*, magnanimous (بزرگ *bozorg* 'big'; the obsolete word منش *maneʃ* 'thinking').

(*c*) A noun and the Present Stem of a verb, e.g.

سرافراز *sarafraz*, exalted, honoured (سر *sar* 'head'; افراشتن *afraʃtan* 'to raise, exalt').

كامياب *kamyab*, successful, prosperous (كام *kam* 'desire'; يافتن *yaftan* 'to obtain').

(*d*) A noun and a Past Participle, e.g.

جهاندیده *jahandide*, experienced, widely travelled (جهان *jahan* 'world'; دیدن *didan* 'to see').

(*e*) An adjective and the Present Stem of a verb, e.g.

تیزرو *tizrou*, fleet (of foot), speedy (تیز *tiz* 'sharp, quick'; رفتن *raftan* 'to go').

(*f*) A noun and a preposition, e.g.

باصفا *basafa*, pleasant, agreeable (با *ba* 'with'; صفا *safa* 'purity').

بی‌صفا *bisafa*, unpleasant, disagreeable (بی *bi* 'without').

بافهم *bafahm*, intelligent (فهم *fahm* 'understanding').

بی‌فهم *bifahm*, unintelligent, stupid.

بی‌کس *bikas*, friendless, forlorn (کس *kas* 'person'; بی *bi* 'without').

زبردست *zabardast*, skilful, quick, able (دست *dast* 'hand'; زبر *zabar* 'above').

برقرار *bar qarar*, settled, fixed, established (بر *bar* 'on'; قرار *qarar* 'settling, establishing').

خانه بدوش *xane be duʃ*, nomadic (خانه *xane* 'house'; دوش *duʃ* 'shoulder, back').

(*g*) Two nouns united by ا *a*, e.g.

برابر *barabar*, equal, opposite (بر *bar* 'breast').

9. Compound Adjectives form their comparative by the addition of تر *-tar* or with بیشتر *biʃtar*, e.g.

باصفاتر *basafatar* } pleasanter.
بیشتر با صفا *biʃtar basafa* }

The superlative is formed in the usual way by the addition of ترین *-tarin*, e.g.

باصفاترین *basafatarin*, pleasantest.

Forms compounded with بی *bi-* do not logically admit of a comparative or superlative.

10. The particle هم *ham* 'like' is used to form compound nouns and adjectives, e.g.

همشهری *hamʃahri*, fellow-townsman.

هماهنگ *hamahang*, harmonious (آهنگ *ahang* 'melody').

همعقیده *hamaqide*, having the same opinion (عقیده *aqide* 'opinion, belief').

11. Adjectival compounds are formed with کم *kam* 'little, less', e.g.

کم‌بضاعت *kambaẓa'at*, of little wealth (بضاعت *baẓa'at* 'merchandise, goods').

کم‌زور *kamẓur*, weak (زور *ẓur* 'power, strength').

12. The negative particle نا *-na* is used to form compound adjectives and nouns, e.g.

نادان *nadan*, ignorant } (دانستن *danestan* 'to know').
نادانی *nadani*, ignorance }

ناهموار *nahamvar*, uneven (هموار *hamvar* 'even').

حق ناشناس *haqqnaʃenas*, ungrateful (حق *haqq* 'right'; شناختن *ʃenaxtan* 'to know, recognize').

ناکس *nakas*, an ignoble, mean person (کس *kas* 'person').

نامرد *namard*, an ignoble, mean person (مرد *mard* 'man').

تغییر ناپذیر *taɣyirnapaẓir*, unchangeable (تغییر *taɣyir* 'change'; پذیرفتن *paẓiroftan* 'to accept').

نارو *narou͡*, treacherous (of a person) (رفتن *raftan* 'to go').

The Imperative affirmative followed by the imperative negative is also used to form compounds, e.g.

کشمکش *keʃmakeʃ*, struggle (کشیدن *kaʃidan* 'to pull').

13. The particle غیر *ɣeir͡* 'other' ('un-') is used to form compounds. It takes the *eẓafe*, e.g.

غیر رسمی *ɣeire͡ rasmi*, unofficial (رسمی *rasmi* 'official').

غیر قابل تحمل *ɣeire͡ qabele tahammol*, insupportable (قابل *qabel* 'worthy, able'; تحمل *tahammol* 'patience, endurance').

14. خود *xod* 'self' is also used to form compounds, e.g.

خودداری *xoddari*, restraint, self-control (داشتن *daʃtan* 'to have, hold').

خودپسند *xodpasand*, conceited (پسند *pasand* 'pleasant, agreeable').

از خود گذشتگی *az xod gozaʃtegi*, self-sacrifice (گذشتن *gozaʃtan* 'to pass by').

بی‌خود *bixod*, in vain (بی *bi* 'without').

15. A rhyming compound is formed, the second part of which is a meaningless word beginning with م *m-* or occasionally with پ *p* and rhyming with the first part of the compound. Such compounds are frequently used in Colloquial Persian, e.g.

بچه مچه *bacce macce* or بچه مچه ها *bacce macceha*, children.

پول مول *pul mul*, money.

قاطی پاتی *qati pati*, mixed.

This type of compound sometimes gives a plural sense as in the first example above. It is also occasionally found in the literary language, e.g.

تار و مار *tar o mar*, destroyed, scattered.

16. Stress on compound nouns and adjectives is carried on the final syllable, e.g.

اعتماد بنفس *eʿtemad be 'nafs*, self-reliance.

سرافراز *saraf'raz*, exalted, honoured.

خانه بدوش *xane be 'duʃ*, nomadic.

پیغامبر *peiɣam'bar*, messenger.

سربازخانه *sarbazxa'ne*, barracks.

Vocabulary

شاه طهماسب Shah Tahmasp (reigned A.D. 1524–76).

انگلیسی *englisi*, English.

انگلستان *englestan*, England.

انتنی جنکینسن Antony Jenkinson.

طرف *taraf*, side; از طرف *az taraf(e)*, on behalf of; طرفین *tarafein*,[1] two parties, sides.

ملکه *maleke*, queen.

[1] For the Arabic dual see Part II, Lesson XIX.

اليزابت Elizabeth.
هجری *hejri*, belonging to the Hejri era (see Appendix III).
سفارت *sefarat*, embassy, mission.
روانه گردیدن *ravane g.*, to set out for.
مزبور *mazbur*, mentioned, aforesaid.
جهت *jehat*, side; reason; *jehat(e)*, for.
پادشاه *padeʃah*, king, ruler.
دایر بر *da'er bar*, depending on, relating to.
ایجاد *ijad*, creation.
دوستی *dusti*, friendship.
حفظ *hefz*, preservation.
مصالح *masaleh* (pl. of مصلحت *maslahat*), interests.
انسانیت *ensaniyat*, humanity, humanitarianism.
منفعت *manfa'at*, benefit (pl. منافع *manafe'*).
ذو الحجة *zol-hejja*,[1] the twelfth month of the Muslim lunar year.
قزوین Qazvin.
آداب *adab* (pl. of ادب *adab*), customs, habits.
رسم *rasm*, custom (pl. رسوم *rosum*).
آشنا *aʃna*, acquainted with.
دولت *doulat*, government, state; دولت متبوع *doulate matbu'* sovereign government (i.e. government to which one is subject).
عهد نامه *ahdname*, treaty, agreement.
منعقد کردن *mon'aqed k.*, to conclude.
ناچار *nacar*, having no remedy.
روسیه *rusiye*, Russia.
بدون *bedun(e)*, without.
حصول *hosul*, acquisition, obtaining.
هیئت *hei'at*, commission, body, group.
جانب *janeb*, side; از جانب *az janeb(e)*, on behalf of.
شرکت *ʃerkat*, company; participation.
مسکو *moskou*, Moscow.
نسبت به *nesbat be*, with regard to, towards.
اجازه *ejaze*, permission.
تجار *tojjar* (pl. of تاجر *tajer*), merchants.
آزاد *azad*, free.
آزادی *azadi*, freedom.
جستن (جو) *jostan* (*ju*), to seek; find.
شوهر *ʃouhar*, husband.

[1] See Appendix III.

روابط ایران و اروپا [1]

در زمان شاه طهماسب یك نفر انگلیسی بنام انتنی جنکینسن از طرف ملکه انگلستان الیزابت در سال ۹٦۹ هجری بعنوان سفارت روانه ایران گردید و نامهٔ از طرف ملکه مزبور جهت شاه طهماسب اول پادشاه صفوی آورد دایر بر ایجاد روابط دوستی و حفظ مصالح انسانیت و منافع طرفین نماینده مزبور در ماه ذوالحجة سال ۹٦۹ بقزوین پایتخت شاه طهماسب آمد ولی چون با آداب و رسوم ایران آشنا نبود نتوانست جهت دولت متبوع خود عهدنامه تجارتی منعقد نماید ناچار برگشت بار دیگر همین نماینده در سال ۹۷۰ از طرف دولت روسیه بایران آمد ولی این دفعه هم بدون حصول نتیجه مراجعت نمود در سال ۹۷۲ هیئتی دیگر [2] از جانب شرکت مسکو بایران آمد و شاه هم نسبت باین هیئت بمهربانی رفتار نمود اجازه دادکه تجار انگلیسی و روسی بآزادی در ایران تجارت و مسافرت نمایند

Exercise 19

1. He has news of his sister. 2. It is a very long time since I have been to (in) England. 3. It was impossible to stay any longer. 4. The man to whom you were speaking this morning is a fellow-townsman of mine. 5. He showed great self-reliance. 6. He brought up his son well. 7. We live the whole year in the country. 8. He would like to live outside the town. 9. I am of the same opinion as you. 10. We decided to stay here because it was pleasanter. 11. He intended to set out for India last week. 12. If he goes by sea his journey will last three weeks. 13. She likes her father-in-law better than her mother-in-law. 14. I tried to come earlier but although I intended to set out at ten o'clock it was eleven before I was ready to start, and as a result it was late when I arrived and you had gone home. 15. Commercial relations between Persia and Europe began in Safavid times. Many envoys came from Europe to Persia and sought to make trade agreements on behalf of their governments with the Persian government and to establish friendly relations. Some of them were successful; others returned to Europe without achieving their object.

[1] اقتباس از تاریخ ایران از مغول تا افشاریه تالیف رضا پازوکی

[2] See Lesson XII, para. 1 (*a*) (iii) for the addition of the Indefinite ی *-i* to the noun instead of to the qualifying adjective.

LESSON XI

Prepositions[1]

1. Prepositions can be divided into two classes: those which take the *ezafe* and those which do not.[2]

2. Prepositions which do not take the *ezafe* include the following:

(*a*) از *az* (from, in, by, through, over, of, than, made of, among, by way of, because, out of, belonging to) denotes direction from, deprivation or liberation; it denotes the material anything is made of; it is used in partitive expressions and to express comparison.

از رفتن صرف نظر میکنم *az raftan sarfe nazar mikonam*, I shall refrain from (give up) going.

از این استفاده کرد *az in estefade kard*, He benefited from this.

از وزارت معزول شد *az vezarat maʿzul ʃod*, He was dismissed from the post of minister (lit. from the ministry).

از خونریزی باید جلوگیری کرد *az xunrizi bayad jelo͡ugiri kard*, Bloodshed must be prevented.

از او اطمینان دارم *az u etminan daram*, I have confidence in him.

از شهر عبور کردیم *az ʃahr obur kardim*, We passed through the town.

از دریافت کاغذتان مسرور گشتم *az daryafte kaɣazetan masrur gaʃtam*, I was made happy by the receipt of your letter.

از فیض دیدار شما محروم ماندم *az fe͡ize didare ʃoma mahrum mandam*, I was deprived of the pleasure of seeing you.

از او خبر ندارم *az u xabar nadaram*, I have no news of him.

[1] See also Part II, Lesson XXI, paras. 14 and 15.

[2] The examples given in the following paras. are intended to serve as an indication of the use of the prepositions in Persian and should not be regarded as exhaustive.

این منزل عبارت است از پنج عدد اطاق	*in manzel ebarat ast az panj adad otaq*, This house consists of five rooms.
این بچه از آن بچه بزرگتر است	*in bacce az an bacce bozorgtar ast*, This child is bigger than that child.
دور باغ دیواری از خشت[1] کشیدند	*doure bay divari az xest kasidand*, They made a brick wall round the garden.
سعدی از شعرای معروف ایران است	*sa'di az so'araye ma'rufe iran ast*, Sa'di is among the famous poets of Iran.
این از عجائب دنیاست	*in az aja'ebe donyast*, This is among the wonders of the world.
اینرا از دلتنگی گفت	*inra az deltangi goft*, He said this out of sadness.
این کتاب از آن من است	*in ketab az ane man ast*, This book is one of my books.

The following verbs take از *az*:

استدعا کردن	*ested'a k.*, to ask, beseech (someone).
استفاده کردن	*estefade k.*, to benefit (from).
استمداد کردن	*estemdad k.*, to ask help (of).
اطمینان داشتن	*etminan d.* } to have confidence (in).
اعتماد داشتن	*e'temad d.* } to have confidence (in).
آمدن	*amadan*, to come (from).
باز داشتن	*baz d.*, to restrain (from).
بر داشتن	*bar d.*, to lift, raise, take away (from).
بر کنار رفتن	*bar kenar raftan*, to go aside, withdraw (from).
بهره بردن	*bahre bordan*, to benefit (from).
پذیرائی کردن	*pazirai k.*, to entertain (someone).
پرسیدن	*porsidan*, to ask (someone).
پرهیز کردن	*parhiz k.*, to refrain (from).
ترسیدن	*tarsidan*, to fear.
تعریف کردن	*ta'rif k.*, to describe, praise.

[1] خشت *xest*, a sun-baked brick.

جلوگیری کردن	*jeloûgiri k.*, to prevent.
خبر داشتن	*xabar d.*, to have news (of).
دوری جستن	*duri jostan*, to avoid (someone).
رد شدن	*radd ʃ.*, to pass (by), overtake.
سؤال کردن	*so'al k.*, to ask (someone).
صرف نظر کردن	*sarfe nazar kardan*, to refrain (from).
عبارت بودن	*ebarat b.*, to consist (of, in).
عبور کردن	*obur k.* } to pass (through, by).
گذشتن	*gozaʃtan* }
محروم بودن (ماندن)	*mahrum b.* (*mandan*), to be deprived of.
مستفیض گشتن	*mostafiz g.*, to derive benefit (from).
مسرور گشتن	*masrur g.*, to be made happy (by).
معذرت خواستن	*ma'zarat xastan*, to ask pardon (from someone).
معزول کردن	*ma'zul k.*, to dismiss (from).

The following compounds of از are also used:

غیر از	*γeîr az*, other than.
بعد از	*ba'd az* } after.
پس از	*pas az* }
قبل از	*qabl az* } before (time).
پیش از	*piʃ az* }
بیرون از	*birun az* } outside.
خارج از	*xarej az* }

(*b*) با *ba* (with, on the responsibility of, to) denotes association with or opposition to.

با او مشورت کردم	*ba u maʃvarat kardam*, I consulted him.
با او آشنا نیستم	*ba u aʃna nistam*, I am not acquainted with him.
با ما بد است	*ba ma bad ast*, He is on bad terms with us, dislikes us.
تصویب آن با هیئت مدیره است	*tasvibe an ba heî'ate modire ast*, Its ratification is the responsibility of the executive committee.

The following verbs take با *ba*:

ارتباط داشتن *ertebat d.*, to have connexions or relations (with).
ازدواج کردن *ezdevaj k.*, to marry.
آشنا بودن *asna b.*, to be acquainted (with a person).
بد بودن *bad b.*, to be on bad terms (with).
حرف زدن *harf zadan*, to talk (with), speak (to).
خوب بودن *xub b.*, to be on good terms (with).
صحبت کردن *sohbat k.*, to talk (with), speak (to).
مخالف بودن *moxalef b.*, to be opposed (to).
مشورت کردن *masvarat k.*, to consult (with).

(*c*) بر *bar* (on, upon, over, about, for, from, of, with, up to = the responsibility of) is used to denote position in a figurative sense or otherwise.

بر دشمنان تاختند *bar dosmanan taxtand*, They attacked the enemy.

بر آنها مستولی گشت *bar anha mostouli gast*, He gained dominion over them (overcame them).

بر این حادثه تأسف خورد *bar in hadese ta'assof xord*, He was sorry about this happening.

بر مردمان عاقل واضح است *bar mardomane aqel vazeh ast*, It is clear to wise persons.

بر من پوشیده نیست *bar man puside nist*, It is not hidden from me.

این بر صحت گفته شما دلالت میکند *in bar sehhate gofteye soma dalalat mikonad*, This is proof of the rightness of what you said.

بر مردم است که اورا مجازات کنند *bar mardom ast ke ura mojazat konand*, It is up to the people to punish him.

بر این کار کمر بست *bar in kar kamar bast*, He girt up his loins to do this work.

پیشنهاد شما مبنی بر سوء تفاهم است *pisnehade soma mabni bar su'e tafahom ast*, Your proposal is based upon a misunderstanding.

The following verbs take بر *bar*[1]:

اعتماد کردن *e'temad k.*, to rely (upon).
افزودن *afzudan*, to increase.
بر خوردن *bar xordan*, to meet (with).
پوشیده بودن *puſide b.*, to be hidden (from).
تاختن *taxtan*, to attack.
تأسف خوردن *ta'assof xordan*, to regret, be sorry (about).
حمله کردن *hamle k.*, to attack.
چیره گردیدن *cire g.*, to obtain dominion (over).
دلالت کردن *dalalat k.*, to be or give proof (of).
رحمت کردن *rahmat k.*, to have mercy (upon).
روا بودن *rava b.*, to be permissible (for).
ریختن (ریز) *rixtan* (*riz*), to pour (over); rush (upon), fall (upon).
شایسته بودن *ſayeste b.*, to be fitting (for).
غالب آمدن *yaleb amadan*, to conquer, overcome.
فرمانروائی کردن *farmanravai k.*, to rule (over a country, etc.).
کمر بستن *kamar bastan*, to gird up one's loins (to do something).
مبنی بودن *mabni b.*, to be based (upon).
مستولی گشتن *mostouli g.*, to gain dominion (over), overcome.
واضح بودن *vazeh b.*, to be clear (to someone).

(*d*) برای *baraye* and its compound از برای *az baraye*, for,[2] e.g.

اینرا برای شما خریدم *inra baraye ſoma xaridam*, I bought this for you.

(*e*) به *be* (to, in, into, at, with, on, upon, of, for, from, as) is used in a wide variety of contexts. It covers motion towards in a figurative sense or otherwise. It shows the relation of an action or state to the limits of space, time or condition. It expresses result, degree, amount and possession. It is also used to form adverbs and in oaths.

اینرا بمن داد *inra be man dad*, He gave this to me.
بما خوش گذشت *be ma xoſ gozaſt*, We enjoyed ourselves.

[1] It will be seen that many verbs admit of a choice between بر *bar* and به *be*.

[2] The ی of برای *baraye* was probably originally an *ezafe*.

باين امر رسيدگی کنيد *be in amr rasidegi konid*, Look into this matter.

باو کمك کردند *be u komak kardand*, They helped him.

باو متوسل شدند *be u motavassel ʃodand*, They had recourse to him.

باطاق وارد شد *be otaq vared ʃod*, He entered the room.

بشما شباهت دارد *be ʃoma ʃabahat darad*, He resembles you.

مطلب باينجا کشيد *matlab be inja kaʃid*, The matter reached this point (here).

بوزارت جنگ منتقل شد *be vezarate jang montaqel ʃod*, He was transferred to the ministry of war.

باين اعتراض کرد *be in e'teraz kard*, He protested at this.

راجع باين باو اعتراض کردم *raje' be in be u e'teraz kardam*, I protested about this to him.

بشهر رسيد *be ʃahr rasid*, He reached (arrived at) the town.

اين بمن مربوط نيست *in be man marbut nist*, This does not concern me.

در راه باو بر خورديم *dar rah be u bar xordim*, We met him on the way.

اين کار باو بر خورد *in kar be u bar xord*, This affair offended him.

بسرما خوردگی مبتلا شد *be sarmaxordegi mobtala ʃod*, He was afflicted with a chill.

باين واقعه واقف بود *be in vaqe'e vaqef bud*, He was aware of this happening.

معروف است بولخرجی *ma'ruf ast be velxarji*, He is known for (his) extravagance.

اينرا بدو ريال ميفروشد *inra be do rial miforuʃad*, He will sell this for two *rials*.

بعضويت هيئت انتخاب شد *be ozviyate hei'at entexab ʃod*, He was chosen as a member of the commission (committee).

باين باغ طمع دارد *be in baɣ tama' darad*, He covets this garden.

بما تعدی کرد *be ma ta'addi kard*, He oppressed us.

باین قایل نیستم *be in qayel nistam*, I do not admit (accept) this.

این رنگ بآن میخورد *in rang be an mixorad*, This colour matches that.

این لباس بشما میاید *in lebas be ʃoma miayad*, This costume suits you.

این هوا بمن میسازد *in hava be man misaȥad*, This climate suits me.

بفارسی *be farsi*, in Persian.

بنظر من *be naȥare man*, in my view.

بعقیده من *be aqideye man*, in my opinion.

بهر حال *be har hal* } in any case.
بهر صورت *be har surat* }

بهمان حال *be haman hal*, in the same condition.

باشتباه *be eʃtebah*, in error.

بقول آنها *be qo͡ule anha*, in their words, according to them.

شمشیر بدست *ʃamʃir be dast*, sword in hand.

بمرور زمان *be morure ȥaman*, in the course of time, with the passing of time.

باین سبب *be in sabab*, for this reason.

بخدا *be xoda*, by God.

The following verbs take به *be*:[1]

احتیاج داشتن *ehteyaj d.*, to be in need (of).

ارسال داشتن *ersal d.*, to send (to).

اعتراض کردن *eʻteraȥ k.*, to protest (to a person), object (to a thing).

اعتماد کردن *eʻtemad k.*, to rely (upon).

انتخاب کردن *entexab k.*, to choose (as).

ایمان آوردن (داشتن) *iman avardan (d.)*, to believe (in).

بر خوردن *bar xordan*, to meet, offend.

بسته بودن *baste b.*, to be dependent (upon something).

تعدی کردن *taʻaddi k.*, to oppress.

[1] It will be seen that many verbs admit of a choice between بر *bar* and به *be*.

تمایل داشتن	*tamayol d.*, to be inclined (to).
حاجت داشتن	*hajat d.*, to be in need (of).
خوش گذشتن	*xoʃ gozaʃtan* (used impersonally), to be enjoyed (by), pass pleasantly.
دادن	*dadan*, to give (to).
در گذشتن (بمرض)	*dar gozaʃtan* (*be maraz*), to die (of an illness).
دعوت کردن	*da'vat k.*, to invite (to).
ربط داشتن	*rabt d.*, to be concerned (with).
رسیدن	*rasidan*, to reach, arrive (at).
رسیدگی کردن	*rasidegi k.*, to investigate, inquire (into).
ساختن	*saxtan*, to suit.
سبقت جستن	*sabqat jostan*, to outstrip, outrun.
شباهت داشتن	*ʃabahat d.* } to resemble.
شبیه بودن	*ʃabih b.* }
طعنه زدن	*ta'ne zadan*, to make insulting insinuations.
طمع داشتن	*tama' d.*, to covet.
فروختن	*foruxtan*, to sell (for a price, to a person).
قایل بودن	*qayel b.*, to admit, accept, affirm.
کشیدن	*kaʃidan*, to lead (to), reach, result (in).
کمك کردن	*komak k.*, to help.
گفتن	*goftan*, to say (to).
مأمور کردن	*ma'mur k.*, to appoint (as).
مایل بودن	*mayel b.*, to be inclined (to).
مبادرت کردن (ورزیدن)	*mobaderat k.* (*varzidan*), to hasten (to do some thing).
مبتلا شدن	*mobtala ʃ.*, to be afflicted (with).
متوسل شدن	*motavassel ʃ.*, to have recourse (to).
مربوط بودن	*marbut b.*, to be connected (with).
مساعدت کردن	*mosa'edat k.*, to help.
مشروط بودن	*maʃrut b.*, to be conditional (upon).
معترض شدن	*mo'tarez ʃ.*, to protest (at), object (to something)
معروفیت داشتن	*ma'rufiat d.* } to be famous (for).
معروف بودن	*ma'ruf b.* }

منتقل شدن *montaqel ʃ.*, to be transferred (to).

نیاز داشتن *niaz d.*, to be in need (of).

واقف بودن *vaqef b.*, to be aware (of).

Certain verbs are followed by the preposition به *be* and the Infinitive. Among them are:

بنا کردن *bana kardan*, to begin (to).

پرداختن *pardaxtan*, to set to work (to).

مشغول شدن *maʃɣul ʃ.*, to become engaged (in), busy (with). شروع کردن *ʃoru' k.*, to begin (to), e.g. شروع کرد بحرف زدن *ʃoru' kard be harf zadan*, he began to speak.

(*f*) بی *bi*, without.

(*g*) تا *ta*, up to, to, e.g.

تا شهر رفتیم *ta ʃahr raftim*, We went to (as far as) the town.

از زمین تا آسمان فرق دارد *az zamin ta asman farq darad*, It is as different as chalk from cheese (from the earth to the sky).

تا یك ساعت دیگر بر میگردیم *ta yak sa'ate digar bar migardim*, We will return in an hour's time.

(*h*) جز *joz* and its compound بجز *bejoz*, except.

(*i*) در[1] *dar* (in, into, at, as, by), shows the relation of an action or state to the limits of space or time in a figurative sense or otherwise. It is also used to express area.

در اطاق نشسته بودیم *dar otaq neʃaste budim*, We were sitting in the room.

در این فکر بودم *dar in fekr budam*, I was thinking of this.

در عین حال *dar eine hal*, at the same time.

در نتیجه *dar natije*, as a result.

شش گز در چهار *ʃeʃ gaz dar cahar*, six *gaz* by four.

(*j*) مگر *magar*, except.

[1] In Classical Persian اندر *andar* 'in, into' is used as a preposition and also as a post-position, e.g. بشهر اندر *be ʃahr andar* in (into) the town.

3. Prepositions taking the *ezafe*, which are derived from primitive adverbs (originally nouns) and nouns, include the following:

بدون *bedun*, without.

برابر *barabar*, opposite.

بهر *bahr* and its compound از بهر *az bahr*, for.

بیرون *birun*, outside.

پائین *pain*, below.

پس *pas* and its compound در پس *dar pas*, behind.

پشت *post* and its compounds در پشت *dar post*, behind and از پشت *az post*, from behind.

پیش *pis* and its compound در پیش *dar pis* (in front of, before, with) are used to denote position and association with, e.g.

پیش او درس میخوانم *pise u dars mixanam*, I have lessons with him (i.e. from him).

کتاب پیش شماست *ketab pise somast*, The book is with you.

اورا پیش وزیر بردند *ura pise vazir bordand*, They took him before the minister.

جلو *jelou*, in front of.

دم *dam*, at, on the edge of, e.g.

دم در ایستاد *dame dar istad*, He stood at the door.

دنبال *dombal*, behind, after, e.g.

دنبال او گشتیم *dombale u gastim*, We went after him (to look for him).

زیر *zir* and its compound در زیر *dar zir*, under.

سر *sar*, at, on, over, e.g.

سر میز مینشستیم *sare miz minesastim*, We were sitting at table.

سر این اشتباه کردند *sare in estebah kardand*, They made a mistake over this.

And its compounds:

بر سر *bar sar*, on.

از سر *az sar*, from, on, off.

پشت سر *poſte sar*, after, behind, e.g.

پشت سر شما میامد *poſte sare ſoma miamad*, He was coming (along) behind you.

کنار *kenar* and its compound بر کنار *bar kenar*, beside.

گرد *gerd*, round, around.

لب *lab*, on the edge of, e.g.

لب دریا *labe darya*, on the seashore.

میان *mian*, between, and its compounds:

در میان *dar mian*, among; between.

از میان *az mian*, from among.

نزد *nazd*, in front of, beside, with, next, and its compounds:

در نزد *dar nazd*, near, beside.

از نزد *az nazd*, from, before.

نزدیك *nazdik*, near.

همراه *hamrah*, together, along with.

بالا *bala* (with the *ezafe* بالای *balaye*), above.

پا *pa* (with the *ezafe* پای *paye*), at the foot of.

پهلو *pahlu* (with the *ezafe* پهلوی *pahluye*), beside, by the side of.

پی *peï* (with the *ezafe* پی *peïye*), after, in pursuit of, and its compounds:

در پی *dar peï*, after; in continuation of.

از پی *az peï*, after.

تو *tu* (with the *ezafe* توی *tuye*), in, into.

جا *ja* (with the *ezafe* جای *jaye*) and its compound:

بجا *beja*, instead of, in place of.

رو *ru* (with the *ezafe* روی *ruye*), on; and its compounds:

از رو *az ru*, from upon, off.

رو برو *ru be ru*, opposite.

سو *su* (with the *ezafe* سوی *suye*), towards; and its compounds:

از سو *az su*, from the direction of.

بسو *be su*, towards.

در باره *dar bare* (with the *ezafe*, *dar bareye*), about, concerning.

Vocabulary

شرلی Sherley.
رابرت Robert.
میلاد *milad*, birth.
میلادی *miladi*, A.D.
قمری *qamari*, lunar.
مطابق *motabeq*, equal to, coinciding with.
اتحاد *ettehad*, union, unity.
ضد *ʒedd(e)*, بر ضد *bar ʒedd(e)*, against.
عثمانی *osmani*, Ottoman.
تحصیل *tahsil*, acquisition; تحصیل کردن *tahsil k.*, to acquire, study.
امتیاز *emteyaʒ*, concession (pl. امتیازات *emteyaʒat*).
همراهان *hamrahan*, companions.
عده *edde*, number.
نظام *neʒam*, order; military affairs.
نظامی *neʒami*, military; a military man.
توپ *tup*, cannon.
توپچی *tupci*, artillery-man.
وضع *vaʒ‘*, situation, condition.
آگاهی داشتن *agahi d.*, to be informed, aware of.
هلند Holland.
اسپانیا *espania*, Spain.
اواخر *avaxer* (pl. of آخر *axer*) = towards the end of (month, year, century, etc.).
قرن *qarn*, century.
شرکت جستن *ʃerkat jostan*, to participate in.
موقع *mo͡uqe‘*, time, situation; موقعیکه *mo͡uqe‘ike*, when.
عباس Abbas.
خراسان *xorasan*, Khurasan, a province in N.E. Persia.
دفع *daf‘*, repelling (noun).
فتنه *fetne*, sedition, rebellion.
تاتار *tatar*, Tartar.
ورود *vorud*, arrival.
پیغام *pe͡iɣam*, message.
فرنگی *farangi*, European.
مایحتاج *ma yahtaj* (Arabic for 'what is needed'), needs, necessities.
نوکر *no͡ukar*, servant.
امثال آن *amsale an*, such like (the likes of that).
مهیا *moha͡iya*, prepared, provided.
بر خلاف *bar xelaf(e)*, contrary to.
خطر *xatar*, danger.
پست *past*, mean (adj.).
ملازمان *molaʒeman*, attendants, retinue.
بریدن *boridan*, to cut (off).
تنگدستی *tangdasti*, being in difficulties, straits.
نعمت *ne‘mat*, bounty.

دریغ داشتن *dariɣ d.*, to grudge.
هنگام *hengam*, time.
گریختن (گریز) *gorixtan* (*goriz*), to flee from.
دربار *darbar*, court.
وزارت *vezarat*, ministry.
وزارت کشور *vezarate keʃvar*, the Ministry of the Interior.
پل *pol*, bridge.
امر *amr* (pl. امور *omur*), matter, affair.
موجب *mouјeb*, cause.
پیشرفت *piʃraft*, advance, progress.
کاهل *kahel*, lazy, negligent, slow.
محتاج *mohtaj*, needing, in need of.
عزت *ezzat*, honour.
مذلت *mazallat*, meanness, ignominy.
نرم *narm*, soft.
دلیر *dalir*, brave, audacious.
سیر *sir*, satiated.
بشر *baʃar*, man, humanity.
گشودن (گشا) *goʃudan* (*goʃa*), to open.
آزمودن (آزما) *azmudan* (*azma*), to try, test.
امید *omid*, hope.
زشت *zeʃt*, ugly.
معذور *ma'zur*, excused.
شر *ʃarr*, evil.

آمدن برادران شرلی بایران[1]

شرلیها دو برادر بودند بنام انتنی و رابرت که در ۱۵۹۷ میلادی مطابق با ۱۰۰۷ هجری قمری با بیست و پنج نفر انگلیسی جهت اتحاد با ممالك اروپا بر ضد دولت عثمانی و تحصیل امتیازات برای تجار انگلیسی از خاك عثمانی و مغرب ایران خودرا بقزوین رساندند (و از همراهان آنها عده نظامی و توپچی بودند که بوضع نظام اروپا بخوبی آگاهی داشته و خود انتنی شرلی هم خدمت سربازیرا انجام داده و در جنگهای هلند و اسپانیا در اواخر قرن شانزدهم میلادی شرکت جسته بود) در این موقع شاه عباس در خراسان مشغول دفع فتنه تاتارها بود چون خبر ورود نمایندگان انگلیسی بشاه رسید پیغام داد که باید از مهمانان فرنگی ما پذیرائی کامل شود و ما یحتاج آنان از اسب و نوکر و امثال آن مهیا باشد و هرکس بر خلاف این فرمان رفتار کند جانش در خطر خواهد بود و هرگاه کسی بپسترین ملازمان ایشان بدرفتاری نماید سرش بریده خواهد شد (نا تمام)

[1] See p. 95, footnote 1.

EXERCISE 20

دوستی مردمرا[1] بدو چیز توان شناخت یکی آنکه چون دوسترا تنگدستی رسد نعمت از او دریغ ندارند و دیگر آنکه هنگام تنگ‌دستی از او نگریزند—این مسافرت بما بسیار خوش گذشت—پاسبان شروع کرد برسیدگی کردن باین موضوع—از وزارت جنگ بوزارت کشور منتقل شد—برادر کوچك شما بیشتر بمادرتان شباهت دارد تا بپدرتان—سر این کار میانشان بهم خورد—اگرچه حق با شماست با وجود این باید از او معذرت بخواهید—این امر با آن امر هیچ ربطی ندارد—دیروز پیش یکی از دوستان شما بودم و خیلی از شما تعریف کرد—پس از آنکه از پل عبور کردم بعده زیادی از مردم بر خوردم—از کاهلی و تن آسانی دوری کنید چه مردم کاهل و تن آسان محتاج این و آنند—توانگری بهنراست نه بمال و بزرگی بعقل است نه بسال—بگفته خود کار کن تا بگفته تو کار کنند—مردمرا بلباس نتوان شناخت—مردن بعزت به از زندگانی بمذلت—بر دوستی پادشاهان اعتماد نشاید کرد[2]—نه چندان نرمی کن که بر تو دلیر شوند و نه چندان درشتی که از تو سیر گردند—آنکه بشر است هرگز زبان بشر نگشاید—تا کسیرا بارها نیازمائید بر وی اعتماد نکنید—بامید هزار دوست یك دشمن مکن—هرگاه کسی از تو زشت گوید ویرا معذورتر از آن کس دان که آن سخن را بتو رساند

EXERCISE 21

1. He came with me to the town and there we separated. 2. He did not return home because he feared his father. 3. He was sent as his country's representative to England. 4. The army attacked the enemy and defeated them. 5. If he had been there we would have asked him. 6. After he had conquered his enemies he ruled over the whole of the country. 7. He sought to avoid us. 8. We besought him to remain. 9. His possessions consist of three houses and two gardens. 10. We consulted together and decided to go. 11. He began to laugh. 12. In my opinion it would be better if you refrained from writing this letter. 13. Among the early English travellers who came to Persia were two brothers, named Sherley; they came to the court of Shah Abbas in the hope of obtaining trade concessions. They stayed a number of years in Persia and entered the service of Shah Abbas. One of them had some knowledge of military affairs, having taken part in several wars in Europe.

[1] See Lesson XII, para. 3.   [2] *Ibid.*

LESSON XII

The various uses of ی *-i*. The use of the *ezafe*. The omission of the *ezafe*. The use of را *-ra*. The use of the plural in ان *-an*. The agreement of nouns of multitude and collective nouns with the verb. Nouns used generically. The Vocative. The use of the comparative degree of adjectives. Repetition. و 'and'.

1. It will be useful here to recapitulate the various uses of ی *-i* and to add some remarks concerning them.

(*a*) Nominal.

(i) The Adjectival ی *-i*= belonging to,[1] e.g.

یزدی *yazdi*, a native of Yazd, belonging to Yazd.

وطنی *vatani*, native, home-made (=made in Persia; from وطن *vatan* 'homeland').

The following relative adjectives should be noted:

ساوجی *saveji*, a man of ساوه Save.

رازی *razi*, a man of ری Rei.

مروزی *marvazi*, a man of مرو Marv.

آوجی *avaji*, a man of آوه Ave.

دهلوی *dehlavi*, a man of دهلی Delhi.

سگزی *sagzi*, a man of Sistan (Segestan).

The Adjectival ی *-i* is not usually added to the name of the tribes, e.g.

نادر شاه افشار *nader ʃah afʃar*[2], Nader Shah, the Afshar,

but it is added to the names of dynasties, e.g.

یعقوب بن لیث صفاری *ya'qub ebne leise saffari*, Ya'qub son of Leis, the Saffarid.

The Adjectival ی *-i* when added to the Infinitive gives the meaning 'fit for, worthy of', e.g.

خوردنی *xordani*, fit to eat, edible.

خواندنی *xandani*, readable, interesting (to read).

دیدنی *didani*, worth seeing.

[1] =The Middle Persian *-ik* > *iy*.

[2] For the omission of the *ezafe* see para. 2 (*f*) below.

This ی -*i* is also added to the Infinitive to form a kind of present participle referring to future time, e.g.

در تهران ماندنی نیستم *dar tehran mandani nistam*, I am not staying in Tehran.

رفتنی هستم *raftani hastam*, I am going.

The Adjectival ی -*i* is capable of wide extension and can be added to almost any word or combination of words, e.g.

اتوموبیل چهار نفری *otomobile cahar nafari*, a four-seater car.

خانه دو طبقه *xaneye do tabaqei*, a two storeyed-house.

(ii) The Abstract ی -*i*,[1] e.g.

مهربانی *mehrabani*, kindness (from مهربان *mehraban* 'kind').

تاریکی *tariki*, darkness (from تاریك *tarik* 'dark').

(iii) The Indefinite ی -*i* (=one),[2] e.g.

مردی *mardi*, a (one) man.

The Indefinite ی -*i* is also capable of extension:

It is used to form adverb equivalents, e.g.

هفته چند *haftei cand*, a few weeks.

سالی دو *sali do*, (for) about two years.[3]

Added to صد *sad* 'hundred' it is used to express percentages, e.g.

صدی سه *sadi se*, 3%.

The Indefinite ی -*i* is also used to emphasize the noun or the quality expressed by the noun or the adjective qualifying the noun, e.g.

بلائی است *balaist*, It is a (great) calamity.

مردی است *mardist*, He is a (fine) man.

مرد خوبی است *marde xubist*, He is a (very) good man.

چنین ملت بزرگی *conin mellate bozorgi*, such a great people.

[1] =The Middle Persian -*ih*.

[2] =The Middle Persian *ē*, *ēv* <Old Persian *aiva*.

[3] A more usual way to express 'about' is to use در حدود *dar hodud(e)* or تقریباً *taqriban*, e.g. در حدود دو سال *dar hodude do sal*, or تقریباً دو سال *taqriban do sal*, about two years.

Used in this way the Indefinite ی *-i* can be added to a plural noun or adjective qualifying a plural noun, e.g.

تلفات بسیاری دادند *talafate besyari dadand*, They suffered (very) many losses.

خانمهای خوبی هستند *xanomhaye xubi hastand*, They are (very) good women.

The ی *-i* added to قدر *qadr*, اندك *andak*, کم *kam* and چند *cand* emphasizes the idea of indefiniteness, e.g.

قدری *qadri*
کمی *kami* } (just) a little.
اندکی *andaki*

The Indefinite ی *-i* is sometimes added to a plural noun to particularize it, e.g.

ملاحظاتی راجع بادبیات در دوره مشروطیت

molahezati[1] *raje' be adabiyat dar doureye masrutiyat*,

some (a few) observations on literature during the period of the Constitution.

With a negative verb the Indefinite ی *-i* conveys the idea of 'none whatever, no special, not very', e.g.

چندان دوام و ثباتی ندارد *candan davam va sabati nadarad*, It is not very firmly established (it has not much permanence or stability).

تعصبی ندارد *ta'assobi nadarad*, He has no fanaticism (whatever).

کاری ندارم *kari nadaram*, I have no (special) work.

The Indefinite ی *-i* used in this way can be further strengthened by the addition of هیچ *hic* 'none' which precedes the noun it governs, e.g.

هیچ عیبی ندارد *hic eibi nadarad*, It has no fault (whatever).

The Indefinite ی *-i* is added to plural nouns qualified by چه *ce* 'what sort of', e.g.

چه کسانی هستند *ce kasani hastand*, What sort of people are they?

[1] Sound feminine plural of ملاحظه *molaheze* (see Part II, Lesson XIX, para. 7).

The Indefinite ی *-i* is also used to convey the idea of 'totality', e.g.

بهم بر مکن تا توانی دلی * که آهی جهانی بهم بر کند

beham bar makon ta tavani deli ke ahi jahani beham bar konad.

Do not disturb a (single) heart as long as you can (avoid it), because a (single) sigh (to God) destroys a (whole) world.

In Lesson III, para. 13, it was stated that the noun and its attributes were regarded as a syntactical whole and the Indefinite ی *-i* was added to the final qualifying word. For the sake of variety, the Indefinite ی *-i* is sometimes added to the noun instead of to the adjective, in which case the *ezafe* is omitted, e.g.

مردی خوب *mardi xub*, a good man.

تنی چند *tani cand*, a few persons.

If two nouns, both indefinite, are united by a preposition, only the first takes the Indefinite ی *-i*, e.g.

سربازی با پاسبان در خیابان ایستاده بود *sarbazi ba pasban dar xiaban istade bud*, A soldier was standing in the street with a policeman.

مردی با بچه در باغ نشسته بود *mardi ba bacce dar bay nefaste bud*, A man was sitting in the garden with a child.

If the intention is to refer to an article in general terms, rather than to differentiate or to particularize it, the Indefinite ی *-i* is not used, e.g.

کاغذ مینویسد *kayaz minevisad*, He is writing a letter.[1]

کتاب میخواند *ketab mixanad*, He is reading a book.

مداد خرید *medad xarid*, He bought a pencil.

اطاق پنجره دارد *otaq panjare darad*, The room has a window (windows).

سیب میخورد *sib mixorad*, He is eating an apple.

[1] = 'he is "letter-writing"', or 'he is writing letters'; کاغذی مینویسد *kayazi minevisad* would mean 'he is writing some letter or other' and کاغذرا مینویسد *kayazra minevisad* 'he is writing the letter'.

Similarly, if a noun is used generically it does not take the Indefinite ی *-i*, e.g.

هنوز وزیر نشده‌است *hanuz vazir nafode ast*, He has not yet become a minister.

هنوز مرد نشده‌است *hanuz mard nafode ast*, He has not yet reached his majority (become a man).

Compare the above with the following:

مردی مثل شما این کاررا نمیکند *mardi mesle foma in karra namikonad*, A man like you would not do this.

(iv) The Relative ی *-i*,[1] e.g.

مردیکه... *mardike*, the (this) man who....

(i) and (ii) carry the stress; (iii) and (iv) are unstressed. Formerly (iii) and (iv) were pronounced *e*.

(*b*) Verbal.

(i) The Personal Ending for the 2nd pers. sing., e.g.

میکنی *mikoni*, Thou dost.

(ii) The Conditional or Continuous ی *-i* which is added to the Preterite, except in the 2nd pers. sing., to form a Conditional Past and an Imperfect, e.g.

گفتی *gofti*, He would have said, used to say, was saying.

کردمی *kardami*, I would have done, used to do, was doing.

The Conditional or Continuous ی *-i* is not used in Modern Persian apart from the form بایستی *bayesti*, which is occasionally found, e.g.

سلطان احمد شبی که صبح آن بایستی بجانب کرمان حرکت کند گفت...

soltan ahmad fabi ke sobhe an bayesti be janebe kerman harakat konad goft....

Soltan Ahmad on the evening before he was to have set out for Kerman said....

2. The principal uses of the *ezafe* have already been given. These are recapitulated below together with certain other uses of the *ezafe*.[2]

[1] = The Pahlavi *i* (*iy*).

[2] Persian grammarians enumerate several different kinds of *ezafe*. These are covered by, although they do not coincide exactly with, the uses of the *ezafe* in para. 2 above.

(*a*) The 'possessive' *ezafe* (to express the genitive), e.g.

کتاب پسر *ketabe pesar*, the boy's book.

در باغ *dare baɣ*, the door of the garden.

(*b*) The 'qualifying' or 'adjectival' *ezafe*, e.g.

مرد خوب *marde xub*, the good man.

بچه کوچك *bacceye kucek*, the small child.

(*c*) The 'prepositional' *ezafe*, e.g.

سر میز *sare miz*, at table.

پشت خانه *poʃte xane*, behind the house.

(*d*) The *ezafe* of 'sonship', e.g.

رستم زال *rostame zal*, Rustam son of Zal.

(*e*) The *ezafe* used to express distance from, e.g.

ده فرسخی اصفهان *dah farsaxiye esfahan*, ten *farsaxs* distant from Isfahan (being a distance of ten *farsaxs* from Isfahan).

(*f*) The *ezafe* is used in many cases in Persian where in English two nouns are used in apposition, e.g.

یعقوب پیغمبر *ya'qube peiɣambar*, Jacob, the prophet.

رود نیل *rude nil*, the River Nile.

محمد خان تاجر *mohammad xane tajer*, Mohammad Khan, the merchant.

Various words meaning 'kind, sort' do not take the *ezafe*. Among them are: نوع *nou'*, طور *tour*, جور *jur*, and قبیل *qabil*, e.g.

این نوع خانه *in nou' xane*, this kind of house.

این قبیل اشخاص[1] *in qabil aʃxas*, people of this kind.

این طور رفتار *in tour raftar*, this kind of conduct.

The Personal Pronouns, with the exception of من *man* 'I', do not take the *ezafe* and must be used in apposition, e.g.

بیچاره شما باید بمانید *bicare ʃoma bayad bemanid*, You, unfortunate one, must remain.

من بدبخت نرفتم *mane badbaxt naraftam*, I, unfortunate one, did not go.

[1] Plural of شخص *ʃaxs*.

همه *hame* 'all' when it means an aggregate without regard to the component parts is used without the *ezafe*, e.g.

همه راه در این فکر بود *hame rah dar in fekr bud*, He was thinking of this the whole way.

همه شب بیدار بود *hame ʃab bidar bud*, He was awake the whole night.

مایل نیستم این همه زحمت بکشید *mayel nistam in hame zahmat bekaʃid*, I do not want you to take all this trouble.

There is no *ezafe* after weights and measures, e.g.

دو متر گودی *do metr goudi*, two metres deep.

سه سنگ آب *se sang ab*, three *sangs* of water.

یك چارك گوشت *yak carak guʃt*, one *carak* of meat.

Similarly

یك لیوان آب *yak livan ab*, a glass of water.

یك فنجان چای *yak fenjan cai*, a cup of tea.

The *ezafe* is not used between a proper name and the titles following it, the two being placed in apposition to each other, e.g.

جناب آقای بهمن نخست وزیر *janabe aqaye bahman naxost vazir*, H. E. Bahman, the Prime Minister.

It has been seen above that when the Indefinite ی *-i* is added to the noun instead of the following qualifying word the *ezafe* falls out. This also happens if the word order is inverted and the adjective precedes the noun it qualifies, e.g.

خوب خانه خرید *xub xanei xarid*, He bought a good house.

Inversion takes place with the words عجب *ajab* 'strange, wonderful' and مرحوم *marhum* 'late, deceased'. The former does not take the *ezafe* whereas the latter does, e.g.

عجب کتابی‌است *ajab ketabist*, It is a strange book.

این شهر عجب هوای خوبی دارد *in ʃahr ajab havaye xubi darad*, This town has a wonderful climate.

مرحوم پدرم *marhume pedaram*, my late father.

3. In Lesson I, para. 6, the use of را *-ra* to mark the definite direct object was described. را *-ra* is also used to express the dative, e.g.

اورا دو پسر بود *ura do pesar bud*, He had two sons (to him were two sons).

شاه وزیررا خلعت داد *ʃah vazirra xelʿat dad*, The Shah gave the minister a robe of honour.

را *-ra* cannot be used to mark both the definite direct object and the indirect object in the same sentence: either the latter must be preceded by به *be* 'to' or the را *-ra* must be omitted after the definite direct object.

The use of را *-ra* to express the dative is a classical rather than a modern usage.

A similar construction is found with certain intransitive verbs in both Classical and Modern Persian, e.g.

این کتاب مرا پسند آمد *in ketab mara pasand amad*, I liked this book (this book came pleasantly to me).

بایستن *bayestan* and شایستن *ʃayestan* are used impersonally with را *-ra* to mean 'it behoves, it is fitting', etc.[1] This construction is classical rather than modern, e.g.

پادشاهرا باید... *padeʃahra bayad*, It behoves the king to....

شمارا شاید... *ʃomara ʃayad...*, It befits you to....

If an adjective or participle used as an adjective is placed in apposition to a noun which is indefinite, the latter, if the object of the verb, takes را *-ra*, e.g.

ظالمیرا خفته دیدم *zalemira xofte didam*, I saw a (certain) tyrant asleep.

سربازیرا در راه کشته دیدم *sarbazira dar rah koʃte didam*, I saw on the road a soldier [who had been] killed.[2]

In Colloquial Persian a certain latitude prevails in the use of را *-ra*, e.g.

کدام کتابرا میخواهید *kodam ketabra mixahid*, Which book do you want?

رفت کتابیرا بخرد *raft ketabira bexarad*, He went to buy a book.

[1] When used thus شاید *ʃayad* takes the negative prefix whereas شاید *ʃayad* 'perhaps' does not, e.g.

نشاید این کاررا کرد *naʃayad in karra kard*, It is not fitting to do such a work.

[2] سربازی کشته در راه دیدم *sarbazi koʃte dar rah didam* would be a more usual construction.

The use of را *-ra* in such a construction gives the force of 'a certain' to the Indefinite ی *-i* and sometimes implies that the sentence is incomplete, some phrase such as که لازم داشت *ke lazem daſt* being perhaps in the speaker's mind in the second of the above examples.

Compare also:

یکی بمن بدهید *yaki beman bedehid*, Give me one.

And یکی‌را بمن بدهید *yakira beman bedehid*, Give me (one of them).

In certain cases را *-ra* is added to an indefinite noun for the sake of clarity, e.g.

شنیدم گوسفندیرا بزرگی رهانید *ſonidam gusfandira bozorgi rahanid*, I have heard that a certain great man set free a sheep.

The words فلان *folan* 'a certain', فلانی *folani* 'so-and-so', همه *hame* 'all', سائر *sa'er* 'other, the rest', تمام *tamam* 'all, the whole', هر یکی *har yaki* 'each one', هردو *har do* 'both', etc., are considered definite and take را *-ra*.

را *-ra* is also used in Classical Persian, though not commonly, to form combinations corresponding to an adverbial phrase in English, e.g.

قضارا *qazara*, by chance.

خدارا *xodara*, for God's sake.

The expression ترا بخدا *tora bexoda* is used between intimate friends to express surprise or to emphasize something.

In Classical Persian the particle مر *mar* is sometimes found preceding a noun or pronoun followed by را *-ra*, e.g.

پادشاه مر عامه‌را بار دادی[1] *padeſah mar ammera bar dadi*, The king used to hold a court for the common people.

4. Two nouns are frequently used in Persian where an adjective and a noun or an adverb and an adjective are used in English, e.g.

کمال امتنانرا دارم *kamale emtenanra daram*, I am extremely grateful (have the perfection of gratitude).

در نهایت سختی زندگی میکند *dar nehayate saxti zendegi mikonad*, He lives in great hardship (in the extremity of difficulty).

با نهایت خوشحالی *ba nehayate xoſhali*, with great (the limit of) happiness.

[1] See above, para. 1 (*b*) (ii) for the Continuous Past in ی *-i*.

5. Adjectives used as nouns denoting rational beings take the plural in ان *-an*, e.g.

بزرگان *bozorgan*, the great.
حسودان *hasudan*, the envious.

Relative Adjectives ending in ی *-i*, however, normally form a plural in ها *-ha*.

Certain words denoting irrational beings or inanimate objects also sometimes form a plural in ان *-an*. Among them are:

لب	*lab*, lip.	بازو	*bazu*, forearm.
چشم	*caʃm*, eye.	گناه	*gonah*, sin.
درخت	*daraxt*, tree.	سخن	*soxan*, word.
آهو	*ahu*, gazelle.	ستاره	*setare*, star.[1]

سرها *sarha* means 'heads'; سران *saran* means 'leaders', e.g.

سران لشکر *sarane laʃkar*, army leaders.

نیا *nia* 'ancestor' and پله *pelle* 'stair' form their plurals نیاکان *niakan* and پلکان *pellekan* respectively.

Words of foreign origin, even if they denote rational beings, do not usually take the plural in ان *-an*, thus خانمها *xanomha*, ladies, انگلیسها *englisha*, the English, but فرانسویان *faransavian*, the French.

6. Nouns of Multitude denoting rational beings are followed by the singular or the plural according to whether the idea of unity or plurality is uppermost in the speaker's mind, e.g.

قشون حمله کرد *qoʃun hamle kard*, The army attacked.

جمعیتی بزرگ در میدان جمع شد *jam'iyati bozorg dar mĕidan jam' ʃod*, A large crowd assembled in the square.

عده متفرق شدند و عده ماندند *eddei motafarriq ʃodand va eddei mandand*, A number dispersed and a number remained (behind).

جمعیت ما از صد نفر تشکیل میشود *jam'iyate ma az sad nafar taʃkil miʃavad*, Our group (society) is composed of one hundred persons.

مردم *mardom* 'people' always takes a plural verb, e.g.

مردم جمع شدند *mardom jam' ʃodand*, The people assembled.

[1] Plural ستارگان *setaregan*.

7. Certain collective nouns take a plural termination when it is intended to signify diversity or variety, e.g.

ایران میوه‌های خوب دارد *iran mivehaye xub darad*, Persia has good fruit (of different kinds).

شرابهای فرانسه معروف است *ʃarabhaye faranse maʿruf ast*, The wine (i.e. the different wines) of France is famous.

انگورهای آذربایجان شیرین است *angurhaye azarbaijan ʃirin ast*, The grapes (i.e. the different kinds of grapes) of Azarbaijan are sweet.

8. Nouns denoting rational beings, when used generically, are usually put in the plural, e.g.

ایرانیها طبع شعر دارند *iraniha tabʿe ʃeʿr darand*, The Persian is poetical.

زنهای دهاتی زیاد کار میکنند *zanhaye dehati ziad kar mikonand*, The country-woman works hard (much).

Nouns denoting irrational beings and inanimate objects, when used generically, are put in the singular, e.g.

سگ تازی برای شکار خوب است *sage tazi baraye ʃekar xub ast*, Salukis are good for hunting.

خربوزه در گرگاب خوب بعمل میاید *xarbuze dar gorgab xub be amal miayad*, Melons grow well in Gorgab.[1]

If a noun used generically forms the predicate it is put in the singular even if the subject of the sentence is plural, e.g.

ما همه بنده خدا ایم *ma hame bandeye xoda im*, We are all servants of God.

این مردها حیوان اند *in mardha heivan and*, These men are (like) animals.

آنها دشمن ما هستند *anha doʃmane ma hastand*, They are our enemies.

If a noun used generically follows another noun which takes the *ezafe* it is put in the plural, e.g.

[1] A village near Isfahan.

این کار کار بچه‌هاست *in kar kare baccehast*, This work is the work of a child.

این مناسب حال بزرگان نیست *in monasebe hale bozorgan nist*, This is not in keeping with the dignity of the great.

مردی با لباس درویشان وارد شهر شد *mardi ba lebase darviʃan varede ʃahr ʃod*, A man in darvish's clothes entered the town.

9. If a series of nouns are united to each other by و *va*, *o*, the plural termination can be omitted, e.g.

وزیر و وکیل و صاحب منصب و آخوند همه حاضر بودند
vazir o vakil o saheb mansab o axund hame hazer budand,
Ministers, deputies, officers and mullas, all were present.

بزرگ و کوچك همه آمدند
bozorg va kucek hame amadand,
Great and small, all came.

گاو و گوسفند و الاغ و اسب در چمن بود
gav o gusfand o olaɣ o asb dar caman bud,
Cows, sheep, asses, and horses were in the meadow.

قلم و مداد و کتاب بین بچه‌ها تقسیم کرد
qalam o medad o ketab beine bacceha taqsim kard,
He distributed pens, pencils and books among the children.

در باغ ما گیلاس و انگور و انجیر خوب پیدا میشود
dar baɣe ma gilas o angur o anjire xub peida miʃavad,
In our garden good cherries, grapes and figs are to be had (found).

10. In certain cases a noun which is logically plural is nevertheless put in the singular, e.g.

روی دوش همه بارهای سنگین بود *ruye duʃe hame barhaye sangin bud*, Heavy loads were on the back(s) of all.

تغییر عقیده دادند *taɣyire aqide dadand*, They changed their minds.

کاغذ مبادله کردیم *kaɣaz mobadele kardim*, We exchanged letters.

11. The vocative is expressed by the particle ای *ei* or (when addressing God or one of the Imams, etc.) یا *ya* preceding the noun or pronoun, e.g.

ای پادشاه *ei padeʃah*, O king!

ای تو که... *ei to ke...*, O thou, who....

12. An ا *-a* can be added to nouns and adjectives to form an interjection, e.g.

خداوندا *xodavanda*, O God!

خوشا بحال شما *xoʃa be hale ʃoma*, O happy your state!

خوشا شیراز *xoʃa ʃiraz*, O happy Shiraz!

If the noun to which this 'interjectory' *alef* is added ends in ا *a* or و *u*, a ی *y* is inserted between the final vowel and the 'interjectory' ا *-a*, e.g.

خدایا *xodaya*, O God!

Personal Pronouns, with the exception of من *man* 'I', do not take the 'interjectory' ا *-a*.

13. Certain nouns are used as adjectives, e.g.

این خانه بسیار راحت است *in xane besyar rahat ast*, This house is very comfortable (راحت = ease, comfort).

14. The comparative degree of adjectives is sometimes used in Persian where the superlative is used in English, e.g.

بهر شهریکه نزدیکتر است بروید *be har ʃahri ke nazdiktar ast beravid*, Go to the nearest town.

The comparative ending is also added to certain nouns, e.g.

این طرفتر بنشینید *in taraftar beneʃinid*, Sit nearer this way (side).

A phrase such as 'he got better and better' is rendered

روز بروز بهتر میشد *ruz be ruz behtar miʃod*,

or

هی بهتر میشد *hei behtar miʃod*.

(See also Lesson XIII, para. 24.)

'The sooner the better' is translated

هر چه زودتر بهتر *har ce zudtar behtar*.

هر قدر *har qadr* can be used instead of هر چه *har ce*, e.g.

هر قدر برودخانه نزدیکتر میشوید زمین حاصلخیزتر است
har qadr be rudxane naʒdiktar miʃavid ʒamin haselxiʒtar ast,
The nearer you get to the river the more fertile the land.

'How much the more' and 'how much the less' are rendered as follows:

اگر آن وقت از او بدتان میامد بطریق اولی[1] باید حالا از او نفرت داشته باشید
agar an vaqt aʒ u badetan miamad be tariqe o͡ula bayad hala aʒ u nefrat daʃte baʃid,
If you disliked him then, how much the more must you dislike him now.

اگر این کتابرا دوست دارید چقدر باید آن یکیرا دوست داشته باشید[2]
agar in ketabra dust darid ce qadr bayad an yakira dust daʃte baʃid,
If you like this book, how much the more must you like that one.

باو نمیشود اعتماد کرد تا چه رسد ببرادرش
be u namiʃavad e'temad kard ta ce rasad be baradaraʃ,
One cannot trust him, much less his brother.

15. In Classical Persian the absolute use of the comparative and superlative is sometimes found, e.g.

قشنگترین *qaʃangtarin*, most beautiful (=very beautiful).
قشنگتر *qaʃangtar*, more beautiful (=very beautiful).

16. Comparison can be expressed by که *ke*, e.g.

مردنت به که مردم آزاری[3] *mordanat beh ke mardom aʒari*, Thy death is better than oppression of the people (it is better that thou shouldst die, than that thou shouldst oppress the people).

This usage is classical rather than modern.

For other methods of expressing comparison see Lesson III, para. 17.

[1] اولی *o͡ula* is the elative of اول *avval*; see Part II, Lesson XVI, para. 16.

[2] For the use of the Subjunctive Past of داشتن *daʃtan* see Lesson XIII, para. 12 (*h*).

[3] From آزردن *aʒordan* 'to oppress'.

17. Many adjectives can be used as nouns. Their use as nouns, however, tends to be more common in the plural than the singular. The use of the plural termination ان *-an* with adjectives used as nouns denoting rational beings has already been noted (see above para. 5).

18. In Persian two nouns or two adjectives with the same or similar meanings are often used together, e.g.

گریه و زاری *gerie o zari*, weeping and wailing.

تك و تنها *tak o tanha*, single and alone.

تر و تازه *tar o taze*, moist and fresh.

خوش و خرم *xoʃ o xorram*, happy and cheerful.

Such combinations are not considered bad style.

19. Repetition of a word indicates:

(*a*) Intensity, e.g.

تند تند بیا *tond tond beya*, Come very quickly.

زار زار گریه میکرد *zar zar gerye mikard*, She was weeping bitterly.

This is also the case where an adjective is repeated with the copula و *o*, or with the *ezafe*, e.g.

تند و تند آمدم *tond o tond amadam*, I came very quickly.

خطرناك خطرناك *xatarnake xatarnak*, very dangerous.

(*b*) Continuation, e.g.

یواش یواش میامد *yavaʃ yavaʃ miamad*, He was coming along slowly.

باران نم نم میامد *baran nam nam miamad*, It kept on drizzling.

(*c*) Grouping, e.g.

كبكها دسته دسته بلند شدند *kabkha daste daste boland ʃodand*, The partridges rose in coveys.

(See also Lesson XIII, para. 3 (*b*) below)

20. و 'and' is derived from two different sources: namely و = *va* from the Arabic and و = *o* from Middle Persian (see p. 38, n. 2). The latter form, in addition to its use in compound numerals and in certain com-

pounds (see Lesson x) tends to be used rather than و = *va* when it connects words or phrases commonly associated together, e.g.

روز و شب *ruz o ʃab*, day and night.

In rapid speech it tends to be used in other contexts also, and in poetry it may be necessitated by the scansion.

و 'and' is used

(*a*) As a copulative, e.g.

آمد و از ما خدا حافظی کرد *amad va az ma xoda hafezi kard*, He came and said good-bye to us.

If a noun is qualified by several adjectives these may be united by و instead of the *ezafe*, e.g.

آدم هوشیار و لایق و صبوری بود *adame huʃyar va layeq va saburi bud*, He was an intelligent, worthy and very patient man,

instead of

آدم هوشیار لایق صبوری بود *adame huʃyare layeqe saburi bud.*

(*b*) To introduce a qualifying phrase, e.g.

سر میز نشسته بود و قلمی بدستش بود *sare miz neʃaste bud va qalami be dasteʃ bud*, He was sitting at the table with a pen in his hand.

(*c*) To mean 'is equal to, accompanied by, is the same as', e.g.

پیری و صد عیب *piri o sad eib*, Old age is accompanied by a hundred defects.

(*d*) To mean 'or', e.g.

گل همین پنج روز و شش باشد *gol hamin panj ruz o ʃeʃ baʃad*, A flower lasts but five or six days.

(*e*) To indicate association, e.g.

من و شراب خوردن چه حرفها میزنید *man o ʃarab xordan ce harfha mizanid*, I—drink wine? What are you saying?

تابستان آینده ما و اصفهان *tabestane ayande ma o esfahan*, Next summer Isfahan for us.

This و is frequently used in poetry, e.g.

که گر جستم از دست این تیر زن * من و کنج ویرانه پیر زن

ke gar jastam az daste in tir zan man o konje veiraneye pir zan,

...saying if I escape the hand of this archer, I will be content with a corner of the old woman's ruined hut.

چو فردا برآید بلند آفتاب * من و گرز و میدان و افراسیاب

co[1] *farda bar ayad boland aftab man o gorz o meidan o afrasiab,*

When tomorrow the sun mounts high (in the heavens) there will I be with my club in the battlefield with Afrasiab.

VOCABULARY

بقیه *baqiye*, remainder.

ترتیب *tartib*, arrangement, arranging.

حکمران *hokmran*, governor.

قسم *qesm*, kind, sort.

وسایل *vasayel* (pl. of وسیله *vasile*), means.

استراحت *esterahat*, rest, repose.

جماعت *jama'at*, group, body, company (of people).

ساختن (ساز) *saxtan* (*saz*), to make.

فراهم *faraham*, available.

حاکم *hakem*, governor.

ناظر *nazer*, overseer, bailiff; a kind of inspector.

استقبال *esteqbal*, going out to give a ceremonial welcome (to someone).

بوسیدن *busidan*, to kiss; روبوسی *rubusi*, kissing on the face.

احترام *ehteram*, respect, honour.

تحف *tohaf* (pl. of تحفه *tohfe*), presents.

هدایا *hadaya* (pl. of هدیه *hadiye*), presents.

لگام *legam*, bridle.

قاطر *qater*, mule.

بخشیدن *baxsidan*, to bestow, give.

سپس *sepas*, then.

ملاطفت *molatefat*, showing favour, kindness.

خدمتگذار *xedmatgozar*, servant, retainer.

صمیمی *samimi*, sincere.

صداقت *sadaqat*, sincerity, faithfulness.

صمیمیت *samimiyat*, sincerity.

معتقد *mo'taqed*, having faith (in), believing (in), convinced (of).

دستیاری *dastyari*, help.

[1] چو *co* is a contraction of چون *cun* used in poetry.

الله وردی خان Allahverdi Khan (one of Shah Abbas' military leaders).

سپهسالار *sepahsalar*, army commander.

فنون *fonun* (pl. of فن *fann*), art.

رنج *ranj*, trouble, vexation; رنج بردن *ranj bordan*, to suffer trouble, vexation.

سپاه *sepah*, army.

سپاهی *sepahi*, soldier.

تهیه *tahie*, preparing, making ready.

پیشنهاد *pisnehad*, proposal.

سفیر *safir*, ambassador, envoy, plenipotentiary.

سلاطین *salatin* (pl. of سلطان *soltan*), rulers, sultans.

متحد *mottahed*, united.

متملق *motamalleq*, a flatterer.

فریفتن (فریب) *fariftan* (*farib*), to deceive.

پشیمانی *pasimani* } regret.
ندامت *nedamat* }

گزیدن *gazidan*, to bite, sting.

قفا *qafa*, nape of the neck; در قفا *dar qafa*, behind.

وجه *vajh*, way, manner.

نیك *nik*, good.

نام *nam*, name.

برتری *bartari*, superiority.

مژده *mozde*, good news.

انوشیروان عادل *anusiravane adel*, Anushiravan the Just (the Sasanian ruler who reigned A.D. 531–78).

خدایتعالی *xodaye ta'ala*, God most high[1].

عدو *adu*, enemy.

حکایت *hekayat*, story.

متفرق کردن *motafarreq k.*, to disperse (trans.).

آمدن برادران شرلی بایران

(بقیه از درس پیش)

با این ترتیب حکمران قزوین از او پذیرائی شایان نمود و همه قسم وسایل استراحت آن جماعترا فراهم ساخت تا آنکه خبر ورود شاه بنزدیکی قزوین بشهر رسید و برادران شرلی و همراهانشان بهمراهی ناظر و حاکم قزوین باستقبال شاه رفتند و شاه هم با آن دو برادر روبوسی کرده با احترام تمام از آنها پذیرائی نمود و تحف و هدایای زیاد (۴۰ اسب با لگام زرین و ۱۰۰ قاطر و ۱۰۰ شتر و مقدار زیادی پول) بآنها و همراهانشان بخشید سپس با آن جماعت بپایتخت (اصفهان) رفت و ششماه در آن شهر از آنها پذیرائی کرد و بقدری نسبت بآنها ملاطفت

[1] تعالی *ta'ala* is an Arabic verbal form (=he is exalted) used here as an adjective.

نمود که خودشانرا از خدمتگذاران صمیمی شاه عباس دانستند و انتنی هم در مدت اقامت در اصفهان شاهرا بصداقت و صمیمیت خود معتقد ساخت و بدستیاری الله وردیخان سپهسالار ایران در آموختن فنون جنگی ایران رنج بسیار برد و ایرانیان فنون جنگرا از شرلی آموختند و سپاهیان مرتب و ۵۰۰ عراده توپ و ۲۰,۰۰۰ تفنگ تهیه کردند سپس انتنی بشاه عباس پیشنهاد کرد که سفیری بدربار سلاطین اروپا فرستد و با ایشان بر ضد دولت عثمانی متحد شود

(نا تمام)

Exercise 22

بسخنان دروغ متملقان فریفته نشوید و از شنیدن آنها بر حذر باشید تا پشیمانی نبرید و انگشت ندامت بدندان نگزید — هرکه در قفای دیگران بد گوید بهیچ وجه دوستیرا نشاید — هرکه‌را در زندگانی کار نیك نباشد پس از مردن نام نیك نباشد — مردمانرا برتری بر جانوران برفتار نیك است و کردار خوب — کسی مژده پیش انوشیروان عادل برد که شنیدم فلان دشمن‌را خدای تعالی بر داشت گفت هیچ شنیدی که مرا خواهد گذاشت

مرا بمرگ عدو جای شادمانی نیست * که زندگانی ما نیز جاودانی نیست

Exercise 23

1. He has gone into the bazaar to buy a book. 2. After he had been two years in the army he became an officer. 3. This story is worth hearing. 4. I do not care for this kind of book. 5. Many kinds of fruit grow in Persia. 6. The people began to assemble in the square; men, women and children were there and did not disperse until after sunset. 7. The women were carrying their children on their backs. 8. The book is both interesting and well written. 9. I am going and nobody can prevent me. 10. It has not done me much good nor any one else either (it had not much benefit for me...). 11. Facilities for rest are available for all the workmen by day and by night. 12. I never spoke or wrote to him. 13. Either he or I must go. 14. He cannot have gone out else he would have told me.

LESSON XIII

The use of the tenses. The Negative. Impersonal Constructions. Continuous Tenses formed with داشتن *daʃtan*. The particle هی *hei*. Certain Classical usages.

1. (*a*) The Infinitive and Short Infinitive are used as nouns, e.g.

دانا شدن توانا شدن است *dana ʃodan tavana ʃodan ast*, To be learned is to be powerful.

گفتن این صلاح نیست *goftane in salah nist*, It is not expedient to say this.

پیشرفت او شایان تحسین است *piʃrafte u ʃayane tahsin ast*, his progress is praiseworthy.

(*b*) The Infinitive is used to express purpose or finality with the preposition به *be*, e.g.

بدیدن برادر خود رفت *be didane baradare xod raft*, He went to see his brother.

شروع کرد بنوشتن *ʃoru' kard be neveʃtan*, He began to write.

بخواندن پرداخت *be xandan pardaxt*, He set to work to read.

If the subordinate verb is a compound verb one part of which is a noun the verbal part can sometimes be omitted, e.g.

شروع کرد بگریه *ʃoru' kard be gerie* (for گریه کردن *gerie kardan*), He began to weep.

شروع کرد بفرار *ʃoru' kard be farar* (for فرار کردن *farar kardan*), He began to flee.

But

شروع کردند بجمع شدن *ʃoru' kardand be jam' ʃodan*, They began to assemble.

(*c*) The Short Infinitive is used after impersonal verbs (see Lesson VI, para. 12), e.g.

میشود کرد *miʃavad kard*, It can be done.

(*d*) In Classical Persian the Infinitive is sometimes used in final clauses where in Modern Persian the Subjunctive would be used, e.g.

لقمان گفت دریغ باشد کلمه حکمت با ایشان گفتن

loqman goft dariɣ baʃad kalameye hekmat ba iʃan goftan,

Loqman said it would be a pity to waste on them (to say to them) words of wisdom.

مصلحت ندیدم از این بیش ریش درونشرا بملامت خراشیدن و نمك پاشیدن

maslehat nadidam az in biʃ riʃe daruneʃra be malamat xaraʃidan va namak paʃidan,

I did not consider it expedient to rub (scratch) his inner wound more than this by reproach or (and) to sprinkle salt upon it.

(*e*) In Classical Persian the Infinitive is sometimes used with the auxiliaries توانستن *tavanestan* 'to be able', خواستن *xastan* 'to want', and بایستن *bayestan* and شایستن *ʃayestan* used impersonally. E.g.

بقیه عمررا از عهده شکر آن بیرون آمدن نتوانم

baqiyeye omrra az ohdeye ʃokre an birun amadan natavanam,

For the rest of (my) life I shall not be able to pay the debt of gratitude I owe for that.

(*f*) In Classical Persian the Infinitive is sometimes used with a preposition to express the passive, e.g.

پادشاه همه‌را بکشتن اشارت فرمود[1] *padeʃah hamera be koʃtan eʃarat farmud*, The king gave a sign for them all to be killed.

2. The Past Participle, apart from its use in conjugating the verb, is used

(*a*) As an adjective, e.g.

آماده باشید *amade baʃid*, Be prepared.

The negative of the Past Participle when it is used as an adjective or a noun (see immediately below) is نا *na-*, e.g.

ناگفته نماند *nagofte namanad*, Let it not remain unsaid.

(*b*) As a noun, e.g.

گفته مرا شنید *gofteye mara ʃenid*, He heard what I said.

The Past Participle is widely used as a noun in the plural referring to human beings, but less frequently in the singular, e.g.

بازداشت شدگان *bazdaʃt ʃodegan*, the internees.

کشتگان *koʃtegan*, the killed.

[1] See Lesson XIV, para. 1 (*c*) for this use of (فرما) فرمودن *farmudan* (*farma*).

(*c*) In apposition in the event of the subject of two co-ordinate sentences being the same and the action of the former of the two preceding the latter, e.g.

نامه شما رسیده خوانده شد *nameye ʃoma raside xande ʃod*, Your letter has been received and read.

If the tenses of the verbs of two or more co-ordinate sentences are the same and their actions concurrent, the Past Participle followed by و *va* can be used in all but the final sentence, provided the subjects are the same.

3. The Present Participle is used:

(*a*) As an adjective, e.g.

خواهان سلامتی شما هستم *xahane salamatiye ʃoma hastam*, I am desirous of your well-being (health).

(*b*) As an adverb, in which case it is usually repeated, e.g.

دوان دوان جلو آمد *davan davan jelōū amad*, He came forward running.

4. The Noun of the Agent, formed by the addition of نده *-ande* to the Present Stem, is also sometimes used as an adjective, e.g.

درخشنده *daraxʃande*, shining (from درخشیدن *daraxʃidan* 'to shine').

مرد بخشنده *marde baxʃandei*, a liberal man (from بخشیدن *baxʃidan* 'to give, bestow').

5. The Preterite is used:

(*a*) For a single definite action in the past, e.g.

دیروز رفت *diruz raft*, He went yesterday.

(*b*) For an action just performed, e.g.

اورا الآن دیدم *ura al'an didam*, I saw him just now.

(*c*) For the anterior of two possible future actions, e.g.

انگلستان که رفتید نامه بمن بنویسید

englestan ke raftid namei be man benevisid,

When you go to England, write a letter to me.

This use is comparable with its use in Present and Future conditions (see Lesson VII, para. 5 (*a*) above).

(*d*) For an action about to be completed, e.g.

آمدم *amadam*=I am coming (in answer to a question or implied question such as 'are you coming?' or a command such as 'hurry up').

رفتم *raftam*=I am going.

(*e*) In one or both parts of a conditional sentence to denote a foregone conclusion, e.g.

اگر رفتی بردی اگر خفتی مردی *agar rafti bordi agar xofti mordi*, If you go you win, if you sleep you die.

(*f*) In narrating past events that closely follow one another where the Pluperfect would be used in English, e.g.

وقتیکه حرف خودرا تمام کرد جواب دادم
vaqtike harfe xodra tamam kard javab dadam,
When he had finished what he had to say, I answered.

(*g*) With certain compound verbs formed with شدن *ʃodan*, indicating a state which began in the past and continues into the present, or a state which has just come to pass, e.g.

حاضر شدم *hazer ʃodam*=I am ready.

تشنه شدم *teʃne ʃodam*=I am thirsty.

پشیمان شدم *paʃiman ʃodam*=I am sorry (repentant).

خسته شدم *xaste ʃodam*=I am tired.

In certain contexts the Preterite of such verbs can refer to the past, e.g.

دیروز گرسنه شدم *diruz gorosne ʃodam*, Yesterday I was hungry.

(*h*) In sentences such as the following where the Perfect or Present is used in English:

کتابمرا فراموش کردم *ketabamra faramuʃ kardam*, I have forgotten my book.

زود آمدید *zud amadid*, You are early.

دیر کردید *dir kardid*, You are late.

جستمش *jostameʃ*, I have found it.

In Colloquial Persian the Preterite بایست *bayest* is sometimes used with a present meaning, e.g.

بایست رفت *bayest raft*=It is time to go.

6. The Imperfect is used:

(*a*) For a continuous action in the past, e.g.

نامهٔ مینوشت *namei minevešt*, He was writing a letter.

باران میامد *baran miamad*, It was raining.

وقتیکه مرا صدا زد کتاب میخواندم *vaqtike mara sada zad ketab mixandam*, When he called me I was reading a book.

میخواستم از شما بپرسم *mixastam az šoma beporsam*, I wanted to ask you.

میخواست برود *mixast beravad*, He wanted to go.

شاید آنها هم دلشان میخواست وسایل راحتی مرا داشتند *šayad anha ham delešan mixast vasa'ele rahatiye mara daštand*, Perhaps they also wished they had the facilities for comfort I had.[1]

(*b*) For habitual action in the past, e.g.

هر سال آنجا میرفتم *har sal anja miraftam*, Every year I went there.

(*c*) For an impossible action or state referring to the past or present (see also Impossible Conditions, Lesson VII, para. 5 (*b*) above), e.g.

اگر میدانست میگفت *agar midanest migoft*, If he had known he would have said;

and in unfulfilled wishes (see below, para. 16).

(*d*) Sometimes with the force of 'to be about to', e.g.

طیاره بر زمین فرود میامد که آتش گرفت

tai̯yare bar zamin forud miamad ke ateš gereft,

The aeroplane was about to land when it caught fire.

The Imperfect of خواستن *xastan* is sometimes used as a kind of auxiliary with this meaning, e.g.

میخواست بنشیند که صداش کردند *mixast benešinad ke sadaš kardand*, He was about to sit down when they called him.

[1] In this example شاید *šayad* does not affect the tense of the main verb. See also para. 12 (*e*) below.

(*e*) In the case of خواستن *xastan*, sometimes in Colloquial Persian in place of the Present, e.g.

کجا میخواستید بروید *koja mixastid beravid* = Where do you want to go?

(*f*) With the force of 'to begin to', e.g.

در اثنای این حال تشنگی بر ملك مستولی شد مرکب هر طرف میتاخت

dar asnaye in hal teʃnegi bar malek mostouli ʃod markab har taraf mitaxt, Meanwhile thirst overcame the king; he began to gallop his horse in every direction.

This usage is literary and is more common in Classical than in Modern Persian.

7. The Perfect is used:

(*a*) For an action in the past the results of which continue to be effective or apparent after the action itself, e.g.

کتاب گم شده است *ketab gom ʃode ast*, The book is lost (i.e. has been lost and is still lost).

شاه عباس این کاروانسرارا بنا کرده است *ʃah abbas in karevansarara bana karde ast*, Shah Abbas built this caravanserai.

The Perfect is thus used when referring to the sayings or writings of famous men (on the assumption that these are still effective and have lived on), e.g.

سعدی گفته است... *sa'di gofte ast*, Sa'di said....

(*b*) To refer to some indefinite time in the past, e.g.

زمانی این سخنرا شنیده‌ام *zamani in soxanra ʃenide am*, I heard these words at some time or other.

تشخیص داده ایم که لازم میباشد *taʃxis dade im ke lazem mibaʃad*, We decided (at some indefinite time in the past) that it was necessary.

(*c*) To refer to the future in the main clause after a temporal clause introduced by تا *ta* 'by the time that', e.g.

تا منزل بر گردید تمام پولتانرا خرج کرده اید

ta manzel bar gardid tamame puletanra xarj karde id, By the time you return home you will have spent all your money.

(*d*) Occasionally with a prefixed می *mi-*, e.g.

کتابهای تاریخ در هر دوره بساده‌ترین طریق نوشته میشده است
ketabhaye tarix dar har doure be sadetarin tariq neveʃte miʃode ast,
Histories, in every period, were written in the simplest style.

8. The Pluperfect is used:

(*a*) To describe the anterior of two actions or states in the past which do not follow one another immediately, e.g.

وقتیکه رسید رفته بودند *vaqtike rasid rafte budand*, When he arrived they had gone.

نامهٔ که نوشته بودید خواندم *namei ke neveʃte budid xandam*, I read the letter which you wrote (had written).

(*b*) In one or both parts of an impossible condition referring to the past (see Lesson VII, para. 5 (*b*) above), e.g.

اگر میدانستم گفته بودم *agar midanestam gofte budam*, If I had known, I would have said (so).

(*c*) To describe unfulfilled wishes in the past (see below, para. 16).

9. The Present is used:

(*a*) For a state or action taking place in the present, e.g.

کاغذ مینویسد *kaɣaz minevisad*, He is writing a letter.

باران میاید *baran miayad*, It is raining.

(*b*) For an action or state beginning in the past and continuing in the present, e.g.

چند وقت است که اینجا هستید *cand vaqt ast ke inja hastid*, How long have you been here?

دو سال است که در ایران هستم *do sal ast ke dar iran hastam*, I have been two years in Persia (and am still there).

از دیروز تا حالا مشغول این کار است *az diruz ta hala maʃɣule in kar ast*, He has been busy with this work (affair) ever since yesterday.

چکار میکنید *ce kar mikonid*, What are you doing, what have you been doing?

(*c*) For something said by a well-known person in the past, e.g.

نویسندگان معروف میگویند... *nevisandegane ma'ruf miguyand...*, Famous writers say....

It is more usual in such cases to use the Perfect (see para. 7 (*a*) above).

(*d*) For the Future, e.g.

فردا باو میگویم *farda be u miguyam*, I will tell him to-morrow.

In compound verbs formed with شدن *ʃodan* of the type mentioned in para. 5 (*g*) above, the present usually has a future meaning, e.g.

خسته میشوید *xaste miʃavid*, You will be tired.

(*e*) In certain cases after اگر *agar* 'if', e.g.

بروید و ببینید احمد درس خودرا میخواند یا نه اگر میخواند خوب است و اگر نمیخواند تنبیهش بکنید

beravid va bebinid ahmad darse xodra mixanad ya na agar mixanad xub ast va agar namixanad tambiheʃ bekonid,

Go and see if Ahmad is doing his lessons or not. If he is doing them it is well, but if not punish him.

It should be noted that there is a tendency in Colloquial Persian to substitute the present indicative for the present subjunctive in the protasis of Possible Conditions referring to future time.

10. The General Present (see Lesson IV, para. 1 (*c*) above) is used for general statements relating to the present or future, e.g.

در آنچه گویم یا نویسم خدا داند که تعصبی ندارم

dar ance guyam ya nevisam xoda danad ke ta'assobi nadaram,

I have no fanaticism—God knows—in whatever I say or write.

هرجا سهوی بینند و خطائی نگرند بگویند

har ja sahvi binand va xatai negarand, beguyand,

Wherever they see a mistake or perceive an error, let them say (so).

هر که شاه آن کند که او گوید * حیف باشد که جز نکو[1] گوید

har ke ʃah an konad ke u guyad heif baʃad ke joz neku guyad,

It is a pity that anyone whose word the king follows should say anything but (what is) good.

[1] For نیکو *niku* 'good'.

In the case of بودن *budan* the general present is frequently used, e.g.

تهران که پایتخت ایران باشد شهر بزرگی‌است
tehran ke pa͡itaxte iran baʃad ʃahre bozorgist,
Tehran, which is the capital of Persia, is a large town.

11. The Subjunctive Present is used:

(*a*) In a subordinate clause to express a state or action about which there is an element of doubt, e.g.

ممکن است که بیاید *momken ast ke beyayad,* It is possible that he may come.

(*b*) To express purpose, with or without که *ke*, e.g.

خواهش میکنم درخواست مرا قبول کنید
xaheʃ mikonam darxaste mara qabul konid,
I ask you to agree to (accept) my request.

تصمیم گرفتند که بروند
tasmim gereftand ke beravand,
They decided to go.

(*c*) After final conjunctions, e.g.

اینرا پنهان کرد تا کسی پیدا نکند
inra panhan kard ta kasi pe͡ida nakonad,
He hid this so that no one would find it.

تا نشان سم اسبت گم کنند * ترکمانا نعلرا وارونه زن
ta neʃane some asbat gom konand torkomana naʿlra varune zan,
O Turkoman, put the horseshoe on back to front so that the print of thy horse's hoof will be lost!

این کاررا حالا بکنید تا زودتر تمام شود
in karra hala bekonid ta zudtar tamam ʃavad,
Do this now so that it will be finished sooner.

In Classical Persian تا *ta* as a final conjunction can be followed by the Indicative to indicate that the action depending upon the main verb has been performed, e.g.

باو فرمود تا رفت *be u farmud ta raft,* He ordered him to go (and he went).

(*d*) After تا *ta* 'by the time that, until' in general statements and when referring to the present or future: e.g.

تا بیائید تاریك خواهد شد
ta beyaid tarik xahad ʃod,
By the time you come it will be dark.

تا اینرا نخوانید نمیفهمید
ta inra naxanid namifahmid,
You will not understand this until you read it.

(*e*) In general relative clauses, e.g.

هر وقتیکه آنرا بخوانم بیاد شما میفتم
har vaqtike anra bexanam be yade ʃoma mioftam,
Whenever I read that I think of you.

(*f*) After the verbs توانستن *tavanestan* 'to be able' and خواستن *xastan* 'to want' (see Lesson VI, para. 7), e.g.

نتوانست بیاید *natavanest beyayad*, He could not come.
میتوانید آنرا باز کنید *mitavanid anra baz konid*, Can you open that?
میخواست برود *mixast beravad*, He wanted to go.
میخواهند شمارا ببینند *mixahand ʃomara bebinand*, They want to see you.

(*g*) After باید *bayad* 'must, ought' referring to the present or future, e.g.

باید برویم *bayad beravim*, We must go.

(*h*) After شاید *ʃayad* 'perhaps' referring to the present or future, e.g.

شاید اینجا باشد *ʃayad inja baʃad*, Perhaps he is here.
شاید بیاید *ʃayad beyayad*, Perhaps he will come.

(*i*) In Conditional Clauses (see Lesson VII, para. 5 (*a*) above), e.g.

اگر وقت بکنیم بگردش میرویم *agar vaqt bekonim be gardeʃ miravim*, If we have time, we will go for a walk.

(*j*) To refer to the 'future with doubt' in the 1st pers. sing., e.g.

بروم یا نروم *beravam ya naravam*, Shall I go or not?
چه بگویم *ce beguyam*, What shall I say?

(*k*) As a Jussive in the 1st and 3rd pers. sing. and pl., e.g.

برویم *beravim*, Let us go.

(*l*) After پیش از آنکه *piʃ az anke* and قبل از آنکه *qabl az anke*, 'before', بجای اینکه *be jaye inke* and در عوض اینکه *dar avaze inke*, 'instead of (this that)', and جز اینکه *joz inke* and غیر از اینکه *ɣeir az inke*, 'except'.

12. The Subjunctive Past is used:

(*a*) To refer to an action or state in the past about which there is an element of doubt, e.g.

گمان میبرم که رفته باشد *gaman mibaram ke rafte baʃad*, I think he may have gone.

(*b*) To describe the anterior of two future actions or states, e.g.

تا دکتر برسد مریض مرده باشد *ta doktor berasad mariz morde baʃad*, By the time the doctor arrives the sick man will have died.

This usage is classical, the Perfect being used rather than the Subjunctive Past in modern usage.

(*c*) To refer to an action presumed to have been already performed, or a state presumed to be in existence, e.g.

میترسم تمام شده باشد *mitarsam tamam ʃode baʃad*, I fear it will have finished.

تصور میکنم تا حالا رسیده باشد *tasavvor mikonam ta hala raside baʃad*, I think he will have arrived by now.

(*d*) After باید *bayad* and بایست *bayest* 'ought, must', referring to past time, e.g.

باید (بایست) رفته باشد *bayad* (*bayest*) *rafte baʃad*, He must have gone.

(*e*) After شاید *ʃayad* 'perhaps', referring to past time unless the action or state referred to is continuous (see para. 6 (*a*) above) or forms the apodosis of an impossible condition in the past (see Lesson VII, para. 5 (*b*) above). E.g.

شاید اینرا خوانده باشید *ʃayad inra xande baʃid*, Perhaps you have read this.

(*f*) After میبایست *mibayest* 'ought to have', e.g.

میبایست دیده باشید *mibayest dide bafid*, You ought to have seen (this).

میبایست این کتابرا خوانده باشد *mibayest in ketabra xande bafad*, He ought to have read this book.

(*g*) In conditional clauses (see Lesson VII, para. 5 (*a*, iii above), e.g.

اگر کرده باشد چه خواهید کرد *agar karde bafad ce xahid kard*, If he has done (it), what will you do?

(*h*) In the case of the verb داشتن *daftan* 'to have' for the Subjunctive Present, e.g.

باید خیلی حوصله داشته باشید *bayad xeili housele dafte bafid*, You must have great patience.

هر چیزی که میل داشته باشید تهیه میکنم *har cizi ke meil dafte bafid tahie mikonam*, I will obtain (prepare) whatever you want.

13. The Future is used:

(*a*) To refer to a future action or state, e.g.

فردا خواهد رفت *farda xahad raft*, He will go to-morrow.

(*b*) To indicate certainty, e.g.

این علی خواهد بود *in ali xahad bud* = This must be 'Ali (said in reply to some such remark as کسی در میزند *kasi dar mizanad* 'someone is knocking at the door').

14. The Imperative is used:

To express a command, e.g.

برو *borou*, go.

15. A form in اد *-ad* (3rd pers. sing.) has a precative sense. It is the sole surviving form of the old Optative.

The prefix بـ *be-* is often added to it, e.g.

برساد *berasad*, May he arrive.

The negative is formed by the prefix مـ *ma-*, e.g.

مکناد *makonad*, May he not do.

This form is seldom, if ever, used in Colloquial Persian.

The precative of بودن *budan* is باد *bad.* مبادا (که) *mabada (ke)* used as a conjunction (=lest) is the negative precative to which the interjectory *alef* has been added (see Lesson XII, para. 12). It is also used in the phrase روز مبادا *ruze mabada*=a rainy day, or (in Classical Persian) the day of judgement.

16. Wishes are expressed by کاشکه *kaʃke* or کاشکی *kaʃki* 'would that' followed by the Subjunctive Present, e.g.

کاشکی بیاید *kaʃki beyayad*, Would that he would come.

The tense in unfulfilled wishes is the Imperfect or the Pluperfect, e.g.

کاشکی میامد (آمده بود) *kaʃki miamad (amade bud)*, Would that he had come.

17. After verbs of saying, thinking, knowing, seeing, etc., the tense of the verb is normally that of direct speech, but the pronoun is not necessarily that of direct speech. The particle که *ke* 'that' sometimes follows the main verb. E.g.

بمن گفت که نمیایم *be man goft ke namiayam*
بمن گفت که نمیاید *be man goft ke namiayad* } He told me that he was not coming.

گفت که اسبها حاضرند *goft ke asbha hazer and*, He said the horses were ready.

باو گفتم که نمیایم *be u goftam ke namiayam*, I told him I was not coming.

دیدیم که اینجا هستند *didim ke inja hastand*, We saw they were here.

فکر کرد که این آسان است *fekr kard ke in asan ast*, He thought this was easy.

افسوس میخورم که چرا آمدم *afsus mixoram ke cera amadam*, I regret that I came.

پرسید کسی منزل هست *porsid kasi manzel hast*, He asked if anyone was at home.

از ما پرسیدند که کیستیم *az ma porsidand ke kistim*, They asked us who we were.

پیغام داد که فردا میایم *peiɣam dad ke farda miayam*, He sent a message to say he would come the next day.

فکر نمیکردم که خواهد آمد *fekr namikardam ke xahad amad*, I did not think that he would come.

Indirect Speech is occasionally used. The last example could thus be rendered:

فکر نمیکردم که بیاید *fekr namikardam ke beyayad.*

قول دادن *qoul dadan* and وعده کردن *va'de kardan* 'to promise' are usually followed by a final clause with the Subjunctive Present, e.g.

وعده کرد که بیاید *va'de kard ke beyayad*, He promised to come.

که *ke* can sometimes be translated by 'saying', e.g.

مدبران ممالك آن طرف در دفع مضرت ایشان مشورت کردند که این طایفه گر[1] هم بر این نسق روزگاری مداومت نمایند مقاومت ایشان ممتنع گردد

modabberane mamaleke an taraf dar daf'e mazarrate ișan mașvarat kardand ke in tayefe gar ham bar in nasaq ruzgari modavamat namayand moqavamate ișan momtane' gardad,

The statesmen of the kingdoms of that region consulted together concerning the repelling of their evil, saying 'if this group (tribe) continues in this way for any (length of) time, it will be impossible to resist them'.

18. Although تا *ta* as a temporal conjunction is capable of five distinct meanings, careful observation of the tenses employed both in the تا *ta* clause and in the main clause will show that in Modern Persian no ambiguity arises, e.g.

(i) 'as long as'

تا باران میاید بیرون نمیرویم

ta baran miayad birun namiravim,

As long as it rains we shall not go out.

تا مدرسه میرفتم چیزی یاد نمیگرفتم

ta madrase miraftam cizi yad namigereftam,

As long as I went to school I learnt nothing.

تا میتوانید آنرا تحمل کنید

ta mitavanid anra tahammol konid,

Bear it as long as you can.

(ii) 'by the time that'

تا برسید دیر میشود

ta berasid dir mișavad,

It will be late by the time you arrive.

[1] For اگر *agar.*

تا دکتر رسید مریض مرده بود

ta doktor rasid mariz morde bud,

By the time the doctor arrived the sick man was dead.

تا برسید ما رفته ایم

ta berasid ma rafte im,

We shall have gone by the time you arrive.

تا سایه‌ور درختی گردد نهالکی * بنگر که چند آب[1] در آید بجویبار

ta sayevar daraxti gardad nehalaki benegar ke cand ab dar ayad be jûbar,

By the time (before) a small sapling becomes a shady tree, see how many times water flows along the stream.

بپایان تا رسد یکشمع صد پروانه میسوزد

be payan ta rasad yak ʃamʿ sad parvane misuzad,

A hundred moths will be burnt by the time (before) a candle burns out.

(iii) 'as soon as'

تا بشهر رسیدید[2] بمن خبر بدهید

ta be ʃahr rasidid be man xabar bedehid,

Let me know as soon as you reach the town.

تا مارا صدا کنید بر میگردیم

ta mara sada konid bar migardim,

We will return as soon as you call us.

تا منزل بر گشتم کاغذرا نوشتم

ta manzel bar gaʃtam kaɣazra neveʃtam,

I wrote the letter as soon as I returned home.

(iv) 'until'

تا آنرا نشنوم باور نمیکنم

ta anra naʃenavam bavar namikonam,

I shall not believe it until I hear (it).

تا اورا ندیدم نمیدانستم که اینجاست

ta ura nadidam namidanestam ke injast,

I did not know he was here until I saw him.

[1] آب *ab* 'water' also means water allowed to flow along an irrigation channel for a specific period of time.

[2] For the use of the Preterite to refer to the Future see above para. 5 (*c*).

من و برادرم تا زن نگرفته بودیم همیشه زیر یك سقف خوابیده و تا
پانزده بیست سال قبل با یکدیگر در زندگی شریك بودیم

man o baradaram ta zan nagerefte budim hamiʃe zire yak saqf xabide va ta panzdah bist sal qabl ba yak digar dar zendegi ʃarik budim,

My brother and I until (before) we married always slept under one roof, and until fifteen or twenty years ago we shared a common life.

(v) 'since'

تا بانگلستان رفته است از او خبری ندارم

ta be englestan rafte ast az u xabari nadaram,

I have no news of him since he went to England.

It should be noted that (*a*) تا *ta* in the sense of 'until' normally requires نه *na* in the تا *ta* clause though usage sanctions such a phrase as تا بیایم صبر کنید *ta beyayam sabr konid* 'wait until I come', and (*b*) تا *ta* as a final conjunction 'in order that' is distinguished from the temporal تا *ta* by the fact that it follows the main clause.[1]

Classical usage with the temporal تا *ta* differs somewhat from modern usage. The Present Subjunctive is used after تا *ta* in the sense of both 'as long as' and 'as soon as' referring to the present and future and in general statements, e.g.

تا صلح توان کرد در جنگ مکوب

ta solh tavan kard dare jang makub,

As long as peace can be achieved, do not knock on the door of war.

مرا تا جان بود امید باشد * که روزی جفت من خورشید باشد

mara ta jan bovad omid baʃad ke ruzi jofte man xorʃid baʃad,

As long as I am alive I have hope that one day my consort may be the sun.

If تا *ta* 'by the time that' refers to the future the Subjunctive Past is used in the main clause, e.g.

[1] In colloquial usage, however, emphasis may require the clause introduced by the temporal تا *ta* to follow the main clause, e.g.

صبر کنید تا بیایم *sabr konid ta beyayam*, Wait until I come (where the emphasis is on 'wait').

تا ترياق از عراق آرند مار گزيده مرده باشد

ta taryaq az eraq arand mar gazide morde bašad,

By the time they bring the antidote from Iraq the person bitten by the snake will have died.

In modern usage also if the verb of the clause introduced by تا *ta* 'as long as' is بودن *budan* 'to be' and refers to the present or future the Present Subjunctive is used, e.g.

تا دولتها اينطور باشند اوضاع خوب نميشود

ta doulatha in tour bašand ouza' xub namišavad,

As long as the governments are like this conditions will not improve.

19. The use of a negative verb with هيچ *hic* and هرگز *hargez* has already been mentioned (see Lesson IV, para. 22 and Lesson VII, para. 1, respectively) and the use of the double negative with تا *ta* 'until' (see Lesson VI, para. 17 (*c*) above).

Certain verbs of prohibition require a negative in the subordinate clause, e.g.

منع كردم كه آنجا نرود *man' kardam ke anja naravad*, I forbade him to go there.

But

ممنوع بود كه كسى آنجا برود *mamnu' bud ke kasi anja beravad*, It was forbidden for anyone to go there.

The word قدغن *qadayan* 'forbidden' requires a negative verb, e.g.

ضمناً قدغن شد كه ديگر بخانه مادرم نروم

zemnan qadayan šod ke digar be xaneye madaram naravam,

Meanwhile it was forbidden for me to go any more to my mother's house.

The Arabic forms اصلاً[1] *aslan* and ابداً[1] *abadan* are used with a negative verb to mean 'not at all' and 'never', e.g.

ابداً آنجا نبودم *abadan anja nabudam*, I was never there.

اصلاً نميخواهم *aslan namixaham*, I do not want (it) at all.

The use of the negative in the following idioms should be noted:

از باغ بيرون نيامده بود كه مرا ديد *az bay birun nayamade bud ke mara did*, He had barely come out of the garden when he saw me.

[1] See Part II, Lesson XXI, para. 16 (*b*) for Arabic Nouns in the accusative used as adverbs.

آفتاب نزده راه افتادیم *aftab nazade rah oftadim*, We set off before sunrise (the sun not having risen).

بمیدان نرسیده کوچه آخر دست راست *be meĭdan naraside kuceye axer daste rast*, the last street on the right before reaching the square (not having arrived at the square).

20. Certain verbs, notably آمدن *amadan* 'to come' and افتادن *oftadan* 'to fall' are used impersonally with or without a preposition governing the logical subject, e.g.

یادم آمد *yadam amad*, I remembered (it came to my mind).
یادش رفت *yadeʃ raft*, He forgot (it went from his mind).
گیرش نیامد *gireʃ nayamad*, He did not obtain (it).
پسندشان نیامد *pasandeʃan nayamad*, They did not like (it).
خوشم آمد *xoʃam amad*, I was pleased (at it).
بما خوش گذشت *be ma xoʃ goẓaʃt*, We enjoyed ourselves.

21. داشتن *daʃtan* is used impersonally in the following constructions:

عیب ندارد *eĭb nadarad* } It does not matter.
ضرر ندارد *ẓarar nadarad* }
احتمال دارد *ehtemal darad*, It is probable.[1]
چاره ندارد *care nadarad*, It cannot be helped (there is no remedy).

22. خواستن *xastan* is sometimes equivalent to 'to need, to make necessary', e.g.

این کار وقت میخواهد *in kar vaqt mixahad*, This affair needs time.

23. In Modern Persian the continuous past and continuous present can be expressed by the Imperfect of داشتن *daʃtan* together with the Imperfect of the main verb and by the Present of داشتن *daʃtan* together with the Present of the main verb respectively, e.g.

داشتم مینوشتم *daʃtam mineveʃtam*, I was in the act of writing.
دارم مینویسم *daram minevisam*, I am in the act of writing.

[1] Also احتمال کلی (تام) دارد *ehtemale kolli* (*tamm*) *darad*, it is very probable, there is every probability.

24. The Particle هی *hei* is also used to express repeated action, e.g.

هی میگفت *hei migoft*, He kept on saying.

هی میگوید *hei miguyad*, He keeps on saying.

25. In Classical Persian the Habitual Past is sometimes rendered by the prefix همی *hami-* in place of می *mi-*, e.g.

همیکردم *hamikardam*, I was doing, used to do, etc.,

or by the suffix ی *-i* added to the Preterite, e.g.

کردمی *kardami*, I was doing, used to do, etc.

This latter form is defective and is only used in the 1st pers. sing. and the 3rd pers. sing. and pl.

26. In Classical Persian a prefix بـ *be-* is sometimes added to the Preterite to give a sense of completion or finality, e.g.

برفت *beraft*, he went.

بگفت *begoft*, he said.

27. In Classical Persian a Conditional Past was formed by adding ی *-i* to the Imperfect or Preterite and a Conditional Present by adding ی *-i* to the Subjunctive Present. These tenses, like the Habitual Past with suffix *-i* (see above, para. 25), are defective, e.g.

تا بدانستمی ز[1] دشمن دوست * زندگانی دو بار بایستی

ta bedanestami ze dosman dust zendegani do bar bayesti,

Life would be needed twice over to know friend from foe.

گر آنها که میگفتمی کردمی * نکو سیرت و پارسا بودمی

gar anha ke migoftami kardami neku sirat o parsa budami,

If I had done those things which I used to say, I would have been of good character and pious.

درخت اگر متحرك شدی ز جای بجای * نه جور اره کشیدی و نی جفای تبر

daraxt agar motaharrek sodi ze jai be jai na joure arre kasidi o nei jafaye tabar,

If a tree could move from place to place it would not suffer the tyranny of the saw and the oppression of the axe.

[1] For از *az*.

اگر مملکترا زبان باشدی * از این دیو و ددها فغان باشدی

agar mamlekatra ʒaban baʃadi aʒ in div o dadha feɣan baʃadi,

If the kingdom had a tongue it would cry out against these demons and wild beasts.

28. In early Classical Persian a passive construction is found with the verb آمدن *amadan* 'to come', e.g.

ذکر هر یکی مختصر کرده آید *ʒekre har yaki moxtasar karde ayad*, Mention of each one will be made briefly.

29. If two or more co-ordinate clauses follow each other, where the same auxiliary verb is used to conjugate the verb, it can be omitted from all but the first or final clause, e.g.

طایفه دزدان عرب بر سر کوه نشسته بودند و منفذ کاروان بسته و رعیت بلدان از مکاید[1] ایشان مرعوب و لشکر سلطان مغلوب بحکم آنکه ملاذی منیع از قله کوهی بدست آورده بودند

tayefeye doʒdane arab bar sare kuh neʃaste budand va manfaʒe karavan baste va ra'iyate boldan aʒ makayede iʃan mar'ub va laʃkare soltan maɣlub be hokme anke malaʒi mani' aʒ qolleye kuhi bedast avarde budand,

A group (tribe) of Arab thieves had established themselves (were sitting) on the top of a mountain and closed the caravan route and the peasants of (these) regions were terrified by their tricks and the sultan's army was defeated by virtue of this that they (the thieves) had obtained possession of an impregnable refuge on the summit of a mountain (where بودند *budand* has been omitted after بسته, مرعوب and مغلوب).

Similarly the verbal part of a compound verb in the first of two or more co-ordinate clauses may be omitted, e.g.

متمنی‌است مبلغ صد ریال بحساب روزنامه ببانک تحویل و نشانی کامل بنویسید تا روزنامه مرتب فرستاده شود

motamannist mablaɣe sad rial be hesabe ruʒname be bank tahvil va neʃaniye kamel benevisid ta ruʒname morattab ferestade ʃavad,

It is requested that you should transfer the sum of 100 rs. to the newspaper's account at the bank and write your full address so that the paper may be sent to you regularly (where دهید *dehid* has been omitted after تحویل).

[1] Plural of مکیده *makide* 'trick, stratagem'.

Vocabulary

ولايات *velayat* (pl. of ولايت), provinces.
آغاز *aɣaz*, beginning.
تسليم *taslim*, surrender; تسليم كردن *taslim k.*, to surrender.
سفرا *sofara* (pl. of سفير *safir*), envoys plenipotentiary.
عيسوى *isavi*, Christian.
مذهب *mazhab*, religion.
جمله *jomle*, collection; sentence; از آن جمله *az an jomle*, among them.
بحر *bahr*, sea; بحر خزر *bahre xazar*, the Caspian Sea.
ابيض *abyaz*, white.
آلمان *alman*, Germany.
ايطاليا *italia*, Italy.
بر عليه *bar aleih(e)*, against.
افتتاح *eftetah*, opening.
ابريشم *abriʃom*, silk.
تقديم *taqdim*, offering; تقديم كردن *taqdim k.*, to offer.
ما بين *ma bein(e)*, between.
نفاق *nefaq*, quarrel, dispute.
بروز *boruz*, appearance; بروز كردن *boruz k.*, to appear, break out.
نواختن (نواز) *navaxtan* (*navaz*), to cherish, favour, patronize.
واقع *vaqe'*, situated; happening, occurring.
عزم *azm*, determination; صاحب عزم *saheb azm*, determined (the owner of determination).
محبت *mohabbat*, love.
جلب *jalb*, attracting; جلب كردن *jalb k.*, to attract.
مأموريت *ma'muriyat*, office, charge.
مجروح *majruh*, wounded.
سردار *sardar*, leader.
هراس *haras*, fear.
بيانات *bayanat* (pl. of بيان *bayan*), explanations, expositions.
اظهار *ezhar*, expressing; expression, manifestation; اظهار داشتن *ezhar d.*, to express.
بدواً *badvan*, at first.
تشجيع *taʃji'*, encouraging, encouragement; تشجيع كردن *taʃji' k.*, to encourage.
عازم *azem*, setting out (for).
بالاخره *belaxere*, at last, finally (see Part II, Lesson XXI, para. 16 (*c*)).
حسين على بك بيات Hosein Ali Bak Bayat.
بعدها *ba'dha*, afterwards.

دهقان *dehqan*, small landowner; peasant.

شکر *ʃokr*, thanks.

خرده گرفتن *xorde gereftan*, to criticize, belittle.

کدو *kadu*, marrow.

بوته *bote*,[1] shrub.

نازك *nazok*, thin, delicate.

بلوط *balut*, sweet chestnut; acorn.

خالق *xaleq*, creator.

مخلوقات *maxluqat*, pl. of مخلوق *maxluq* 'what is created'.

خلاف *xelaf(e)*, contrary to.

فراز *faraz*, top.

دماغ *demaɣ*, brain; *damaɣ*, nose.

جاری *jari*, flowing.

ضعف *za'f*, weakness.

رأی *ra'i*, *raî*, judgement, opinion.

سستی *sosti*, looseness, slackness, weakness.

تدبیر *tadbir*, counsel, plan, administration.

نگریستن (نگر) *negaristan* (*negar*), to look, see.

جسارت *jesarat*, boldness.

پوزش *puzeʃ*, forgiveness.

استغفار *esteɣfar*, asking pardon.

فرصت *forsat*, chance, opportunity; فرصترا غنیمت شمردن *forsatra ɣanimat ʃomordan*, to seize a chance (esteem the chance booty).

دلتنگ *deltang*, distressed, sad; دل ما برای شما تنگ شد *dele ma baraye ʃoma tang ʃod*, we miss you.

تکذیب *takzib*, denial; تکذیب کردن *takzib k.*, to deny.

رستن (رو) *rostan* (*ru*), to grow (of things).

تنبیه *tambih*, punishment; تنبیه کردن *tambih k.*, to punish.

آمدن برادران شرلی بایران (بقیه از درس پیش)

شاه که در این زمان میخواست با دولت عثمانی از در جنگ در آید و ولایاتیراکه در آغاز پادشاهی خود بآن دولت تسلیم کرده بود باز گیرد باین ترتیب سفرائی[2] بدربار تمام پادشاهان عیسوی مذهب اروپا فرستاد از آن جمله انتنی شرلیرا بهمراهی حسینعلی بك بیات باروپا جهت نمایندگی روانه کرد و آنها هم از راه بحر خزر و مسکو و دریای ابیض و دریای شمال و آلمان بایطالیا وارد

[1] This word is pronounced *bote* not *bute* (see Introduction to Part I, Alphabetical Table).

[2] Note the use of ی *-i* with the plural (see Lesson XII, para. 1 (*a*) (iii) above).

شدند و در تمام ممالك بین راه نامه‌های دوستانه شاه عباس دایر بر اتحاد با ایران بر علیه عثمانی و افتتاح روابط تجارتی برای فروش ابریشم ایرانرا با هدایائیکه شاه داده بود تقدیم کردند و در ایطالیا مابین حسینعلی بك بیات و انتنی شرلی نفاق بروز کرد و انتنی از او جدا شده باسپانیا رفت و دیگر بایران بر نگشت اما رابرت شرلی برادر انتنی که در خدمت شاه عباس مانده بود مورد نوازش واقع گشت[1] و چون از آمدن انتنی خبری نشده شاه عباس نسبت باو بی‌لطف گشت ولی رابرت شرلی چون جوانی صاحب عزم و نیکو رفتار بود باز محبت شاهرا نسبت بخود جلب کرد اولین مأموریتی که از طرف شاه عباس برابرت شرلی داده شد انتخاب او بریاست دستهٔ از سپاه و فرستادن وی بجنگ با عثمانی بود و همچنین در جنگهائیکه شاه عباس در سالهای ۱۰۱۳ و ۱۰۱٤ هجری با عثمانی کرد شرکت نمود و سه مرتبه مجروح شد و در جنگی عده زیادی از سپاه عثمانیرا کشته و سرداران آنهارا اسیر گرفت و در یك جنگ که با عثمانیها روبرو شد پس از مرتب کردن سپاه خود چون دید سربازانش از زیادی عدد دشمن در هراسند رو بدیشان کرده بیاناتی اظهار داشت سپس خود بدواً بطرف دشمن حمله برد و سپاهیانش هم تشجیع شده باین ترتیب عثمانیهارا شکست داده مورد نوازش شاه عباس واقع گشت و بعدها از طرف شاه عباس در ۱۰۱٦ هجری (۱٦۰۸ میلادی) از اصفهان عازم اروپا شد و پس از مسافرت طولانی و انجام مأموریت خویش در سال ۱۰۲۰ هجری بانگلستان رفت و بالاخره پس از هشت سال مسافرت در سال ۱۰۲٤ بایران برگشت (پایان)

Exercise 24

دهقانی ناشکر بر خدای تعالی خرده میگرفت که چرا کدوی بزرگرا بر بوته نازکی سبز نموده و بلوط کوچکرا بر درختی بلند رویانیده است من اگر خالق مخلوقات بودم بر خلاف این کار میکردم دهقان در این اندیشه بود که بلوطی از فراز درخت چنان بر دماغش خورد که خون جاری شد دهقان با خود گفت ضعف رأی و سستی تدبیر من بنگر اگر این بلوط کدو میشد مرا کشته بود پس از جسارت خویش پوزش خواست و استغفار کرد

[1] Literally 'he became situated (in) the place of favour'. مورد *mŏured*, originally drinking-place, is used in Persian in certain stereotyped phrases to mean 'place, site' in general.

EXERCISE 25

1. I do not understand how it occurred. 2. Not even his enemies were unkind to him, let alone his friends. 3. The house is uninhabitable in summer let alone in winter. 4. Seize the chance, else you will regret it. 5. I miss him, yet I am glad he went (although I miss him...). 6. He is always ill; nevertheless he is always cheerful. 7. He is living in great hardship; meanwhile his brother on the contrary is living in the greatest comfort. 8. The factory caught fire last night; it was completely destroyed and on that account many workmen will be unemployed. 9. The work had to be done; accordingly we did it. 10. There was no one there so I went away. 11. It is best that he should go. 12. His best friends will not deny that he was in error. 13. My only terror is that my father should follow (come after) me. 14. It is probable that he will come to-day. 15. It is not known which road he took (by which road he went). 16. It is immaterial whether he comes or goes. 17. Such books as this and such men as he are rare.

LESSON XIV

Polite Conversation. Some discrepancies between the spoken and the written word. دیگر *digar* and که *ke*.

1. Politeness requires the use of certain honorifics and phrases in formal conversation.

(*a*) Personal Pronouns. The 1st pers. sing. من *man* is sparingly used. بنده *bande* (lit. 'slave') is used in place of من *man* 'I' if the speaker wishes to indicate humility towards a person of equal or higher rank. بنده منزل *bande manzel* means 'my house'. Politeness does not require that mention of oneself should be made last if more than one pronoun is used, or a noun or nouns and the pronoun. The 1st pers. usually comes first, e.g.

من و شما *man o ʃoma*, you and I.

من و برادرم *man o baradaram*, my brother and I.

The use of the 3rd pers. pl. for the 3rd pers. sing. is common when reference is being made to a person of equal or superior rank.[1]

[1] It is probably due to this custom that آنها *anha* has come to be used in Modern Persian for the 3rd pers. pl. of the Personal Pronoun ایشان *iʃan*.

The 2nd pers. sing. is used only to children, intimate friends and servants.

سرکار *sarkar* is often used in place of شما *ʃoma* in referring to an equal or superior.

(*b*) Formerly many honorific titles were in use and strict rules governed their employment. Most of these have fallen into disuse. The only officially recognized honorific title is جناب *janab*, which is accorded to ministers and high officials, e.g.

جناب نخست وزیر *janabe naxost vazir*, H.E. the Prime Minister.

The term جناب عالی *janabe ali* or حضرت عالی *hazrate ali* is sometimes used to address a person of superior (or equal) rank.

The Shah is referred to as اعلیحضرت *a'la hazrat*[1] and the Queen as علیا حضرت *olia hazrat*.

(*c*) When referring to what a person of equal or higher rank has said it is customary to use the verb فرمودن *farmudan* 'to command' rather than گفتن *goftan* 'to say', e.g.

چه فرمودید *ce farmudid*, What did you say?

فرمودن *farmudan* is substituted for کردن *kardan* and certain other verbs used to form compound verbs when reference is to a person of equal or higher rank, e.g.

خواهش میکنم وقترا تعیین بفرمائید *xaheʃ mikonam vaqtra ta'yin befarmaid*, Please (I request you) appoint the time.

نامهٔرا که مرقوم فرموده بودید رسید *nameira ke marqum farmude budid rasid*, The letter you wrote arrived.

فرمایش داشتن *farmayeʃ daʃtan* is similarly used for 'to want, desire', e.g.

چه فرمایش دارید (داشتید) *ce farmayeʃ darid (daʃtid)*, What do you want?

or

چه فرمایشی دارید (داشتید) *ce farmayeʃi darid (daʃtid)*.

When referring to oneself, if speaking to a person of equal or higher rank, it is customary to use the verb عرض کردن *arz kardan* 'to make a petition' instead of گفتن, e.g.

عرض کردم... *arz kardam*, I said....

[1] Usually pronounced *ala hazrat*.

عرض میشود *arz̧ miʃavad* is similarly prefixed to an expression of opinion or statement.

The following compounds are used when reference is to a person of equal or higher rank. They must never be used when referring to oneself:

تشریف داشتن *taʃrif daʃtan*, to be in, be present.
تشریف بردن *taʃrif bordan*, to go, depart.
تشریف آوردن *taʃrif avardan*, to come, arrive.

E.g.

آقا تشریف دارند *aqa taʃrif darand*, Is (your) master in?
فردا تشریف میاورند *farda taʃrif miavarand*, He (they) will come to-morrow.
بشهر تشریف بردند *be ʃahr taʃrif bordand*, He has (they have) gone to the town.

When accepting an invitation on one's own behalf from a person of equal or higher rank or arranging to call upon such a person, the verb شرفیاب شدن *ʃarafyab ʃodan* 'to become a recipient of honour' is used or خدمت رسیدن *xedmat rasidan* 'to arrive at the service of', e.g.

فردا شرفیاب میشوم *farda ʃarafyab miʃavam*, I will come to-morrow.
خدمت شما میرسم *xedmate ʃoma mirasam*, I will come to see you.

These expressions must not be used when referring to anyone other than oneself.

خدمت *xedmat* is also used in place of به *be* 'to' and پیش *piʃ* = with, and در خدمت *dar xedmat* = با *ba* 'with', when referring to a person of equal or superior rank, e.g.

خدمت شما عرض میکنم *xedmate ʃoma arz̧ mikonam*, I will tell you.
خدمت وزیر بودم *xedmate vaz̧ir budam*, I was with the minister.
در خدمت ایشان باصفهان رفتم *dar xedmate iʃan be esfahan raftam*, I went with him to Isfahan.

مرحمت کردن *marhamat kardan* is used in place of دادن *dadan* 'to give' when reference is to a person of equal or higher rank. It must never be used with reference to oneself.

کتابرا مرحمت کنید *ketabra marhamat konid*, Give (me) the book.

ملتفت شدن *moltafet ʃodan* is used rather than فهمیدن *fahmidan* for 'to understand'.

(*d*) The most usual formula of greeting is سلام علیکم *salam aleikom* 'peace be upon you', which is repeated in answer by the person to whom the greeting is given.

احوال شما چطور است *ahvale ʃoma ce tour ast* 'how are you' is a common formula used when inquiring after someone's health. شریف *ʃarif* 'noble, noble person' can be substituted for شما *ʃoma* and مزاج *mezaj* 'disposition', وجود *vojud* 'existence', or حال *hal* 'state' for احوال *ahval*. The answer to such an inquiry is الحمد لله *al hamdo lellah* 'Praise be to God'.

صبح شما بخیر *sobhe ʃoma be xeir* '(may) your morning (be) good' is an alternative greeting which can be used in the morning. عاقبت شما بخیر *aqebate ʃoma be xeir* '(may) your end (be) good' is sometimes said in reply to this.

On a feast-day or holiday, such as New Year's Day, the usual greeting is عید شما مبارك *ide ʃoma mobarak* 'may your feast be blessed'.

(*e*) The phrase خوش آمدید *xoʃ amadid* 'welcome' is used to welcome someone to one's house. If a long time has elapsed since the previous visit of the visitor the phrase چه عجب *ce ajab* 'what a wonder (that you have at last honoured me)' is sometimes used. The phrase عجب بجمال شما *ajab be jamale ʃoma* 'the marvel is at your kindness' may be said in reply.

(*f*) A variety of expressions are used on taking leave. On wishing to terminate a meeting or visit it is customary to ask one's host's permission to leave by some such phrase as مرخص میفرمائید *moraxxas mifarmaid*, or اجازه میفرمائید *ejaze mifarmaid* 'do you give me permission to depart' or by indicating that one has troubled one's host long enough by a phrase such as زحمت کم کنم *zahmat kam konam* 'let me make the trouble (given by me) less'.

If one's host then deprecates such an intention by saying زود است *zud ast*, it is customary to stay a few more minutes and then once more ask permission to depart. As a guest leaves he can say زحمت دادم *zahmat dadam* 'I have given (you) trouble' to which his host replies زحمت کشیدید *zahmat kaʃidid* 'you have taken trouble (in coming)'; if one's host says first زحمت کشیدید *zahmat kaʃidid* the answer is زحمت دادم *zahmat dadam*. As the guest departs the host may say to him, if he (the guest) is of equal or higher rank, مشرف فرمودید *moʃarraf farmudid* 'you have conferred honour (on me).'

On parting from someone it is usual to use some phrase such as لطف شما زیاد *lotfe ʃoma ziad*, التفات شما زیاد *eltefate ʃoma ziad* 'your favour (was) great', لطف فرمودید *lotf farmudid* 'you have conferred honour on me', لطف عالی کم نشود *lotfe ali kam naʃavad* 'may the high favour not grow less', or سایه شما کم نشود *sayeye ʃoma kam naʃavad* 'may your shadow never grow less'. مبارك *mobarak* can be substituted for شما *ʃoma* in the last phrase but is more formal.

خدا حافظ *xoda hafez* or خدا حافظ شما *xoda hafeze ʃoma* 'may God be your protector' is also used, especially when the person to whom it is said is going on a journey. The answer to this is باامان خدا *be amane xoda* 'in the protection of God'.

شب بشما خوش *ʃab be ʃoma xoʃ* or شب بخیر *ʃab be xeir* 'good-night' is used, but not widely.

(*g*) بفرمائید *befarmaid* is used for 'please do, please come in, please sit down', etc.

(*h*) چه عرض کنم *ce arz konam* is an expression used when the speaker does not know the answer to a question or wishes to give a non-committal reply.

(*i*) بی زحمت *bi zahmat* 'without trouble' is an expression prefixed to a request asking someone to do something, e.g.

بی زحمت اینجا تشریف بیاورید *bi zahmat inja taʃrif beyavarid*, Please come here.

بی زحمت آنرا بمن بدهید *bi zahmat anra be man bedehid*, Please give that to me.

(*j*) دست شما درد نکند *daste ʃoma dard nakonad* 'may your hand not pain you' is said to someone who has, for example, fetched something or done something for one involving some degree, however slight, of physical effort. In answer to this is sometimes heard

سر شما درد نکند *sare ʃoma dard nakonad* 'may your head not pain you'.

(*k*) چشم *caʃm* '(upon my) eye' is said in answer to a request or command and signifies an intention to comply with the request.

(*l*) 'Excuse me (=forgive me)' is translated by ببخشید *bebaxʃid*, to which the answer خدا ببخشد *xoda bebaxʃad* 'may God forgive (you)' is sometimes given.

(*m*) 'Please (=I pray you)' can be translated by خواهش میکنم *xaheʃ mikonam* 'I request (you)' or استدعا میکنم *ested'a mikonam* 'I beseech (you)'.

(*n*) اختیار دارید *exteyar darid* 'you have the choice (=you are free to make such a statement, but. . .)' is said by way of remonstrance or protest at a remark.

(*o*) The phrase ان شاء الله *en ʃa allah* 'if God wills' is often prefixed to an expression of an intended action or of hope concerning some future state or action. It is also used alone to mean 'yes' or 'I hope so' in answer to a question regarding one's intentions or some future possibility,[1] e.g.

فردا تشريف مياوريد *farda taʃrif miavarid*, Are you coming to-morrow?

ان شاء الله *en ʃa allah*, I hope so.

(*p*) It is customary to prefix the phrase ما شاء الله *ma ʃa allah* 'what God wills' to an expression of praise of anyone's belongings, etc., or of some action, in order to avert the evil eye, popularly supposed to be stimulated by praise to fall upon an object or person, e.g.

ما شاء الله پسر خوبيست *ma ʃa allah pesare xubist*, He is a good boy.

ما شاء الله خوب درس ميخواند *ma ʃa allah xub dars mixanad*, He studies, learns his lessons, well.

(*q*) The phrase خدا نكند *xoda nakonad* 'may God not do (it)' is customarily prefixed to mention of the possible occurrence of some undesirable event, e.g.

خدا نكند مريض بشويد... *xoda nakonad mariẓ beʃavid*, If, God forbid, you should fall ill....

(*r*) چشم ما روشن *caʃme ma ro͞uʃan* 'our eye (is) bright' is an expression used to express pleasure on seeing someone who has been absent for a time, for example, on a journey. The use of the plural arises from a belief or assumption that the speaker, as an individual, is too insignificant to express pleasure on his own behalf alone. A similar idea lies behind the use of the plural in the phrase هميشه دعاگو هستيم *hamiʃe do'agu hastim* 'we are always praying (for you)' sometimes said in reply to a question from a person of equal or higher rank such as چكار ميكنيد *ce kar mikonid* 'what have you been (are) you doing?'

(*s*) تبريك گفتن *tabrik goftan* and تسليت گفتن *tasliat goftan* mean 'to offer congratulations' and 'to offer condolences' respectively. عرض كردن *arẓ kardan* may be substituted for گفتن *goftan*.

[1] This phrase is also used when the speaker has little or no intention of performing the action referred to.

(*t*) زیارت کردن *ziarat kardan* 'to make a pilgrimage' is used for 'to visit' (an equal or person of higher rank), e.g.

میل دارم سرکاررا زیارت کنم *meil daram sarkarra ziarat konam*, I should like to visit you.

(*u*) زیارت رفتن *ziarat raftan* means 'to go on a pilgrimage'. مشرف شدن *mosarraf sodan* 'to be the recipient of honour' means to have performed a pilgrimage, i.e. to have visited a shrine and carried out the necessary rites. On meeting someone on the road returning, or who has returned, from a pilgrimage the phrase زیارت قبول *ziarat qabul* '(may your) pilgrimage (be) acceptable' is used, to which the answer is خدا حافظ شما *xoda hafeze soma* '(may) God (be) your protector'.[1] On meeting someone who is going to perform a pilgrimage the phrase التماس دعا *eltemase do'a* '(I) beseech (your) prayer' may be said, to which the reply is محتاج دعا *mohtaje do'a* '(I) need (your) prayer'.

2. In the Introduction the vowel system and its relation to the written word was described. Although this relation is remarkably constant certain discrepancies are found. Some of these have already been noted in the Introduction and in Lesson v, para. 2. Certain other tendencies in Colloquial Persian should be noted:

(*a*) ا *a* followed by ن *n* tends to become *u*, e.g.

نان *nan* 'bread' becomes *nun*.

آن *an* 'that, it' becomes *un*.

(*b*) In certain words ا *a* followed by ن *n* tends to become a relatively short vowel intermediate between *a* and *o*.[2] It has this quality in the word خانم *xanom* 'lady' (see also Lesson v, para. 2) and دانگ *dang* (see Lesson v, para. 17). This 'shortened' *a* is frequently nasalized.

In certain Turkish words the written ا has a similar quality, even when not followed by ن *n*, e.g. the first *a* of باطلاق *batlaq* 'swamp'.

را *-ra* sometimes becomes *-ro*, the *o* of *-ro* being somewhat prolonged, and approximating to *ou*.

(*c*) است *ast* 'is' is often replaced by *e*, e.g. خوب است *xub ast* 'it is good' becomes *xub e*.

(*d*) Certain verbs, notably دادن *dadan* 'to give' and گفتن *goftan* 'to say' and گذاشتن *gozaftan* 'to place, put, allow', tend to contract, the

[1] جای شما خالی *jaye soma xali* 'your place (was) empty' is also said.

[2] This modified *a* is also used in the recitation of poetry.

eh, *u(y)* and *go* respectively of tenses formed from the Present Stem being elided, e.g.

میدهم *mideham* 'I give' becomes *midam*.
میگویم *miguyam* 'I say' becomes *migam*.
میگوئید *miguid* 'you say' becomes *migid*.
میگذارید *migozarid* 'you put', etc., becomes *mizarid*.

(*e*) Instances of vowel harmony have already been given, namely in the case of the Imperatives of certain verbs, the Present Stem of which ends in *ou* (see Lesson IV, para. 5). The *a* of the Present Stem of رفتن *raftan* 'to go' and شدن *ʃodan* 'to become' when followed by the Personal endings ی *-i*, ایم *-im* and اید *-id* tends to become *e*, e.g.

میرویم *miravim* 'we are going' becomes *mirevim*.

The verbal prefix *na* when followed by *mi* tends to become *ne*, e.g.

نمیکنم *nemikonam* rather than *namikonam*.
هیچ کس tends to become *hic kes* rather than *hic kas*.

3. The words دیگر *digar* (sometimes pronounced *dige*) and که *ke* are used in Colloquial Persian as catchwords with no specific meaning. دیگر *digar* sometimes adds a slight degree of finality to the sentence; it may also convey a slight suggestion of protest that the person addressed should not be aware of, or should not believe, the statement made by the speaker, e.g.

منزل بودم دیگر *manzel budam digar*, I *was* at home.
منزل نبودم دیگر *manzel nabudam digar*, I was *not* at home.
نرفتم که *naraftam ke*, I did not go.
او که مرد *u ke mord*, he, he's dead.

4. In Colloquial Persian there is a tendency to add the Pronominal Suffix ش *-eʃ* (*-aʃ*) to the 3rd pers. sing. of intransitive verbs, especially when this is composed of one syllable[1], e.g.

بودش *budeʃ*, he was (there).
نیستش *nisteʃ*, he is not there.
مردش *mordeʃ*, he died.
رفتش *rafteʃ*, he went.

[1] This usage is occasionally found in Classical Persian also.

Vocabulary

کمپانی *kompani*, Company.
هند *hend*, India.
شرقی *ʃarqi*, east (adj.).
شاه صفی Shah Safi (ruled Persia A.D. 1629–42).
جانشین *janeʃin*, successor.
حقوق *hoquq* (pl. of حق *haqq*), rights.
شعبان *ʃaʿban*, the 8th month of the *hejri* year (see Appendix III).
مساعدت *mosaʿedat*, help.
اتباع *atbaʿ* (pl. of تابع *tabeʿ*), subjects.
مودت *movaddat*, friendship.
اساسًا *asasan*, essentially.
قسمت *qesmat*, portion, part.
مهم *mohemm*, important.
توسعه *tou͡seʿe*, extension, expansion; توسعه یافتن *tou͡seʿe yaftan*, to be extended, expanded, to spread.
رقابت *reqabat*, rivalry.
تأسیس *taʿsis*, founding; تأسیس کردن *taʿsis k.*, to found.
همایونی *homayuni*, blessed, august.
عمومی *omumi*, general.
عفو *afv*, pardon; عفو عمومی *afve omumi*, general amnesty.
ستاد *setad*, military staff.
ارتش *arteʃ*, army; ستاد کل ارتش *setade kolle arteʃ*, the General Staff.
لشکر *laʃkar*, army; division (of an army).
فرماندهی *farmandehi*, command (of an army, etc.).
عشایر *aʃayer*, tribes.
کلیه *kolliye*, all, the totality.
رئیس *raʿis*, head, chief, director; (pl. رؤسا *roʿasa*).
ایلات *ilat* (pl. of ایل *il*), tribes.
ابلاغ کردن *eblaɣ k.*, to send, convey, notify.
اطلاع *ettelaʿ*, information.
بقرار *be qarar(e)*, according to.
ضمن *ẓemn(e)*, in the course of, while.
اسلحه *aslehe*, arms, firearms.
مسلح *mosallah*, armed.
بشرط آنکه *be ʃarte anke*, on condition that.
پروانه *parvane*, licence, permit.
مخصوص *maxsus*, special.
علاوه بر *alave bar*, in addition to.
اطمینان *etminan*, assurance, confidence.
دشت *daʃt*, plain, field, steppe.
تماشا *tamaʃa*, sight, spectacle; تماشا کردن *tamaʃa k.*, to watch, look at.
باك *bak*, fear.

تنبلی *tambali*, laziness.
محکم *mohkam*, firm, strong.
مقصود *maqsud*, aim, object.
حدت *heddat*, vehemence, force.
قرنطینه *qarantine*, quarantine.
توقف *tavaqqof*, stopping, delay, pause.
مسافر *mosafer*, traveller (pl. مسافرین *mosaferin*).
قانون *qanun*, law, rule (pl. قوانین *qavanin*).
صرف و نحو *sarf o nahv*, grammar and syntax.
تلخ *talx*, bitter; اوقات او تلخ شد *ouqate u talx ʃod*, he became angry (lit. his times became bitter).
صفت *sefat*, quality (pl. صفات *sefat*).
شك *ʃakk*, doubt.
سوء قصد کردن (بر علیه کسی) *su'e qasd k.* (*bar aleihe kasi*), to make an attempt on the life (of someone).
رایج *rayej*, current, in use.
کفیل *kafil*, substitute, deputy, acting (for someone else).
نائب *na'eb*, substitute; assistant.
وبا *vaba*, cholera.
مختل *moxtall*, disorganized, confused.
بر عکس *bar aks*, on the contrary.
اصطلاح *estelah*, expression, idiom.
عنصر *onsor*, element (pl. عناصر *anaser*).
تن در دادن (به) *tan dar dadan* (*be*), to submit (to).
فاسد *fased*, corrupt.

ایران و انگلیس

بعد از شاه عباس بزرگ در سال ۱۰۳۸ کمپانی تجارتی هند شرق انگلیس فرمان تازه در باب تجارت ابریشم از شاه صفی جانشین وی گرفتند ولی نتوانستند تمام امتیازات و حقوق‌را که در زمان شاه عباس بزرگ تحصیل کرده بودند بار دیگر بدست آورند و با آنکه از طرف چارلز اول پادشاه انگلیس در ماه شعبان ۱۰۳۹ (۱۶۳۰) نماینده و نامه برای کمك و مساعدت بتجار و اتباع انگلیسی در ایران برای شاه صفی آمد و از طرف پادشاه ایران هم بخوبی این اظهار مودت و دوستی پذیرفته شد ولی در زمان این پادشاه اساسًا قسمت مهم تجارت ایران بدست تجار هلندی بود و بار دیگر چارلز اول برای کمك بشرکت هند شرق انگلیس نامهٔ دیگر برای شاه صفی فرستاد و از طرف پادشاه صفوی هم این نامه بخوبی پذیرفته

شد و نامه دوستانه هم برای پادشاه انگلستان فرستاد و بالاخره در ۱۰۵۳ (۱٦٤۳) شرکت تجارتی هند شرق انگلیس برای خود تجارتخانه در بصره تأسیس کردند در این ضمن روز بروز تجارت هلندیها در ایران توسعه می‌یافت و با انگلیسها برقابت میپرداختند (ناتمام)

عفو عمومی عشایر

بنابر پیشنهاد ستاد لشکر جنوب و تصویب اعلیحضرت همایونی فرمان عفو عمومی نسبت بکلیه عشایر فارس صادر شد و این فرمان از طرف فرماندهی لشکر برؤسای ایلات و عشایر ابلاغ گردیده است بقرار اطلاع از ستاد کل ارتش ضمن ابلاغ این فرمان اعلام شده است که ایلات و عشایر میتوانند اسلحه با خود داشته و مسلح شوند بشرط آنکه پروانه مخصوصی دریافت دارند علاوه بر ابلاغ عفو عمومی بکلیه عشایر و ایلات از طرف دولت از هر جهت اطمینان داده شده و آنانرا بکمکهای لازم از طرف دولت امیدوار نموده است

آرزو[1]

بچه بودم تابستان بییلاق رفته بودیم هر روز عصر بچه‌ها بدنبال گوسفندان از کوه میامدند میگفتند نزدیك قله دشت سبزی است آبهای زیاد دارد از آن بالا شهر و دنیارا میشود تماشا کرد تا نبینی نمیشود گفت دلم میخواست من هم به بیباکی و توانائی آنها بودم شاید آنها هم دلشان میخواست وسایل تنبلی مرا داشتند یك روز بکدخدا گفتم من فردا با بچه‌ها بدشت میروم تا آنجا چقدر راه است خندیده گفت خیلی باید رفت تا آنجا برسی و خیلی خسته میشوی گفتم اگر دشت پشت این کوه باشد برای من دور نیست مگر تا آنجا چقدر راه است گفت پنج ساعت تمام باید سربالا رفت از ترس دلم فرو ریخت اما کار گذشته بود فردا با قدمهای محکم با کدخدا و بچه‌ها بطرف مقصود روانه شدم با خود گفتم تا جان دارم خستگی نشان نمیدهم هنوز در حدت تصمیم بودم کدخدا گفت رسیدیم دشت اینجاست از خوشحالی چند قدمی دویده گفتم من حاضرم تا قله بروم اما شما گفتید پنج ساعت راه است دو ساعت و نیم است که حرکت کرده‌ایم گفت اگر میگفتم دو ساعت راه است خسته باینجا میرسیدی پنج ساعت گفتم که دو ساعت راه آسان بیائی

[1] اقتباس از آئینه تألیف محمد حجازی

EXERCISE 26

1. He often becomes angry; for all that we like him and he has some good qualities. 2. There was no doubt that his life would be aimed at. 3. Whatever he talks about will be interesting. 4. It is immaterial whether he comes himself or he sends a substitute. 5. I always considered him my best friend. 6. The cholera scare has produced (been the cause of) a severe quarantine that has upset all commercial relations, to say nothing of the interruption of passenger traffic. 7. I have not nearly finished my work; on the contrary I have only just begun. 8. The expression is contrary to the rules of grammar; all the same it is part of the common tongue. 9. In every society, however seemingly corrupt, there are those who have not submitted to the evil elements. 10. Since its formation some years ago, this company has made large profits. 11. I wish you had come yesterday; then you would have seen my brother before he set out.

PART II

THE ARABIC ELEMENT

Introduction[1]

1. There is a large Arabic element in Persian. This element is an indispensable part of the spoken and written word. The student will have already come across many Arabic words in the vocabularies—nouns, adjectives, adverbs, prepositions and conjunctions. The Arabic words incorporated into the Persian language have become Persianized. Many of them have acquired a meaning other than their present-day meaning in Arabic-speaking countries or have retained the meaning which they held at the time when they were incorporated into the Persian language. Not only have a large number of Arabic words been incorporated into Persian, but many Arabic phrases also. Persian literature abounds in quotations from Arabic writings, especially from the *Qor'an* and religious works such as the *Nahj ol-Balaghe*.

2. In the following lessons an attempt will be made to describe the formation of the main derivative Arabic forms which are used in Persian. The Arabic language is built up on triliteral and quadriliteral roots, of which the former are the more common. By addition to the root of one or more of the letters ا, ت, س, م, ن, و or ى (known as servile letters) or by altering the vowel pattern the full conjugation of the verb can be formed. The servile letters are also found in their own right, as it were, forming one or more of the letters of the triliteral or quadriliteral root.

3. The letters ت, ث, د, ذ, ر, ز, س, ش, ص, ض, ط, ظ, ل and ن are known as 'sun letters' (اَلْحُرُوفُ اَلشَّمْسِيَّة). When the Arabic definite article ال is prefixed to a word beginning with one of the sun letters, the *l* is assimilated to the sun letter, e.g.

اَلسُّلْطَان *as-soltan*, the Sultan.

4. The other letters of the alphabet are known as 'moon letters' (اَلْحُرُوفُ اَلْقَمَرِيَّة) and the *l* of the article is not assimilated to them.

5. The value of the consonants and vowels in Arabic differs from their value in Persian, but Arabic words and phrases, when used in Persian,

[1] In this and the following chapters I am indebted to W. Wright's *Grammar of the Arabic Language* (C.U.P.). The student is advised to consult further this or some other reputable Arabic Grammar.

are usually Persianized and hence no attempt will be made in the following pages to differentiate between Arabic and Persian values (see also para. 12 below). The long vowels *i*, *a*, and *u* are indicated by placing the *kasre*, *fathe* and *zamme* before the letters ی, ا, and و respectively; in which case these letters are called 'letters of prolongation' (حُرُوفُ ٱلْمَدّ). In some common words *a* is indicated merely by *fathe* or by a stroke written perpendicularly to resemble a small *alef*, e.g. اَللّٰه God, لٰكِن but.

6. ا *alef*, و *vav* and ی *ye* are 'weak letters' (حُرُوفُ ٱلْعِلَّة) so called because they undergo certain changes according to their phonetic context.

7. *Tanvin* (nunation). At the end of nouns and adjectives when these are indefinite, the vowel signs ُ (*o*) and ِ (*e*) are written double, thus ٌ and ٍ, and pronounced *on* and *en* respectively. The vowel sign َ (*a*) is also written double and pronounced *an*. It then takes an *alef* unless the word ends in ة (*t*)[1] or *hamze*, in which case it is written ةً and ءً respectively. E.g.

وَالِدٌ *valedon*, father (nom.).

وَالِدٍ *valeden*, father (gen.).

وَالِدًا *valedan*, father (acc.).

دَفْعَةً *daf'atan*, once.

اِبْتِدَاءً *ebteda'an*, in the beginning.

8. ء *hamze* in Arabic is of two kinds; هَمْزَةُ ٱلْقَطْع and هَمْزَةُ ٱلْوَصْل respectively. The former cannot be dropped, whereas the latter is omitted under certain circumstances.

The following rules govern the writing of the هَمْزَةُ ٱلْقَطْع:

(*a*) At the beginning of a word it is always written with *alef*, e.g.

أَمْر order. إِبِل camel. أُفُق horizon.

In Persian the sign ء in an initial position is omitted: thus امر.

[1] The feminine ending (see Lesson XVI, para. 5 et seq.) is written ة.

(*b*) In a medial position, three cases arise:

(i) *hamze* is unvowelled. It is then borne by the letter cognate with the *preceding* vowel, i.e. by ا *alef* if the vowel is *a*, by و *vav* if the vowel is *o*, and by ی *ye* if the vowel is *e* (written without dots).

E.g. رَأْس head. مُؤْمِن believer. بِئْر well.

(ii) *hamze* is vowelled and follows a *sokun* not marking a long vowel or diphthong. It is then borne by the letter cognate with the *following* vowel, e.g.

مَسْأَلَة question. مَسْؤُول responsible. مَرْئِی visible.

(iii) *hamze* is vowelled and follows a short or a long vowel. If *either* of the vowels is *e* or *i* the bearer is ـ *ye* without dots; if not, but either is *o* or *u*, the bearer is و *vav*, otherwise the bearer is ا *alef*, unless the first vowel is *a*, when there is no bearer.

E.g. خَطِیئَة	sin.	سُئِل	He was asked.
وَسَائِل	means.	طَاؤُوس	peacock.
سُؤَال	question.	تَأَمُّل	thought, consideration.
سَأَل	He asked.	قِرَاءَة	reading.

For *hamze* in a medial position both Arabic and Persian admit deviations from the rule to avoid two consecutive *vavs* or *yes*. For this purpose (i) ؤ may change to ئ, e.g. مَسْئُول, and (ii) both ؤ and ئ may be written without the bearer, either between two letters or above the ligature joining two letters, e.g. رُؤُوس, heads, مَشِیئَة wish. Two consecutive *alefs* are always so avoided (as in قِرَاءَة, in (iii) above). أ may even be changed to ئ when there is no such compulsion, as in مَسْئَلَة (the usual form of the word in Persian). It is improper, though by no means unknown, for *hamze* to be written over a letter of prolongation which should follow it, e.g. طَاؤُس (for طَاؤُوس). In such cases the long vowel must be retained in pronunciation.

(*c*) In a final position:

Preceded by a *sokun* or a long vowel it has no bearer, e.g.

ضَوْء light, brightness. شَیْء thing. سُوء evil.

Otherwise it follows the same rules as the *hamze* in a medial position. In a final position the sign ـٔ is often omitted in Persian.

هَمْزَةُ ٱلْوَصْلِ occurs at the beginning of some words but does not represent an essential part of the word itself. When such a word follows another word the هَمْزَةُ ٱلْوَصْلِ with its vowel is dropped and the sign ـٱ known as وَصْلَة replaces the *hamze*, and the *alef* which supported the *hamze*, while preserved in writing, is not represented in pronunciation, e.g.

عَبْدُ ٱلْقَادِر Abd ol-Qader (a proper name).

The *hamze* of the definite article ال, the Imperative of the I form of the verb and of the Perfect, Imperative and Verbal Noun of the VII, VIII, IX and X forms of the verb is a هَمْزَةُ ٱلْوَصْلِ, as also is the *hamze* of the following words:

اِبْن	son.	اِبْنَة	daughter.
اِثْنَان	two (m.).	اِثْنَتَان	two (f.).
اِمْرُؤ	man.	اِمْرَأَة	woman.

If the word preceding a هَمْزَةُ ٱلْوَصْلِ does not end in a vowel, the final consonant generally receives a *kasre* (*e*) except مِن 'from' which takes a *fathe* (*a*) before the article, e.g.

مِنَ ٱلْوَلَد from the boy.

The Personal Pronouns هُم 'they', كُم 'you' and أَنْتُم 'ye', the personal ending تُم of the 2nd pers. pl. of the Perfect and the preposition مُذ 'since' take a *zamme* (*o*) before a هَمْزَةُ ٱلْوَصْلِ, e.g.

لَعَنَهُمُ ٱللّٰه may God curse them.

If the word preceding a هَمْزَةُ ٱلْوَصْلِ ends in ا (*a*) و (*u*) or ى (*i*) the vowels *a*, *u* and *i* become short. In Persian they are pronounced *a*, *o* and *e* respectively, e.g.

أَبُو ٱلْبَشَر *abol-baʃar*, the father of humanity (a proper name).

فِى ٱلْفَوْر *fel-fōur*, immediately.

In certain expressions the هَمْزَةُ ٱلْوَصْل is omitted in writing, e.g.

بِسْمِ ٱللّٰه (for باسم الله) in the name of God.

It is also omitted from the word إِبْن 'son' when this comes between the name of the son and his father, provided it is not at the beginning of a line, e.g.

زيد بن على *zeid ebne ali*,[1] Zeid son of Ali,

and from the article ال when this is preceded by لِ 'to, for' or the particle لَ 'verily', e.g.

لِلرَّجُل to the man. لَلحَقّ verily the truth.

If the noun begins with ل then the ل of the article also falls out, e.g.

لِلَّيْلَة for the night. لِلّٰه to God.

9. In a medial position a *hamze* in Arabic words is pronounced in Persian as a glottal plosive and is represented in the transcription by the sign ', e.g.

رئيس *ra'is*, chief, director.

Initial or final *hamze* is not represented in the transcription; final *hamze* is not usually pronounced. There are, however, certain exceptions to this rule, among them جزء *joz'* 'part, portion' and سوء *su'* 'evil', the final *hamze* of which is pronounced and therefore represented in the transcription. In words which have, in Arabic, a final *hamze* preceded by an *alef*, the *hamze* being usually omitted in Persian, the *ezafe* when added to such words is written as ى, e.g.

اقتضاى وقت *eqtezaye vaqt*, the exigency of the time.

10. A stroke resembling a *madde* is generally put above abbreviations. The following abbreviations are in common use in Persian:

صَلَّى ٱللّٰهُ عَلَيْهِ وَسَلَّمَ = صٓ God bless him and give him peace (used after the name of Muhammad).

عَلَيْهِ ٱلسَّلَامُ = عٓ Upon him be peace (used after the names of the prophets).

[1] The transcription gives the Persian pronunciation, which differs from Arabic usage.

رَضِيَ ٱللّٰهُ عَنْهُ = رضی May God be pleased with him (used after the names of the Companions of Muhammad).

رَحِمَهُ ٱللّٰهُ = رح May God have compassion on him (used after the names of the dead).

11. The Arabic ة is written in Persian ت (*t*) or ه. The tendency is for it to become ت if it occurs in the following forms of the Verbal Noun of the I form: فَعُولَة, فَعَالَة, فِعَالَة, فَعَالِيَة (see Lesson XV, para. 4) or in the Abstract Noun of Quality (see Lesson XVI, para. 13). If it is the feminine ending it is written ه. In pronunciation it falls away and the *fathe* preceding the ة in Arabic is changed in Persian to *e*,[1] thus وَالِدَة 'mother' becomes والده *valede*. The ة of Verbal Nouns of the II and III forms is also usually changed to the 'silent' *h*.

Sometimes both forms are found with a different meaning, e.g.

اراده *erade*, will.

ارادت *eradat*, respect for, devotion to (someone).

امنیه *amniye*, gendarmerie.

امنیت *amniyat*, security, public order.

12. It was stated above that Arabic words and phrases were usually Persianized when used in Persian. There are a few exceptions. The case of numerals has already been noted (see note to para. 11 above). In the following phrases the Arabic *kasre* preserves its Arabic value, that is it approximates to the vowel in the English word 'bit':

بِسْمِ ٱللّٰه in the name of God.

اَلْحَمْدُ لِلّٰه Praise be to God.

مِنْهَا the formula used to perform subtraction (see above, Lesson V, para. 12).

[1] This does not apply to numerals used in dates. The ة in such cases is preserved in the orthography, but is not pronounced, and the *fathe* or a of the Arabic preserved. In the names of the months ذُو ٱلْحِجَّة and ذُو ٱلْقَعْدَة the *fathe* is also preserved.

In the expression عَيْنُهُ (in Persian) 'exactly like', the *zamme* also preserves its Arabic value, that is it approximates to the Persian vowel *u* but its articulation time is less. These differences are not shown in the transcription.

ـِیّ in Arabic words is represented in the transcription as *iy*,[1] e.g.

رعیت (for رَعِیَّة) *ra'iyat*, peasant.

بلدیه (for بَلَدِیَّة) *baladiye*, municipality.

ـَیّ becomes *aiy*, e.g. مُهَیَّا *mohaiya*, prepared.

ی followed by ا *a* in some Arabic words (notably the Verbal Noun of the VII and VIII form of Hollow Verbs, see Lesson XVIII, para. 4) is represented in the transcription by *ey*, but this *e* approximates to the vowel in the English word 'bit' (and not to the *e* in the English word 'bed'), e.g.

اِمْتِیاز *emteyaz*.

This does not apply to ی followed by ا in Persian words, e.g.

شیرازیان *ʃirazian*, people of Shiraz.

LESSON XV

The Triliteral Root.

1. The Arabic verbal root contains three radical letters or four,[2] e.g.

فَعَلَ to do (of which the radical letters are ف, ع and ل).

تَرْجَمَ to translate (of which the radical letters are ت, ر, ج and م).

2. The triliteral root is the more common of the two. In the 3rd pers. sing. Perfect Active the first and third radicals always have an *a* as their vowel. The medial radical may have *a*, *e* or *o*, e.g.

فَعَلَ to do. حَزِنَ to be sad. حَسُنَ to be beautiful.

[1] It is thus differentiated from یَة (یه) *ie* in the form تفعله when the third radical is ی.

[2] Arabic dictionaries give the verb under the 3rd pers. sing. masc. of the Perfect Active of the root form. This is given in Arabic-English dictionaries as the infinitive, thus فَعَلَ 'to do' and تَرْجَمَ 'to translate'; the real meaning of these forms is 'he did' and 'he translated' respectively. The derived forms must be looked up in Arabic dictionaries under the root form.

3. From the simple or root form are derived fourteen forms. Only nine of these are in common use and only these will be given in this and the following lessons. All ten forms seldom occur in one root. The Arabic dictionaries give only those forms which are in use.

4. The Active and Passive Participles and the Verbal Noun of the Arabic verb are used in Persian. Only these forms together with the 3rd pers. masc. sing. of the Perfect Active will be given in the tables in this and the following lessons.[1] The verb فَعَلَ is commonly used by Arabic grammarians as a paradigm. The derivative forms are formed by the addition of servile letters (see p. 181, para. 2 above), vowel permutations and the doubling of the 2nd and 3rd radical letters, as follows:

Form	3rd pers. sing. Perfect Active	Active Participle	Passive Participle
I	فَعَلَ	فَاعِل	مَفْعُول

E.g.

كَتَبَ	he wrote.	كاتب	scribe.	مكتوب	written; letter.

There are some forty forms of the Verbal Noun of the root form of the verb. Only those in more frequent use will be given here:

فَعْل e.g.:

فَهْم	understanding	from	فَهِمَ	to understand.

فَعَل e.g.:

فَرَح	joy	„	فَرِحَ	to be glad.

فُعُول e.g.:

جُلُوس	accession	„	جَلَسَ	to sit.

فُعُولَة[2] e.g.:

سُهُولَت	ease	„	سَهُلَ	to be easy.

[1] There are a few cases in Persian of other Arabic verbal forms, e.g. يَعْنِي, used in Persian to mean 'namely', is the 3rd pers. sing. of the Imperfect Active of عَنَى 'to mean'. أَعْنِي, also used to mean 'namely', is the 1st pers. sing. of the Imperfect Active of the same verb.

[2] Usually written with ت in Persian.

فَعَالَة[1] e.g.:

سَعَادت	prosperity	from	سَعَدَ	to be auspicious.

فُعْل e.g.:

شُغْل	occupation	,,	شَغَلَ	to be occupied.

فِعْل e.g.:

قِسْم	part	,,	قَسَمَ	to divide.

فِعَال e.g.:

لِقَاء	meeting	,,	لَقِیَ[2]	to meet.

فِعَالَة[1] e.g.:

خِلَافت	caliphate	,,	خَلَفَ	to succeed.

فُعَال e.g.:

سُؤَال	question	,,	سَأَلَ[3]	to question.

فَعَال e.g.:

خَلَاص	liberation	,,	خَلَصَ	to be freed (from).

فَعْلَى e.g.:

دَعْوَى	claim	,,	دَعَا	to call out, etc.

فُعْلَان e.g.:

غُفْرَان	pardon	,,	غَفَرَ	to forgive.

فِعْلَان e.g.:

عِرْفَان	mysticism	,,	عَرَفَ	to know.

فَعُول e.g.:

قَبُول	acceptance	,,	قَبِلَ	to accept.

[1] Usually written with ت in Persian.

[2] For the rules governing the formation of the derived forms of weak verbs see Lesson xviii.

[3] For the rules governing the formation of the derived forms of hamzated verbs see Lesson xvii.

فَعِيل e.g.:

رَحِيل	departure, journey	from	رَحَلَ	to depart (from).

فَعَالِيَة[1] e.g.:

صَلَاحِيت	competence	„	صَلُحَ	to be honest.

مَفْعَلَة[2] e.g.:

مَقَالَة	treatise	„	قَالَ[3]	to say.

5. The meanings of the derived forms are modifications of the meaning of the root form as follows:

II. فَعَّلَ intensive; makes intransitive verbs transitive. E.g. ضَرَبَ to beat, ضَرَّبَ to beat violently; فَرَقَ to separate (intrans.), فَرَّقَ to disperse (trans.).

III. فَاعَلَ the relation of the action of I to another person, e.g. قَتَلَ to kill, قَاتَلَ to fight with.

IV. أَفْعَلَ causative; brings about the condition or action implied in I, e.g. عَلِمَ to know, أَعْلَمَ to inform (someone of something); بَلُغَ to be eloquent, أَبْلَغَ to speak eloquently.

V. تَفَعَّلَ Reflexive of II; describes the consequences of II, especially with reference to oneself, e.g. فَرَّقَ to disperse (trans.), تَفَرَّقَ to be dispersed; خَوَّفَ to terrify, تَخَوَّفَ to be afraid.

VI. تَفَاعَلَ Reflexive of III; expresses the consequences of III; reciprocal. E.g. رَامَى to throw (at the same time as another), تَرَامَى to throw oneself down; خَادَعَ to try to outwit, تَخَادَعَ to pretend to be deceived; قَاتَلَ to fight with, تَقَاتَلَ to fight with one another.

[1] Usually written with ت in Persian.

[2] Usually written with ه in Persian, the ه being then treated like the 'silent' *h*.

[3] For the rules governing the formation of the derived forms of weak verbs see Lesson XVIII.

VII. إِنْفَعَلَ Passive; being affected by I especially from the point of view of the person initiating action for his own ends, e.g. كَسَرَ to break off, إِنْكَسَرَ to be broken; هَزَمَ to put to flight, إِنْهَزَمَ to let oneself be put to flight, to flee.

VIII. إِفْتَعَلَ Reflexive of I; reciprocal, e.g. ضَرَبَ to beat, اِضْطَرَبَ[1] to move oneself to and fro, to be agitated; قَتَلَ to kill, إِقْتَتَلَ to fight with one another.

IX. إِفْعَلَّ used for colours and physical defects, e.g. إِسْوَدَّ to be black, إِحْوَلَّ to squint.

X. إِسْتَفْعَلَ Reflexive of IV; desiring, seeking, asking for, considering or thinking a thing possesses the qualities expressed by I, e.g. أَوْجَبَ to make it necessary for others, إِسْتَوْجَبَ to make something necessary for oneself; غَفَرَ to pardon, إِسْتَغْفَرَ to ask pardon, غَاثَ to help, إِسْتَغَاثَ to call for help, حَسُنَ to be comely, إِسْتَحْسَنَ to think beautiful.

6. Arabic Verbal Nouns are abstract and denote the state, action or feeling indicated by the verb.

7. The Active Participle is used as an adjective or noun referring to a continuous action, habitual state or permanent quality, e.g.

عَالِمٌ learned, a learned man.

مُعَلِّمٌ teacher.

The tendency in Persian is for the Active Participle of the I form to be used as an adjective in the singular rather than as a noun, but to be widely used as a noun in the plural.

8. The Passive Participle is used as an adjective or noun, e.g.

مَعْلُومٌ known.

مَكْتُوبٌ letter (what is written).

[1] See below, para. 9.

Form	3rd pers. sing. Perfect Active		Active Participle		Passive Participle		Verbal Noun	
II	فَعَّلَ		مُفَعِّل		مُفَعَّل		تَفْعِيل	or تَفْعِلَة[1]
E.g.	عَلَّمَ	to teach	مُعَلِّم	teacher			تَعْلِيم	teaching
	فَرَّقَ	to separate	مُفَرِّق	discriminative	مُفَرَّق	dispersed	تَفْرِقَه	separation, disunity
III	فَاعَلَ		مُفَاعِل		مُفَاعَل		فِعَال	or مُفَاعَلَة[2]
E.g.	كَاتَبَ	to correspond	مُكَاتِب	correspondent			مُكَاتَبه	correspondence
	حَافَظَ	to observe carefully	مُحَافِظ	guardian			مُحَافَظه	preservation, defence
	قَاتَلَ	to wage war against	مُقَاتِل	fighter, warrior			قِتَال	battle
IV	أَفْعَلَ		مُفْعِل		مُفْعَل		إِفْعَال	
E.g.	أَحْسَنَ	to do good	مُحْسِن	beneficient			إِحْسَان	beneficence
V	تَفَعَّلَ		مُتَفَعِّل		مُتَفَعَّل		تَفَعُّل	
E.g.	تَكَبَّرَ	to magnify oneself	مُتَكَبِّر	proud			تَكَبُّر	pride

VI	تفاعل		متفاعل		متفاعل		تفاعل	
E.g.	تعاهد	to make a mutual compact	متعاهد	contracting party			تعاهد	a mutual agreement
VII	انفعل		منفعل		منفعل[3]		انفعال	
E.g.	انكسر	to be broken	منكسر	broken			انكسار	fracture, rupture
VIII	افتعل		مفتعل		مفتعل		افتعال	
E.g.	امتنع	to be inaccessible	ممتنع	impossible			امتناع	abstention
IX	افعلّ		مفعلّ				افعلال	
E.g.	احمرّ	to be red	محمرّ	red			احمرار	redness
X	استفعل		مستفعل		مستفعل		استفعال	
E.g.	استقبل	to come forward	مستقبل	one who goes to meet (someone)	مستقبل	future (tense)	استقبال	going to meet

Usually written with ه in Persian.

[2] In Persian this usually becomes ه and the *fathe* of the ع frequently becomes a *kasre*, thus محافظه *mohafeze* but مكاتبه *mokatabe*.

[3] The Passive Participle of this form where the latter is Passive in meaning (see above, para. 5) does not occur.

9. The inserted ت of the VIII form undergoes the following changes:

(*a*) If the first radical of the root is ت this unites with the inserted ت, e.g.

اِتِّبَاع submission, obedience (from تَبِعَ).

(*b*) If the first radical is د or ز the inserted ت changes into د which unites with the radical د, e.g.

اِدِّرَاك attainment (from دَرَكَ).

اِزْدِحَام crowding (from زَحَمَ).

(*c*) If the first radical is ذ the inserted ت changes into ذ and unites with the radical ذ, e.g.

اِذِّخَار hoarding (from ذَخَرَ).

(*d*) If the first radical is ص, ض or ط the inserted ت is changed into ط, which unites with the radical ط, e.g.

اِطِّلَاع information (from طَلَعَ).

اِصْطِلَاح expression (from صَلُحَ).

اِضْطِرَاب anxiety (from ضَرَبَ).

10. Arabic forms are used in Persian not only standing alone, but also combined with Persian words and particles to form compounds. Many examples of Compound Verbs thus formed have been given in Lesson IX, para. 2. Persian particles and suffixes are also added to Arabic forms to form compounds, e.g.

حاجتمند *hajatmand*, needy (حاجت need).

شعله‌ور *ʃo'levar*, blazing (شعله flame).

اولین *avvalin*, first (اول first).

نامعلوم *nama'lum*, unknown (معلوم known).

ناصالح *nasaleh*, dishonest (صالح good, just).

عاقلانه *aqelane*, wise; wisely (عاقل wise, reasonable).

ایران و انگلیس (بقیه از درس پیش)

در زمان پادشاهی شاه عباس دوم نفوذ انگلیسها بمراتب کمتر از سابق گردید و بر عکس تسلط و نفوذ هلندیها در ایران و خلیج فارس زیاد میگشت و بطوری از پیشرفت کار خود در ایران گستاخ شده بودند که حتی با کشتیهای جنگی خود در بصره دار التجاره‌های انگلیسیرا ویران کردند ولی بعدًا در نتیجه جنگی که در اروپا میان دو دولت فوق الذکر روی داد روابط تجارتی ایشان در هندوستان و ایران مختل شد و دولت ایران هم از موقع استفاده کرده از نفوذ و امتیازات آن دو دولت در ایران کاست از آنجمله از ادای مبلغی که هر ساله از بابت در آمدهای گمرکی بندر عباس بانگلیسها داده میشد خودداری کرد و شرکت هند شرقی هم بپادشاه انگلستان که در آنزمان چارلز دوم بود توسل جست و او در سال ۱۰۸۱ بشاه سلیمان[1] در این باب نامه نوشت و تا اواخر قرن دوازدهم هجری نفوذ هلندیها در خلیج بمراتب بیشتر از انگلیسها بود ولی در اواخر این قرن بعضی حوادث تازه که در اروپا اتفاق افتاد مایه ضعف هلندیها گردید و در همین موقع هم بواسطه اختلافاتیکه در میان شرکای هند شرقی روی داد دولت انگلیس در سال ۱۱۲۰ هجری (۱۷۰۸ میلادی) تمام شرکتهای قدیمرا با یکدیگر متحد نموده شرکتی بزرگ بنام شرکت تجار انگلیسی برای تجارت هند شرقی تأسیس کرد و ضمنًا پادشاه انگلستان هم رؤسای شرکترا بمقامات قنسولی و سفارت در دربار پادشاهان هندوستان گماشت و نفوذ آنان افزون گشت پایان

طهران

طهران هنوز ببزرگی امروزه نشده بود و بیشتر خیابانهائی که اکنون هرکس از اهالی شهر اسم آنرا میداند و مایه جلال پایتخت شده بوجود نیامده بود هنوز در دروازه‌هارا موقع اذان غروب میبستند عبور و مرور از داخل بخارج و در خود شهر از اول شب قطع میشد زمستانها که آفتاب زودتر غروب میکرد در دروازه‌هارا هم زودتر میبستند در این اوقات بود که یکی از سفرا تا صبح بیرون دروازه ماند و در میان چاروادارها بیتوته کرد همین اوقات بود که در چند قدمی دروازه‌ها دزدان برای چند تومان مردمرا سر میبریدند

[1] Shah Soleiman ruled from A.H. 1077 to 1105.

Exercise 27

1. The Prime Minister was both detested and despised. 2. He has treated me badly and yet I wish to do him justice. 3. He has an enemy, namely his own brother. 4. A great deal of the forest of the west is Crown land, and to prevent it from being wasted the government has decreed that no one can cut down the trees without permission. 5. He said 'All that I have is at your disposal'. 6. It was that which killed him. 7. He always does that which the hour demands, not that which he would like to do. 8. I have made such alterations as occurred to me. 9. He is the same man that we met yesterday. 10. That is the reason why he cannot succeed. 11. I know that he has come. 12. I feared that it might anger him. 13. Take the money, there is no saying but you will need it. 14. No one doubts that he will be successful.

LESSON XVI

The Declension of Nouns. The Gender of Nouns. The Noun of Place. The Noun of Instrument. Abstract Nouns. Diminutives. Adjectives.

1. Arabic has three cases, nominative, genitive and accusative. If the noun is not defined by the definite article ال the case endings are generally ـٌ *on*, ـٍ *en* and ـًا *an*, e.g.

Nom. وَالِدٌ
Gen. وَالِدٍ } father.
Acc. وَالِدًا

For certain classes of nouns, known as diptotes, the accusative ending is used also for the genitive when the noun is indefinite.

2. If the noun is defined by the definite article the case endings for all nouns are ـُ *o*, ـِ *e* and ـَ *a*, e.g.

Nom. ٱلْوَالِدُ
Gen. ٱلْوَالِدِ
Acc. ٱلْوَالِدَ

3. If a word is in the construct state[1] and definite it does not take the article, e.g.

صَاحِبُ ٱلْبَيْتِ the owner of the house.

حُبُّ ٱلْوَطَنِ patriotism (love of the country).

4. In Persian the case endings fall away when a word stands alone, but in phrases such as those given in para. 3 above, which are used in Persian as compounds, the nominative ending of the first part is retained, thus

وَالِدٌ father (nom.) becomes in Persian والد *valed.*

حُبُّ ٱلْوَطَنِ patriotism becomes in Persian حبّ الوطن *hobb ol-vatan.*

5. Arabic has two genders: masculine and feminine. Most masculine words can be made feminine by the addition of ة, e.g.

وَالِدٌ father.

وَالِدَةٌ mother (in Persian والده *valede*).

6. Many words singular in form have a collective meaning in Arabic. To indicate a single object the feminine ending ة is added, e.g.

شَجَر tree (trees in general).

شَجَرَة a tree.

7. Words denoting males and ending in ة are masculine, e.g.

خَلِيفَة caliph (in Persian خليفه *xalife*).

8. Adjectives qualifying a feminine noun or pronoun also take the feminine ending ة unless they have special feminine forms (see below),[2] e.g.

كَبِيرٌ great (m.).

كَبِيرَةٌ great (f.) (in Persian كبيره *kabire*).

[1] I.e. in the form of the substantive used when standing before another having an attributive (or genitive) relation to it.

[2] In Arabic certain adjectives which refer only to women do not take the feminine ending. This rule is not always observed in Persian e.g. حامِل 'pregnant' becomes in Persian حامله *hamele.*

9. Broken plurals (see Lesson XX) are feminine[1] and therefore take a feminine adjective. This agreement is sometimes preserved in Persian, e.g.

امور مهمه *omure mohemme*, important matters (امور being the broken plural of امر *amr*).

10. A Noun of Place is formed on the measure مَفْعَل, مَفْعِل, مَفْعَلَة or مَفْعِلَة, e.g.

مَقْصَد destination.

مَسْجِد mosque.

مَدْرَسَة school (in Persian مدرسه *madrase*).[2]

مَقْبَرَة cemetery (in Persian مقبره *maqbere*).

Nouns of Place from the derived forms of the Triliteral Verb are identical in form with the Passive Participle.

11. A noun denoting the Instrument is formed on the measure مِفْعَال, مِفْعَل or مِفْعَلَة, e.g.

مِفْتَاح key.

مِبْضَع lancet.

مِشْرَبَة copper bowl used in the *hammam* (in Persian مشربه and pronounced *meʃrabe* or *maʃrabe*).

12. Nouns denoting professions and trades are formed on the measure فَعَّال, e.g.

نَجَّار carpenter.

خَبَّاز baker.

13. Abstract Nouns of Quality are formed by adding the feminine termination ة to Relative Adjectives (see below, para. 18). This becomes ت or the 'silent' *h* in Persian.

[1] Certain other classes of words are feminine in Arabic, but since they are not so regarded in Persian they will not be mentioned here.

[2] مدرسه is usually pronounced *madrese* in Persian.

This form is used to denote the abstract idea of the thing as distinguished from the concrete thing itself; and also to represent the thing or things signified by the primitive noun as a whole or totality, e.g.

إِنْسَانِيَّة humanity (in Persian انسانيت *ensaniyat*; إِنْسَان human being).

نَصْرَانِيَّة what constitutes being a Christian (in Persian نصرانيت *nasraniyat*; نَصْرَانِى a Christian).

This termination is occasionally added to Persian nouns, e.g.

خريت *xariyat* stupidity (from خر *xar* ass, donkey).

This form is also occasionally used in Persian to denote a dynasty; in this case the ة becomes the 'silent' *h*, e.g.

قاجاريه *qajariye*, the Qajar Dynasty.
صفويه *safaviye*, the Safavid Dynasty.

14. Diminutives are formed on the measure فُعَيْل, e.g.

طُفَيْل a little child (from طِفْل child).[1]

حُسَيْن Hosein (diminutive of Hasan).

If the noun has a feminine ending this is attached to the diminutive, e.g.

قُلَيْعَة a small fortress (from قَلْعَة).

15. Adjectives are formed on a variety of measures. Among them are:

(*a*) فَعِيل e.g.

شَرِيف noble. مَرِيض sick.

When derived from transitive verbs this form has a passive meaning, e.g.

أَسِير captive.

(*b*) فَعْلَان, fem. فَعْلَى, e.g.

سَكْرَان drunk (m.); سَكْرَى (f.).

(*c*) فَعْل e.g.

صَعْب difficult.

[1] طفيل *tofeil* is used in Persian to mean 'parasite'.

(*d*) فَعَل e.g.

حَسَن beautiful.

(*e*) the following forms intensive in meaning:

فَعُول e.g.

صَبُور (very) patient (in Persian usually pronounced *sabur*).

جَهُول (very) ignorant (in Persian usually pronounced *jahul*).

فَعَّال e.g.

عَلَّام very learned. فَعَّال very active.

فِعِّيل e.g.

صِدِّيق very sincere.

فُعُّول e.g.

قُدُّوس very holy.

16. The Elative is formed on the measure أَفْعَل, fem. فُعْلَى,[1] e.g.

أَكْبَر greater, greatest (m.) (from كَبِير great).

كُبْرَى greater, greatest (f.).

The Arabic elative is used in Persian as an adjective and follows the noun it qualifies, e.g.

پسر ارشد *pesare arʃad*, the eldest son.

It can also be used as a noun, e.g.

اشرف انبيا *aʃrafe ambia*, the most illustrious of prophets.

The elative اعلَى *a'la* is also used to mean 'excellent, first-rate' as well as 'the highest', e.g.

کشمش اعلى در ايران پيدا ميشود *keʃmeʃe a'la dar iran pĕida miʃavad*, Excellent raisins are found in Persia.

[1] The Persian comparative and superlative endings are sometimes added to an Arabic elative, e.g. أَوْلَى (from أَوَّل 'first') and اولى تر *ŏulatar*, better, superior.

17. Adjectives denoting a colour or physical defect are also formed on the measure أَفْعَل. The feminine is formed on the measure فَعْلاء; the alternate form فَعْلَى is rare, e.g.

أَصْفَر yellow (m.). صَفْراء (f.).

18. Relative Adjectives are formed by the addition of ى to the noun. In Arabic this ى has a *tašdid*, but in Persian it becomes *i*, e.g.

دِمِشْقى an inhabitant of Damascus or person born in Damascus (دِمِشْق).

Certain nouns to which this ى is added undergo various changes:

(*a*) The feminine ending ة is omitted, e.g.

حَقِيقى real, true (from حَقِيقة truth, reality).

طَبِيعى natural (from طَبِيعة nature).

صِناعى industrial (from صِناعة industry).

(*b*) The feminine termination ى (or ا) of the form فُعْلَى is omitted or changed into و, e.g.

دُنْيَوى worldly (from دُنْيا = world, fem. of the elative أَدْنَى lower, lowest).

(*c*) The termination ة falls away if the word ends in ية, e.g.

إِسْكَنْدَرى a native of Alexandria (from إِسْكَنْدَرِيَّة).

(*d*) If the final radical is a ى, و or *alef hamze*, this is changed into و, e.g.

مَعْنَوى spiritual (from مَعْنَى meaning).

عَلَوى an Alid (from عَلى Ali).

سَماوى heavenly (from سَماء heaven).

(*e*) If the noun contains more than four letters (radicals together with servile letters), the final being ى, the latter is omitted, e.g.

مُصْطَفى pertaining to the chosen (from مُصْطَفَى chosen).

(*f*) Certain words such as أَب 'father' and أَخ brother are defective, having lost the final weak radical. In the adjectival form this reappears as و, e.g.

أَبَوِى paternal.[1] أَخَوِى fraternal.[2]

Cf. also لُغَوِى dialectical (from لُغَة, Pers. لغت word, dialect).

19. Certain nouns form relative adjectives in ـَانِى, e.g.

جِسْمَانِى bodily, corporeal (from جِسْم body).

رُوْحَانِى spiritual (from رُوح spirit).[3]

برنامه دولت

برنامه دولت که در مجلس شورای ملی مورد مذاکره قرار گرفت از این قرار است — (۱) در سیاست خارجی دولت با رعایت کامل مصالح کشور مقتضی میداند با دولتهائیکه منافع ایران با منافع آنها ارتباط دارد همکاری نزدیك داشته باشد — (۲) اصلاح و رفع نقصهای قوانین دادگستری برای تکمیل امنیت قضائی و نیز تجدید نظر در قوانین دیگریکه با مقتضیات امروز وفق نمیدهد — (۳) تجدید نظر در سازمان قوای تأمینیه و تکمیل وسائل امنیت — (٤) اهتمام مخصوصی در تأمین خواربار لازم برای کشور — (٥) تجدید نظر در قوانین استخدام کارمندان دولت — (٦) اصلاح در امور اقتصادی و مالی کشور از قبیل تعدیل مالیاتها برای تخفیف تحمیلات مالیاتی و جلوگیری از هزینه‌هائیکه مقتضای اوضاع کنونی کشور نیست در موقع تهیه بودجه سال آینده تجدید نظر در مقررات بازرگانی و الغای انحصارهای غیر ضروری که تاکنون ملغی نشده است و اهتمام در پائین آوردن قیمت زندگی — (۷) توجه مخصوص بپیشرفت کار کشاورزی و بهبود زندگی کشاورزان و توسعه امور آبیاری منع تدریجی کشت و استعمال تریاك تجدید نظر در قوانین عمران و اجرای برنامه کشاورزی — (۸) ترقی و تکمیل صنایع بقدر امکان با تمایل باین که کارخانه‌ها بدست افراد شرکتهای غیر دولتی اداره شود و اهتمام در بهبود زندگی کارگران — (۹) تکمیل

[1] Used in Persian to mean 'father'. [2] Used in Persian to mean 'brother'.

[3] Also pronounced *rōuhani* in Persian.

راه‌ها و راه‌آهن در حدود استطاعت کشور — (۱۰) اصلاح قانون تقسیمات کشور و توجه باینکه اهالی در اداره امور محلی خود شرکت داشته باشند — (۱۱) تکمیل و ترقی تأسیسات فرهنگی و اهتمام در اصلاح اخلاق عمومی — (۱۲) توسعه سازمان بهداری و توجه مخصوص ببهداشت عمومی

آمیزش زبانها[1]

در عالم هیچ زبانی نیست که بتواند از آمیختگی با زبان دیگر خودرا برکنار دارد مگر زبان مردمی‌که هرگز با مردم دیگر آمیزش نکنند و این نیز محال است چه بوسیله تجارت و سفر و معاشرت و حتی بوسیله شنیدن افسانه‌ها و روایات ملل دیگر لغاتی از آن مردم در این مردم نفوذ میکند و همه زبانهای عالم از این رو دارای لغتهای دخیل است باید دید از آمیختن زبانی با زبان دیگر چه نتایجی حاصل میشود آمیختن زبانها بر چند قسم است یکی اینکه زبانی هر چه‌را ندارد بالطبع از همسایه یا جای دورتر بستاند و ملایم بلهجه و سلیقه خویش نماید یعنی آن لغترا فرو برده و نشخوار کرده و قابل هضم سازد و از حالات و اختصاصات اصلی آنرا بیندازد و حتی بمیل خود آنرا گاهی قلب کند گاهی تصحیف کند گاهی مفهوم آنرا تغییر دهد اگر جامد است مشتق کند و اگر مشتق است جامد کند الی آخر چنانکه عربان بلغات بیگانه همین کاررا کرده و میکنند و ما هم با برخی از لغات عربی و لغات ترکی و فرنگی این عملرا نموده‌ایم ولی این کار در میان ما عمومیت نداشته است

[1] سبک شناسی تألیف محمد تقی بهار (ملک الشعرا)

Exercise 28

1. What changes we make in our plans will be announced later. 2. The enemy devastated the country as they retreated. 3. You ought to have told me instead of I you. 4. The more money he makes the more he wants. 5. So long as the nation retains its vigour its language never grows old. 6. I doubt whether he was there. 7. I do not know whether he (his condition) is better or worse. 8. I asked him whether he would come himself or send a substitute. 9. Little did she foresee what a difference this would make. 10. I insist upon it that he should go. 11. I came as soon as I heard of it. 12. I shall come as soon as ever I can. 13. When your work is done let me know. 14. I shall be ready by the time you get back.

LESSON XVII

Doubled Verbs. Hamzated Verbs.

1. In Lesson xv an example of the 'sound' Triliteral Verb was given. Certain additional rules have to be borne in mind in the formation of the derived forms of 'doubled' verbs, i.e. verbs whose second and third radical is the same, 'hamzated' verbs, i.e. verbs one of whose radicals is a *hamze*, and 'weak' verbs, i.e. verbs one of whose radicals is و or ی.

2. The following rules will enable the reader to find the Verbal Nouns and Participles of 'doubled' verbs and their derived forms.

(*a*) If the first and third radicals are vowelled, the second radical rejects its vowel (unless it is itself doubled), unites with the third and forms a doubled letter.

(*b*) If the first radical is vowelless and the third vowelled, the second radical gives up its vowel to the first, combines with the third and forms a doubled letter.

(*c*) When the second radical is separated from the third by a long vowel no contraction takes place.

مَدَّ to stretch out

Form	3rd pers. sing. masc. Perfect Active	Active Participle	Passive Participle	Verbal Noun
I	مَدَّ	مَادّ	مَمْدُود	مَدّ
II	مَدَّدَ	مُمَدِّد	مُمَدَّد	تَمْدِيد
III	مَادَّ	مُمَادّ	مُمَادّ	مِدَاد
IV	أَمَدَّ	مُمِدّ	مُمَدّ	إِمْدَاد
V	تَمَدَّدَ	مُتَمَدِّد	مُتَمَدَّد	تَمَدُّد
VI	تَمَادَّ	مُتَمَادّ	مُتَمَادّ	تَمَادُد (or تَمَادّ)
VII	اِنْفَلَّ[1]	مُنْفَلّ		اِنْفِلَال
VIII	اِمْتَدَّ	مُمْتَدّ		اِمْتِدَاد
IX	Seldom occurs	—	—	—
X	اِسْتَمَدَّ	مُسْتَمِدّ	مُسْتَمَدّ	اِسْتِمْدَاد

[1] اِنْفَلَّ to be notched (a sword), broken (a tooth). The VII form of مَدَّ does not occur.

3. The following rules, in conjunction with those given in the Introduction to Part II for the writing of *hamze*, will enable the reader to form the Verbal Nouns and Participles of 'hamzated' verbs and their derived forms. It should be remembered that the *hamze* is a consonant and like other consonants may be vowelled or vowelless.

(*a*) If a *hamze* with *a* is prefixed, as in the IV form, to the first radical and this is a *hamze*, the two come together and are written آ.

(*b*) If a *hamze* with *e* or *o* is prefixed to the first radical and this is a *hamze*, the *hamze* of the radical is changed to ی (*i*) or و (*u*) respectively. Exceptionally the VIII form of أَخَذ 'to take' is اِتَّخَذ.

(*c*) The Verbal Noun of the II form is formed on the measure تَفْعِلَة if the third radical is a *hamze*.

Form	3rd pers. sing. masc. Perfect Active	Active Participle	Passive Participle	Verbal Noun
I	اَسَرَ[1]	آسِر	مَأْسور	أَسْر
II	أَثَّرَ[2]	مُؤَثِّر	مُؤَثَّر	تَأْثیر
III	آثَرَ	مُؤاثِر	مُؤاثَر	إثار
IV	آثَرَ	مُؤْثِر	مُؤْثَر	إیثار
V	تَأَثَّرَ	مُتَأَثِّر	مُتَأَثَّر	تَأَثُّر
VI	تَآثَرَ (or تَوَاثَرَ)	مُتَآثِر	مُتَآثَر	تَآثُر (or تَوَاثُر).
VII	Does not occur	—	—	—
VIII	اِیتَثَرَ	مُؤْتَثِر	مُؤْتَثَر	اِیتِثار
IX	Does not occur	—	—	—
X	اِسْتَأْثَرَ	مُسْتَأْثِر	مُسْتَأْثَر	اِسْتِئْثار

[1] أَسَرَ to take captive, bind. [2] أَثَّرَ to leave a trace.

Form	3rd pers. sing. masc. Perfect Active	Active Participle	Passive Participle	Verbal Noun
I	سَأَلَ[1]	سَائِل	مَسْؤُول	سُؤَال
II	لَأَّمَ[2]	مُلَئِّم	مُلَأَّم	تَلْئِيم
III	لَاءَمَ	مُلَائِم	مُلَاءَم	مُلَاءَمَة
IV	أَلْأَمَ	مُلْئِم	مُلْأَم	إِلْآم
V	تَلَأَّمَ	مُتَلَئِّم	مُتَلَأَّم	تَلَؤُّم
VI	تَلَاءَمَ	مُتَلَائِم	مُتَلَاءَم	تَلَاؤُم
VII	اِنْجَأَثَ[3]	مُنْجَئِث	مُنْجَأَث	اِنْجِئَاث
VIII	اِلْتَأَمَ	مُلْتَئِم	مُلْتَأَم	اِلْتِئَام
IX	Does not occur	—	—	—
X	اِسْتَلْأَمَ	مُسْتَلْئِم	مُسْتَلْأَم	اِسْتِلْآم
I	بَرَأَ[4], خَطِئَ[5], دَنُؤَ[6]	بَارِئ	مَبْرُوء	بَرْء
II	بَرَّأَ	مُبَرِّئ	مُبَرَّأ	تَبْرِئَة
III	بَارَأَ	مُبَارِئ	مُبَارَأ	مُبَارَأَة
IV	أَبْرَأَ	مُبْرِئ	مُبْرَأ	إِبْرَاء
V	تَبَرَّأَ	مُتَبَرِّئ	مُتَبَرَّأ	تَبَرُّؤ

[1] سَأَلَ to ask.

[2] لَأَّمَ to dress (a wound); to solder.

[3] اِنْجَأَثَ to be split (a tree).

[4] بَرَأَ to create.

[5] خَطِئَ to fail, make a mistake.

[6] دَنُؤَ to be mean.

Form	3rd pers. sing. masc. Perfect Active	Active Participle	Passive Participle	Verbal Noun
VI	تَبَارَأَ	مُتَبَارِئٌ	مُتَبَارَأٌ	تَبَارُؤٌ
VII	اِنْسَبَأَ [1]	مُنْسَبِئٌ	مُنْسَبَأٌ	اِنْسِبَاءٌ
VIII	اِهْتَنَأَ [2]	مُهْتَنِئٌ	مُهْتَنَأٌ	اِهْتِنَاءٌ
IX	Does not occur	—	—	—
X	اِسْتَبْرَأَ	مُسْتَبْرِئٌ	مُسْتَبْرَأٌ	اِسْتِبْرَاءٌ

بهداری راه آهن

در کارهای ساختمانی مانند هر نوع کار بزرگ و کوچك دیگر بهداشت و تندرستی کارگرانرا از آغاز باید مورد توجه قرار داد پس از آزمایشهای بسیار دانسته‌اند چنانچه تمام اسباب و افزار کار فراهم گردد ولی مهندس و استاد و ناظر و سر عمله و عمله ناتوان و رنجور باشند کاری از پیش نمیرود از همین جهت در پیشرفتهای ساختمانی مسئله بهداشت کارگران یکی از عوامل مؤثر کار بشمار میاید سازمانهای بزرگ ساختمانی که در شهر بکار مشغولند شاید چندان نیازمند بنگاه‌های بهداری نباشند چه بنگاه‌های بهداری شهرداریها و غیره مراقب تندرستی مردم شهرنشین میباشند ولی کارگرانیکه در راه‌ها و نقاط دور از آبادی براه سازی مشغولند بدوا و درمان دسترسی ندارند باین جهت چنانچه در بهداشت این قبیل کارگران اندکی مسامحه شود پیشرفت کارها از نظم بیرون شده و تندرستی هزاران تن بمخاطره خواهد افتاد اداره بهداری ساختمان راه آهن که برای آسایش کارگران راه آهن تأسیس شده ضامن تندرستی آنهاست سازمان این اداره در تمام راه‌ها بدستیاری شعب مخصوصی که برای حفظ تندرستی کارگران دارد از سه راه اقدام مینماید (۱) تدابیر احتیاطی برای جلوگیری از سرایت بیماریهای مسری (۲) مداوای کارگران بیمار (۳) کمك بآسیب دیدگان چون مقاطعه کاران ساختمانی بنابر مفاد تعهدات خود موظفند خانه و آب مشروب و خواربار کارگرانرا مطابق اصول بهداشت آماده سازند اداره بهداری برای حفظ کارگران از بیماریهای

[1] اِنْسَبَأَ to be flayed. [2] اِهْتَنَأَ to administer carefully.

واگیری انجام شدن تعهداترا مراقبت نموده و بوسیله مأمورین و بازرسهای فنی رسیدگی لازم و بموقع بعمل میاورد بعلاوه هنگام ضرورت بکارگرانیکه در نزدیکی نقاط بیماریهای مسری مشغول کار هستند مایه ضد بیماری تلقیح نموده و بوسیله پخش گنه گنه در تهیه موجبات تندرستی آنان اقدام مینماید

علم ادب[1]

موضوع علم ادب کلام منظوم و منثور و بعبارت دیگر سخنان پیوسته و پراکنده است که در این علم از آنها بحث کنند غرض از علم ادب آن است که سخنان پیوسته و پراکنده در هر رشته که باشد با رعایت اصول فصاحت و بلاغت انشاء شده و مطابق روش سخنسنجان و دانشمندان ترکیب یابد و پایه نثر و نظم دبیر یا شاعر بجائی رسد که عقلرا از آن لذت و اهتزاز دست دهد و دلرا فرح و گشایش حاصل گردد فائده علم ادب آن است که مردرا از لغزش نادانی نگاه دارد و درشتی طبیعت‌را هموار سازد و اخلاق‌را روشنی و پاکیزگی بخشد و حس فتوت و مردانگی‌را بر انگیزد و همت مردرا بسوی کسب افتخار براند و بکارهای نیک و مقاصد بزرگ ارشاد و رهنمونی کند چه مرد ادیب ناگزیر باشد که در آثار بزرگان و استادان و سخنان حکیمان و دانشمندان بر رسی و کنجکاوی فراوان کند و از هر خرمنی خوشه‌ای بر دارد پس از هر سخنی پندی فرا گیرد و از هر نکته سودی بدست آورد و چون چنین کند ناچار از آنچه فرا گرفته است در نفس وی نقشی باز ماند و در خاطر وی نشاط و گشایشی پدیدار گردد و در خویهای وی تهذیب و تأثیری بسزا متمکن شود

[1] آئین نگارش تالیف حسین سمیعی (ادیب السلطنه)

Exercise 29

1. I visit him as often as I can. 2. As he grew richer he grew more ambitious (he had more ambition). 3. In proportion as the writer's aim comes to be the transcribing, not of the world of mere fact, but of his sense of it, he becomes an artist, his work fine art. 4. His efforts were so far successful (successful up to this limit) as they reduced the number of those suffering from infectious diseases. 5. This proposal, so far as it interests the general public, is well known. 6. Run there as fast as you can. 7. He was not so cross as he had the right to be (as was his right). 8. It is better that ten criminals should escape than that one

innocent man should be hanged.   9. She is better than when I last wrote
to you.   10. The English love their liberty even more than their kings.
11. He dared not stir lest he should be seen.   12. Of course, if I were
rich, I would travel.   13. We should have arrived sooner but that we
had a collision.

LESSON XVIII

Weak Verbs. Assimilated Verbs. Hollow Verbs. Defective Verbs.

1. 'Weak' verbs can be divided into three classes: 'Assimilated' verbs,
i.e. those the first radical of which is و or ى, 'Hollow' verbs, i.e. those
the second radical of which is و or ى, and 'Defective' verbs, i.e. those
the third radical of which is و or ى.

2. The following changes are undergone by a verb the first radical
of which is و:

(a) If the first radical is vowelless and preceded by e, the و of the
first radical is changed into ى; thus the Verbal Noun of the IV form of
وَجَدَ 'to find' is اِيجَاد and the Verbal Noun of the X form of وَجَبَ 'to
become binding, obligatory' is اِسْتِيجَاب.

(b) If the first radical is vowelless and preceded by o, the و of the
first radical is assimilated to the o and becomes u.

(c) In the VIII form the و is assimilated to the inserted ت. The
Verbal Noun of the VIII form of وَصَلَ 'to arrive' is thus اِتِّصَال and the
Active Participle مُتَّصِل.

3. The following changes are undergone by a verb the first radical
of which is ى:

(a) If the first radical is vowelless and follows o, it is changed into u;
thus the Active Participle of the IV form of يَسَرَ 'to become gentle,
tractable' is مُوسِر.

(b) In the VIII form the ى is assimilated to the inserted ت; thus the
Verbal Noun of the VIII form of يَسَرَ is اِتِّسَار and the Active Participle
مُتَّسِر.

4. The 3rd pers. sing. masc. past tense of 'Hollow' verbs is usually written with *alef* as the medial letter. This *alef* may represent a radical و or ی.

(*a*) The forms II, III, V, VI and IX are conjugated like the strong verb. In the remaining forms

(*b*) If the و or ی is vowelled and the first radical is vowelless the vowel of the و or ی is given to the first radical and becomes *a* or *i* respectively.

(*c*) If the first and third radicals are vowelled, the former with an *a*, this with the radical و or ی becomes ا *a*.

(*d*) If the first and third radicals are vowelled, the former with an *o*, this with the radical و or ی becomes ی *i*.

(*e*) The Verbal Nouns of the IV and X forms drop the second radical and add ة after the third radical.

(*f*) In the Active Participle of the I form the و or ی is changed to *hamze*.

(*g*) In the Passive Participle of the I form, if the second radical is و, one of the two و's is usually dropped.

(*h*) In the Passive Participle of the I form, if the second radical is ی, the و is usually dropped.

(*i*) 'Hollow' verbs denoting colours and physical defects retain the و or ی in the IX form.

قَالَ to speak; سَارَ to go, travel

Form	3rd pers. sing. masc. Perfect Active	Active Participle	Passive Participle	Verbal Noun
I	سَارَ ;قَالَ	سَائِر ;قَائِل	مَبِيع[1] ;مَقُول	سَيْر ;قَوْل
II	سَيَّرَ ;قَوَّلَ	مُسَيِّر ;مُقَوِّل	مُسَيَّر ;مُقَوَّل	تَسْيِير ;تَقْوِيل
III	سَايَرَ ;قَاوَلَ	مُسَايِر ;مُقَاوِل	مُسَايَر ;مُقَاوَل	مُسَايَرَة ;مُقَاوَلَة
IV	أَقَالَ	مُقِيل	مُقَال	إِقَالَة
V	تَسَيَّرَ ;تَقَوَّلَ	مُتَسَيِّر ;مُتَقَوِّل	مُتَسَيَّر ;مُتَقَوَّل	تَسَيُّر ;تَقَوُّل

[1] بَاعَ to buy.

Form	3rd pers. sing. masc. Perfect Active	Active Participle	Passive Participle	Verbal Noun
VI	تَسَایَرَ ; تَقَاوَلَ	مُتَسَایِر ; مُتَقَاوِل	مُتَسَایَر ; مُتَقَاوَل	تَسَایُر ; تَقَاوُل
VII	اِنْشَالَ[1]	مُنْشَال		اِنْشِیَال
VIII	اِقْتَالَ	مُقْتَال		اِقْتِیَال
IX	اِیبْضَّ[3] ; اِسْوَدَّ[2]			اِیبْضَاض ; اِسْوِدَاد
X	اِسْتَقَامَ[4]	مُسْتَقِیم	مُسْتَقَام	اِسْتِقَام

5. The following rules will enable the reader to find the Verbal Nouns and Participles of 'Defective' verbs and their derived forms. In the Infinitive the final radical is sometimes written ا, which represents an original ی.

(*a*) If the second and third radicals are vowelled with an *a* and no letter is added after the last radical, this combination is reduced to ا (-*a*).

(*b*) If the second radical is vowelled with an *e* and the third is و and vowelled with an *a* and no letter is added after the last radical this combination becomes ـَی.

(*c*) In the derived forms the third radical of 'Defective' verbs always appears as ی.

(*d*) In the Active Participles the final و or ی unites with *tanvin* and is written ـٍ. If the article precedes the Participle the final radical reappears as ی; this is also the case with the Verbal Nouns of the V and VI forms.

(*e*) In the Passive Participles the third radical appears as ی and the *tanvin* is written ـً over the medial radical, e.g. مُنْقَضًی *monqaẓan*. In Persian this is written منقضی *monqaẓa*, i.e. the form used in Arabic with the article.

(*f*) In the Passive Participle of the I form, if the third radical is و, the و of the third radical and the inserted و coalesce and are written with a *tašdid*.

[1] اِنْشَالَ to be lifted.

[2] اِسْوَدَّ to be black.

[3] اِیبْضَّ to be white.

[4] اِسْتَقَامَ to be straight; to rise.

(*g*) In the Passive Participle of the I form, if the third radical is ى, the و of the Participle form is changed into ى and assimilated to the ى of the radical.

(*h*) The Verbal Noun of the II form is on the measure تَفْعِلَة.

(*i*) In the Verbal Nouns of the IV, VII, VIII and X forms, where the third radical follows ا (*a*), the ى is changed into a *hamze*, which is written without a bearer.

(*j*) In the Verbal Nouns of the V and VI forms, the final ى is dropped unless the noun is defined by the article.

Form	3rd pers. sing. masc. Perfect Active		Active Participle	Passive Participle	Verbal Noun
I	نَدَا	to call	نَادٍ	مَنْدُوّ	نَدْو
	رَمَى	to throw	رَامٍ	مَرْمِيّ	رَمْى
	رَضِىَ	to be satisfied	رَاضٍ	—	رِضًا, رِضْوَان
		قَضَى to decide			
II	قَضَّى		مُقَضٍّ	مُقَضًّى	تَقْضِيَة
III	قَاضَى		مُقَاضٍ	مُقَاضًى	مُقَاضَاة, قِضَاء
IV	أَقْضَى		مُقْضٍ	مُقْضًى	إِقْضَاء
V	تَقَضَّى		مُتَقَضٍّ	مُتَقَضًّى	تَقَضٍّ
VI	تَقَاضَى		مُتَقَاضٍ	مُتَقَاضًى	تَقَاضٍ
VII	اِنْقَضَى		مُنْقَضٍ	مُنْقَضًى	اِنْقِضَاء
VIII	اِقْتَضَى		مُقْتَضٍ	مُقْتَضًى	اِقْتِضَاء
IX	Wanting				
X	اِسْتَقْضَى		مُسْتَقْضٍ	مُسْتَقْضًى	اِسْتِقْضَاء

6. In Persian the Active Participles and the Verbal Nouns appear in the form which they would have in Arabic if preceded by the article.

7. The final radical of the Verbal Noun of the VI form is usually written ا in Persian, e.g.

تماشا *tamaʃa* (for تَمَاشٍ and اَلتَّمَاشِی) beholding, a spectacle, show.

8. In Persian if the *ezafe* is added to the Passive Participle of the derived forms of a 'Defective' verb the final ى is changed into ا, e.g.

منتهای کوشش *montahaye kuʃeʃ*, the utmost effort (for مُنْتَهَی).

فرهنگ امروز

یکی از مشخصات بر جسته و امتیازهای نمایان فرهنگ امروز وجود آزمایشگاه‌های مختلف بنگاه‌های فرهنگی‌است در پیش آنچه‌را دانش‌آموزان و دانش جویان رشته های گوناگون فرا میگرفتند منحصر بهمان نکات و مسائل کتابچه های درسی ویا کتابهای چاپی بود اما اصول و روش فرهنگ امروز با گذشته از این حیث متفاوت و بلکه برتر است که دانش‌آموزان و دانش‌جویان آنچه‌را در کتابها میخوانند و بذهن میسپارند در آزمایشگاه‌ها طرز کار و روش اعمال آنرا نیز بچشم دیده و میاموزند و این روش تازه راهنمایان اصول آموزش و پرورشرا برآن داشته که حتی در تدریس اصول تاریخ و علم شناسائی ادوار باستانی ملل و اقوام نیز این اصول‌را بکار برده و برای اثبات مدعای تاریخی دانشجویانرا بموزه‌ها و خرابه‌های زیر زمینی بکشانند

در فن انشاء[1]

اکنون از آنچه بفن انشاء و دبیری اختصاص دارد شمه باز گوئیم و باز نمائیم که انشاء چیست و از آن چه خواهند انشاء در لغت شروع کردن و بوجود آوردنرا گویند و در اصطلاح علمی است که بدان علم راه در یافت معانی و تعبیر از آن معانی بالفاظ و عبارات پسندیده و دلپذیر چنانکه گوارای طبیعت و نزدیك بفهم خواننده و روشن کننده مقصود نویسنده باشد شناخته شود و این فن دبیری بود و دبیر ناچار بفرا گرفتن بسی از دانشها نیازمند است و باید که در کار دبیری از فنون گوناگون استفاده کند و یاری جوید چه دبیر سخنسنج همیشه در

[1] آئین نگارش

يك موضوع سخن نراند و بر يك نسق چيز ننويسد بل اختلاف سخن او باندازه اختلاف مبحث‌ها و موضوعهائی است که ویرا پیش آید و ناگزیر باید که از هر چیز بهره‌ای بسزا داشته باشد تا بتواند در همه گونه سخنها وارد شود و در هر باب سخنوری کند نحو صرف منطق معانی بیان بدیع تاریخ قصص لغت امثال اخلاق رجال انساب محاضرات و بسی دیگر از این گونه دانشها همه از عوامل علم ادب و بویژه از اسباب و ابزار فن دبیری شمرده شده و دبیر و نگارنده از آموختن آنها ناگزیر باشد و بی این دانشها و آگاهیها نتواند بهنر نگارش دست یافته در هر باره که خواهد چیز نویسد چون غرض من از تمهید این مجموعه گفتگو و بررسی در علم ادب و اصول و فروع آن نیست و تنها ببخشی از آن که دبیری و انشاء است میپردازم در باره دانشهای نامبرده و ارتباط آنها با علم ادب وارد شرح و تفصیل نمیشوم و از آنچه استادان فن در این باب نگاشته اند که کدام یك از علوم جزو اصول ادب است و کدام یك جزو فروع و تأثیر هر یك از آنها در ادبیات بچه اندازه است و مدخلیت کدام بیشتر در میگذرم و همینقدر میگویم که از این اشارات بخوبی میتوان درجه ارتباط و پیوستگی علم ادب‌را بتمام معارف بشری بدست آورد و خدمات بزرگیرا که بتمام دانشهای صوری و معنوی انجام میدهد معلوم داشت

Exercise 30

1. I have stood it as long as I can; my patience is now exhausted. 2. He spends his money as fast as he gets it. 3. Nothing could be more distasteful to me than that I should have to go. 4. I do not say that he has been in any way negligent or that he has been dishonest. 5. He is speaking so loudly that I hear him even from here. 6. He is so badly injured that he must die. 7. He is so badly injured he will probably die. 8. He is so badly injured that he may die. 9. The crops failed because it was a dry year. 10. He cannot be tired since he has walked only a short way.

LESSON XIX

Quadriliteral Verbs. The Dual. The Sound Masculine Plural. The Sound Feminine Plural.

1. Quadriliteral Verbs are formed on the measure فَعْلَلَ, e.g.

تَرْجَمَ to translate

3rd pers. sing. masc. Perfect Active	Active Participle	Passive Participle	Verbal Noun
تَرْجَمَ	مُتَرْجِم	مُتَرْجَم	تَرْجَمَة

There are three derived forms, of which the following two are more commonly found:

3rd pers. sing. masc. Perfect Active		Active Participle	Verbal Noun
تَسَلْطَنَ	to become sultan	مُتَسَلْطِن	تَسَلْطُن
اِطْمَأَنَّ	to be at rest	مُطْمَئِنّ	اِطْمِئْنَان

2. Arabic has three numbers: singular, dual and plural.

3. The dual is formed by adding the termination اَنِ in the nominative and اَيْنِ in the oblique cases, e.g.

Nom.	مَلِكَانِ	two kings.	مَلِكَتَانِ	two queens.
Gen. and Acc.	مَلِكَيْنِ		مَلِكَتَيْنِ	
Nom.	كَبِيرَانِ	great (m.)	كَبِيرَتَانِ	great (f.).
Gen. and Acc.	كَبِيرَيْنِ		كَبِيرَتَيْنِ	

The dual is occasionally used in Persian, usually in the oblique cases, e.g.

از طرفین *az tarafein*, from both sides.

والدین *valedein*, parents.

4. The plural is of two kinds: sound and broken.

5. The sound plural masculine of nouns and adjectives is formed by adding ـُونَ in the nominative and ـِينَ in the oblique cases, e.g.

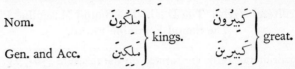

Nom.	مَلِكُونَ	kings.	كَبِيرُونَ	great.
Gen. and Acc.	مَلِكِينَ		كَبِيرِينَ	

6. The sound plural masculine is used for:

(*a*) Masculine proper names, except those ending in ة.

(*b*) Diminutives denoting rational beings.

(*c*) Participles.

(*d*) Nouns of the measure فَعَّال (denoting workers in a trade or profession).

(*e*) Relative Adjectives.

(*f*) Adjectives of the form أَفْعَل denoting elatives.

7. The sound plural of feminine nouns and adjectives is formed by changing ة[1] into اتٌ in the nominative and اتٍ in the oblique cases, e.g.

Nom.	مَلِكَاتٌ	queens.	كَبِيرَاتٌ	great.
Gen. and Acc.	مَلِكَاتٍ		كَبِيرَاتٍ	

8. The main types of word for which the sound feminine plural is used are:

(*a*) Feminine proper names.

(*b*) Class names ending in ة.

(*c*) The feminine of adjectives the masculine of which takes the sound masculine plural.

(*d*) Verbal Nouns of the derived forms.[2]

(*e*) Diminutives denoting irrational beings and things.

(*f*) Foreign words.

(*g*) Certain masculine nouns, e.g.

حَيْوَان animal. حَيْوَانَات animals.

[1] In Persian this may be ت or ه. In either case the plural is ات, e.g. ملاحظه *molaheẓe* 'consideration, view, etc.' pl. ملاحظات *molaheẓat*.

[2] The Verbal Nouns of the II and IV forms also have Broken Plurals (see Lesson xx).

9. The sound feminine plural is sometimes added to Persian nouns, e.g.

فرمایشات *farmayeʃat*, orders, commands.
نگارشات *negareʃat*, writings.
باغات *baɣat*, gardens.

دهات *dehat* (from ده *deh* 'village') is used as a singular to mean 'country (as opposed to town)'.

A plural on the analogy of the sound feminine plural is also sometimes formed from Persian and Arabic words ending in ه -*e*, this being changed into ج before the termination of the sound feminine plural, e.g.

میوجات *mivejat*, fruits.
نوشتجات *neveʃtejat*, writings.
کارخانجات *karxanejat*, factories.
روزنامجات *ruznamejat*, newspapers.
حوالجات *havalejat*, transfers.
قبالجات *qabalejat*, title-deeds.

باغ فلاحتی

در دو کیلومتری شهر اهواز در سمت مغرب رود کارون باغ بسیار بزرگی که دارای انواع و اقسام درختهای متناسب با آب و هوای خوزستان است تأسیس و با موتور از کارون برای مشروب ساختن اشجار اقدام بآبیاری آن باغ وسیع نموده‌اند و انواع و اقسام اشجار خرما انار زیتون موز و غیره در آن باغ غرس حتی گیاه‌ها و نهالهای گرمسیری نیز برای نمونه در اراضی زراعتی باغ مزبور کاشته و ملیونها تومان خرج باغ و خرید لوازم و اثاثیه برای کشاورزی و وارد کردن نهال اشجار از خارجه شده است

ملاحظاتی راجع بادبیات در دوره مشروطیت[1]

ظهور مشروطیت که فرمان آن در سال ۱۳۲٤ قمری صادر شد نتیجه یك سلسله مقدمات سیاسی و علمی و ادبی بود که شرح و بسط آنرا کتابی جداگانه باید اجمالاً توان گفت که در این دوره ادبیات ایران گذشته از دوام در موضوعات

[1] تاریخ ادبیات ایران تالیف دکتر رضازاده شفق

و طرزهای قدیم تازگیهائی نیز پیدا کرد و ممکن است آنهارا بطریق ذیل تلخیص نمود (۱) زبانهای بیگانه خاصه زبان فرانسوی در ایران که از اوایل دوره قاجاریه شروع بانتشار نموده بود رواج یافت و راه آمدوشد بین ایران و فرنگستان بیشتر از سابق باز شد و تصانیف ادبی آن سرزمین از نظم و نثر و داستان و رمان در این دیار معروف گردید در نتیجه این اختلاط نه تنها عدهای از کتب فرنگی بفارسی ترجمه و مقداری لغات فرنگی داخل زبان فارسی شد بلکه برخی نویسندگان جدید در معانی و الفاظ تا حدی سبك و روش و طرز فکر مغرب زمینرا اقتباس کرده و گاهی در این خط دورتر رفته از شیوه زبان فارسی خارج شدند (۲) از موضوعات تازهای که داخل ادبیات گردید افکار آزادیخواهانه و عقاید اجتماعی و سیاسی و فکر تساوی حقوق سیاسی و مسئله آزادی افکار و حریت مطبوعات و احساسات وطنپرستانه است که الحق در نظم و نثر جلوه خاصی نمود و شعرای توانای خوش قریحه و نویسندگان قابلی ظهور کرده و با بهترین الفاظ بتعبیر این سنخ افکار پرداختند حتی اینگونه افکار بلطف قریحه شاعرانه مانند عارف قزوینی بشکل تصنیف ملی در میان عامه انتشار پیداکرد از شاعران ایندوره میتوان برای نمونه از میان گذشتگان ادیب الممالك فراهانی و ادیب پیشاوری‌را نام برد و از عالم بانوان پروین اعتصامی‌را ذکر کرد و از زندگان آقای محمد تقی بهار (ملك الشعرا) را نامید که در طرز قصیده و تتبعات تاریخی و ادبی استاد است در واقع شاعران و گویندگان و نویسندگان سخنور ادب‌پرور زیادی در عصر ما ظهور کرده‌اند که الحق نظم و نثر فارسیرا زنده نگهداشته وآنرا گویاتر و شیواتر نموده و معانی تازه در آن دمیده و خودرا اخلاف صدق بزرگان قدیم نشان داده‌اند (۳) نظم و نثر فارسی از مقام شامخ ادبی قدیم که معمولاً از حیات مردم دور و از ذوق و احتیاجات عامه مهجور بود کمی بپائین آمده و بذهن و زندگی توده نزدیك شده و بر حسب احتیاجات جامعه در مضامین تازگی پیداکرده و بمطالب اجتماعی گرویده است و نویسندگان در ادای این موضوعات بیشتر از زینت الفاظ و استعمال جمله‌های دور و دراز متوجه بادای مطلب و بیان مقصود شده اند

(نا تمام)

Exercise 31

1. The fault is not mine for the simple reason that I was not present and had nothing to do with the affair. 2. He refused to participate on the ground that he was not interested in the matter. 3. To be sure the present law has not remained in force in as much as the universities contain teachers who have never believed in these principles. 4. You can have it for a few days on condition you return it some time next week. 5. I do not attach any importance to it so long as you are satisfied. 6. Nothing would content him but I must come. 7. He was everywhere except in the right place. 8. I walk every day unless it rains. 9. Foolish though he may be he is kind of heart. 10. We sometimes expect gratitude when we are not entitled to it. 11. However we may assess (judge) the merits or defects of Greek philosophy, it must always form an interesting subject. 12. Whether he succeeds or fails, we shall have to do our part.

LESSON XX

Broken Plurals.

1. In addition to the sound plurals, which are used for certain forms only, there are the so-called Broken Plurals, of which there are some thirty measures. Broken plurals maintain the radicals of the singular in their original order but change the vowel pattern. They may in addition add a consonant at the beginning or end or both. The consonants so used are أ at the beginning and ن, ء or ة at the end. The following table gives the plural measures from triliteral roots and the singular measures from which they are derived. Those forms which are more commonly used in Persian are marked with an asterisk.

2. Measures for Broken Plurals from triliteral roots.

*1. فُعَل from

*(a) فُعْلَة (b) فُعْلَى [1] (c) فَعْلَة

2. فُعْل from

(a) أَفْعَلُ [2] (b) فَعْلَاءُ [3]

[1] Feminine of the elative. [2] Not the elative.

[3] The feminine of أَفْعَلُ, not the elative.

*3. فُعُل from

*(a) فِعَال[1] *(b) فَعِيل[2] *(c) فَعِيلَة[2]

*(d) فَعُول[2] (e) فَعْل

*4. فِعَل from

*(a) فِعْلَة (b) فَعْلَة

*5. فِعَال from

*(a) فَعْل[3] *(b) فِعْل[3] *(c) فَعُل

*(d) فَعَل[1] *(e) فَعَلَة[1] *(f) فَعِيل[4]

(g) فُعْلَة *(h) فَعْلَة

*6. فُعُول from

*(a) فَعْل *(b) فِعْل *(c) فُعْل

(d) فَعَل *(e) فَعِل *(f) فَاعِل[1]

7. فُعَّل from

فَاعِل

*8. فُعَّال from

فَاعِل

9. فَعَلَة from

فَاعِل[5]

[1] Not from roots the second radical of which is doubled or the third radical of which is و or ى.

[2] Not from roots the third radical of which is و or ى.

[3] Not from roots the first or second radical of which is ى.

[4] Verbal adjectives not having a passive significance.

[5] If it denotes a rational being and the third radical is not و or ى.

*10. فُعَلَة from

فَاعِل[1]

11. فِعْلَة from

(a) فَعْل (b) فَعَل (c) فَعَال

(d) فُعَال (e) فَعِيل

12. أَفْعُل from

(a) فَعْل (b) فِعْل (c) فُعْل

(d) from feminine words which do not end in ة and have a long vowel between the second and third radicals.

*13. أَفْعَال from

*(a) فَعْل[2] *(b) فُعْل *(c) فِعْل

(d) فَعَل

*14. أَفْعِلَة from

*(a) فَعَال *(b) فِعَال *(c) فَعِيل[3]

(d) فُعَال *(e) فَعُول

*15. فَوَاعِل from

*(a) فَاعِل *(b) فَاعِلَة

*16. فَعَائِل from

feminine nouns which have a long vowel between the second and third radicals.

[1] If it denotes a rational being and the third radical is و or ى.

[2] Especially if the first radical is و or the middle radical is و or ى.

[3] Especially adjectives the second radical of which is doubled or the third radical of which is و or ى.

17. فِعْلَان from

(a) فَعَل (b) فُعْل[1] (c) فُعَال

(d) فَعَال (e) فَعِيل (f) فَاعِل

18. فُعْلَان from

(a) فَعَل (b) فَاعِل[2] (c) فُعَال

(d) أَفْعَل[3]

*19. فُعَلَاءُ from

*(a) فَعِيل[4] (b) فَاعِل[4]

*20. أَفْعِلَاءُ from

فَعِيل[5]

21. فَعْلَى from

(a) فَعِيل[6] (b) فَعْلَانُ

22. فَعَالِى[7] from

(a) فَعْلَاءُ (b) فَعْلَى

23. فَعَالَى from

(a) فُعْلَى[8] (b) فَعْلَانُ (c) فَعِيلَة[9]

(d) فَاعِلَة[10]

[1] From roots with a medial و.

[2] When used as a noun, but not from roots with a medial و or ى.

[3] Denoting colours and physical defects.

[4] Denoting male persons, but not words with a doubled second radical or those the third radical of which is و or ى.

[5] Especially from roots with a doubled second radical or of which the third radical is و or ى.

[6] Usually with a passive meaning.

[7] In Arabic فَعَالٍ unless preceded by the article, or in construct.

[8] Feminine but not of the elative.

[9] If the third radical is و or ى.

[10] From words of which the medial radical is و or of which the third radical is و or ى.

24. فُعُولَة from

(a) فَعْل[1] (b) فَعَل

25. فَعَالَة from

(a) فَعَل (b) فَاعِل

26. فَعَل from

فَاعِل

Examples:[2]

1\. (a) رُتْبه rank, رُتَب; صُورَت face, form, صُوَر; اُمَّت community, اُمَم

(b) اُخْرَى last (f.), اُخَر; كُبْرَى greatest (f.) كُبَر

(c) دَوْلَت state, دُوَل

2\. (a) اَزْرَق blue, زُرْق

(b) زَرْقَاء blue (f.), زُرْق

3\. (a) كِتَاب book, كُتُب

(b) طَرِيق way, road, طُرُق

(c) مَدِينه city, مُدُن; صَحِيفه book, page, صُحُف

(d) رَسُول prophet, رُسُل

(e) سَقْف roof, سُقُف

4\. (a) حِكْمَت wisdom, حِكَم; مِلَّت people, nation, مِلَل; نِعْمَت beneficence, plenty, نِعَم

(b) خَيْمه tent, خِيَم

[1] When the second radical is doubled.

[2] The customary spelling in Persian is used in the examples, e.g. اُمّت for اُمَّة, but vocalization has been added.

5. (*a*) كَلْب dog, كِلاب; ثَوْب clothes, ثِياب

(*b*) رِيح wind, رِياح

(*c*) رَجُل man, رِجال

(*d*) جَبَل mountain, جِبال

(*e*) رَقَبَت neck, رِقاب

(*f*) كَرِيم generous, كِرام; كَبِير great, كِبار

(*g*) رُقْعه piece of paper, رِقاع; قُبّه dome, قِباب

(*h*) قَلْعه fortress, قِلاع

6. (*a*) قَلْب heart, قُلُوب

(*b*) عِلْم knowledge, science, عُلُوم

(*c*) جُنْد army, militia, جُنُود; بُرْج tower, sign of the Zodiac, بُرُوج

(*d*) اَسَد lion, اُسُود

(*e*) مَلِك king, مُلُوك

(*f*) شاهِد witness, شُهُود

7. حاكِم governor, judge حُكَّم

8. حاكِم governor, judge, حُكّام; كاتِب scribe, كُتّاب; جاهِل ignorant, جُهّال; تاجِر merchant, تُجّار

9. كاتِب scribe, كَتَبه; طالِب student (of a school devoted to the study of religious sciences), طَلَبه

10. والِی governor, وُلات; قاضِی judge, قُضات

11. (*a*) ثَوْر ox, ثِيَرَت
(*b*) اَخ (for اَخَو) brother, اِخْوَت
(*c*) غَزَال gazelle, غِزْلَت
(*d*) غُلَام slave, غِلْمَت
(*e*) صَبِى boy, صِبْيَت

12. (*a*) بَحْر sea, اَبْحُر; عَيْن eye, اَعْيُن; نَفْس soul, اَنْفُس
(*b*) رِجْل foot, اَرْجُل
(*c*) قُفْل lock, اَقْفُل
(*d*) ذِرَاع arm, اَذْرُع; يَمِين oath, اَيْمُن

13. (*a*) شَخْص person, اَشْخَاص; وَقْت time, اَوْقَات; يَوْم day, اَيَّام
(*b*) رُوح soul, اَرْوَاح
(*c*) طِفْل child, اَطْفَال; جِسْم body, اَجْسَام
(*d*) سَبَب cause, reason, اَسْبَاب goods, chattels; حَال condition, state, اَحْوَال

14. (*a*) طَعَام food, اَطْعِمه; دَوَاء medicine, اَدْوِيه drugs, spice; زَمَان time, اَزْمِنه
(*b*) سِلَاح weapon, اَسْلِحه; اِمَام imam, اَئِمّه; اِنَاء vessel, vase, آنِيه; لِسَان tongue, اَلْسِنه
(*c*) دَلِيل proof, اَدِلّه; عَزِيز dear, precious, اَعِزّه; حَبِيب friend, اَحِبّه
(*d*) تُرَاب dust, اَتْرِبه
(*e*) عَمُود column, اَعْمِده

15. (*a*) فَارِس rider, فَوَارِس; سَاحِل shore, سَوَاحِل

(*b*) حَادِثه happening, حَوَادِث; فَاکِهه fruit, فَوَاکه; عَامّه common, عَوَامّ (for عَوَامِم) the common people; خَاصّه noble, خَوَاصّ (for خَوَاصِص); نَاحِیه neighbourhood, نَوَاحِی; جَارِیه slave-girl (f.), جَوَارِی; نَادِره rarity, نَوَادِر; فَائِده benefit فَوَائِد

16. عَجُوز old woman, عَجَائِز; رِسَاله treatise, letter, رَسَائِل; عَجِیبه wonder, عَجَائِب; جَزِیره island, جَزَائِر; وَسِیله means, وَسَائِل

17. (*a*) نَار (for نَوْر) fire, نِیرَان; اَخ (for اَخَو) brother, اِخْوَان; جَار neighbour, جِیرَان

(*b*) حُوت large fish, حِیتَان

(*c*) غُلَام slave, غِلْمَان

(*d*) غَزَال gazelle, غِزْلَان

(*e*) صَبِیّ (for صَبِیو) boy, صِبْیَان

(*f*) حَائِط wall, حِیطَان

18. (*a*) بَلَد city, بُلْدَان

(*b*) فَارِس rider, فُرْسَان; شَابّ young man, شُبَّان

(*c*) شُجَاع brave, شُجْعَان

(*d*) اَعْرَج lame, عُرْجَان

19. (*a*) وَزِیر minister, وُزَرَا; فَقِیر poor, فُقَرَا; رَئِیس head, chief, رُؤَسَا

(*b*) شَاعِر poet, شُعَرَا; عَالِم learned, عُلَمَا

20. صَدیق friend, اَصْدقا; طَبیب doctor, اَطبّا; غَنی rich, اَغْنیا; قَریب relative, اَقْربا; نَبی prophet, اَنْبیا; وَلی vicegerent, اَوْلیا

21. (*a*) قَتیل killed, قَتْلی; جَریح wounded, جَرْحی; مَیّت (for مَویت) dead, مَوْتی

(*b*) کَسْلان lazy, کَسْلی

22. (*a*) عَذْرا virgin, عَذاری; صَحْرا plain, صَحاری

(*b*) فَتْوی legal decision, فَتاوی; دَعْوی dispute, claim, دَعاوی

23. (*a*) حُبْلی pregnant, حَبالی

(*b*) کَسْلان lazy, کَسالی

(*c*) هَدیّه present, gift, هَدایا; رَعیّت peasant, subject, رَعایا[1]; بَلیّه calamity, بَلایا

(*d*) زاویه corner, angle, زَوایا

24. (*a*) عَمّ paternal uncle, عُمومه

(*b*) عَلَف fodder عُلوفه

25. (*a*) حَجَر stone, حِجاره

(*b*) صاحِب friend, owner, صَحابه

26. خادِم servant, خَدَم; حارِس guard, حَرَس

3. Broken plurals from quadriliteral roots are formed on the following measures. Nouns formed from triliteral roots by prefixing م, ت or ا form their plurals on the same measures as nouns from quadriliteral roots.

*(i) فَعالِل e.g.

کَوْکَب star کَواکِب

جَوْهَر jewel جَواهِر

[1] Sometimes pronounced *ro'aya*.

تَجْرِبَة (in Persian تجربه) experience تَجَارِب[1]

مَنْزِلَة (in Persian منزلت) stage, resting-place مَنَازِل

مَدْرَسَة (in Persian مدرسه) school مَدَارِس

أَقْرَب nearest أَقَارِب relations, relatives

أَكْبَر greatest أَكَابِر

*(ii) فَعَالِيل and فَوَاعِيل from nouns which have a long vowel before the last radical, e.g.

تَصْوِير picture تَصَاوِير

مِفْتَاح key مَفَاتِيح

إِرْجَاف rumour[2] أَرَاجِيف

جَامُوس buffalo جَوَامِيس

قَانُون law قَوَانِين

دِينَار dinar (a coin) دَنَانِير

دِيوَان divan (a collection of poems, etc.) دَوَاوِين

تَارِيخ history تَوَارِيخ

أُسْتَاد master, teacher أَسَاتِيد

(iii) فَعَالِلَة

from (*a*) relative adjectives, e.g.

أَرْمَنِى Armenian أَرَامِنَة (in Persian ارامنه)

(*b*) from certain quadriliteral nouns (especially foreign ones) denoting persons, e.g.

تِلْمِيذ student (of a school where religious sciences are taught) تَلَامِذَة (in Persian تلامذه).

[1] In Persian pronounced *tajarob*. [2] See para. 10 below.

4. In nouns that contain five or more radicals (exclusive of ة and long vowels) one of the radicals is rejected in the plural, generally the last, e.g.

عَنْكَبُوت spider عَنَاكِب

5. From the foregoing paragraphs it will be seen that some words can form their plural on more than one measure. In a few cases the meaning of the plural varies with the measure used, e.g.

عَيْن eye; spring; notable person	أَعْيُن / عُيُون	eyes; springs.
	أَعْيَان	notables.
بَحْر sea; poetical metre	بُحُور	metres.
	بِحَار ; أَبْحُر	seas.
بَيْت house; couplet	بُيُوت	houses.
	أَبْيَات	couplets.
أَمْر affair, command	أُمُور	affairs.
	أَوَامِر	commands.
شَاهِد witness, evident example	شُهُود	witnesses.
	شَوَاهِد	examples.

6. A number of words form their plural irregularly. Among them are:

إِبْن son بَنِى

خَلِيفَة (in Persian خليفه) caliph خُلَفَاء

ضَمِير mind ضَمَائِر

لَيْل night لَيَالِى

أَهْل people أَهَالِى

أَرْض earth أَرَاضِى fields, lands

إِنْسَان man نَاس

فم mouth أَفْواه

ماء water مِياه

سَماء sky, heaven سَمَاوَات

حَاجَة (in Persian حاجت) need حَوائِج

A broken plural خوانين *xavanin* is irregularly formed in Persian from خان *xan* 'khan' (a courtesy title).

7. A few Arabic broken plurals are used in Persian with a singular meaning, e.g.

عمله (for عَمَلَة, pl. of عامِل) workman (pl. عَمَلَجات).

أَرْباب (pl. of رَبّ) master; owner of a landed estate (pl. اربابان).

بِلَاد (pl. of بَلَد) country, region.

ادويه (for أَدْوِيَة, pl. of دَوَاء) spice (pl. أَدَوِيجَات).

نِيرَان (pl. of نار) fire.

فُتُوح (pl. of فَتْح) conquest (pl. فُتُوحَات).

8. In addition to the above plurals of plurals, certain Arabic nouns are used with a double plural in Persian, a sound feminine plural being made of the broken plural, or a broken plural of a broken plural, e.g.

جَوْهَر jewel جَواهِر جَواهِرات

بَيْت house بُيُوت بُيُوتَات = an office in charge of Crown property, etc.

مَكَان place أَمْكِنَة (in Persian امكنه) أَمَاكِن

لَازِم necessary لَوَازِم necessities لَوَازِمَات

9. Broken plurals are extensively used in Persian. The Persian plural terminations ان *-an* and ها *-ha* are also added to the singular of Arabic nouns to form the plural.

10. Certain Arabic words are used in the plural in Persian but are rare in the singular. Among them are:

مزخرفات *mozaxrafat*, nonsense (the singular مزخرف *mozaxraf* is used only as an adjective 'nonsensical, absurd').

مهملات *mohmalat*, nonsense (the singular مهمل *mohmal* is used only as an adjective 'absurd').

موهومات *mouhumat*, superstition(s) (the singular موهوم *mouhum* is used only as an adjective 'fanciful, imaginary').

اراجیف *arajif* (pl. of ارجاف *erjaf*), rumours.

اولاد *oulad* (pl. of ولد *valad*), children.

حشرات *hasarat* (pl. of حَشَرَة), insects.

اسباب *asbab* means 'utensils, goods, chattels, luggage' in the plural; the singular سبب *sabab* means 'cause'.

حکومت مرکزی

هیچ کشور و هیچ جماعتی اداره نمیشود مگر اینکه نقطه اتکاء مرکزی مقتدری داشته باشد یك معنی امنیت همین است که حکومت مرکزی قدرت داشته باشد مفهوم مخالف این اصل نیز مؤید و مثبت همین اصل است یعنی در هر کشور و هر جماعتی که قدرت مرکزی ضعیف گردد و آن نقطه اتکاء سست و متزلزل شود آن کشور و آن جماعت اداره نمیشود معنی اداره نشدن یك کشور یا زندگی یك جماعت و قوم هرج و مرج و عدم امنیت است و بزرگترین وظیفه سیاسی هر دولتی در داخله حفظ انتظامات است عدالت و دادگستری محض حفظ امنیت است و امنیت باعتبار وجود عدالت دوام و استقرار پیدا میکند

ملاحظاتی راجع بادبیات در دوره مشروطیت

(دنباله از درس پیش)

(٤) احداث مدارس جدید و روزنامه‌ها و مجلات بتوسیع و تعمیم معارف خدمت بزرگی کرده و ادبیات نسبت به عامه بیشتر مأنوس و در دسترس واقع گشته و توجه بعلم و ادب زیادت گرفته (٥) تمایلی در مردم و طبقه دانشمندان و مؤلفان نسبت بتألیفات علمی و ادبی متقدمان ایران پدید آمده نیز از طرف وزارت فرهنگ توجهی نسبت بتألیف کتابهای درسی و ترجمه تألیفات علمی

مغرب‌زمین پیدا شده و بخصوص تصحیح و طبع مؤلفات گذشتگان ایرانی در نظم و نثر مورد نظر خاص واقع گشته و مقدار مهمی از نوادر آثار و تصانیف گذشته باهتمام دانشمندان بطرز تصحیح جدیدی بحلیه طبع در آمده و احیا گردیده (۶) درج مطالب علمی و تاریخی بطرز تحقیقی و انتقادی و رجوع باصول و اسناد از روی نظام فکری و تتبع کامل ترقی شایانی کرده و در واقع شیوه بعضی مولفان بزرگ اسلامیکه در قدیم نسبت بزمان آنان معمول بود احیا گردیده و در این امر از روش انتقادی دانشمندان مغرب‌زمین نیز استفاده کامل شده است و در حقیقت تالیفات و تحقیقات خاورشناسان مغرب‌زمین از این حیث در نهضت جدید ادبی ایران تاثیر خاص داشته و در میل و رغبت ایرانیان نسبت باحیای آثار گذشتگان نیز در سلیقه و راه و رسم پژوهش مطالب علمی عاملی مهم بوده‌است و توان گفت در میان دانشمندان ایران پیشرو عمده در این فن آقای محمد قزوینی بوده است (۷) نهضتی بر ضد عبارت پردازیهای بی‌لزوم و مبالغه‌ها و مضامین و تشبیهات غیرطبیعی و پیچیدهٔ قسمتی از ادبیات قدیم شروع کرده و در این مورد برخی ترك اغلب مضامین و تشبیهات و اسلوب و معانی قدیمرا میخواهند و موضوعهای تازه پیدا میکنند و اوزان و اشکال نو بکار میبرند و در نثر مخالف جمله‌بندی تازی‌منش و استعمال کلمات زیاد عربی هستند و باحیاء شیوه ایرانی و استعمال لغات فارسی اهتمام دارند حتی بعضی دورتر رفته باستعمال جمله های فارسی خالص میکوشند در ضمن توان گفت ایندوره از یك لحاظ یعنی بیشتر از لحاظ موضوع و هدف و طرز تعبیرات ادبی دوره تحول و انقلاب است موازین قدیم تا حدی متزلزل شده و اصول جدید هم سر و صورتی کامل پیدا نکرده و ادبیات بطور کلی یك سیر تکامل مینماید در هر صورت برخی گویندگان جدید آثار زیبای دلربائیکه نوید سبك عالیتریرا میدهد بوجود آورده‌اند

Exercise 32

1. In spite of his youth he was not only fit to benefit from university education, but carried to the university a literary taste and stock of learning which would have done honour to a graduate. 2. There is not only conciseness in these lines but also elegance. 3. It will be my endeavour to relate the history of the people as well as the history of the government. 4. The wolf is hard and strong and withal one of the cleverest of animals. 5. Take a few of them, say a dozen or so. 6. How strong is the influence which universities and schools together have upon

public opinion, to what an extent their influence dominates the men who in turn are entrusted with the administration of the country, may be judged by the following statement. 7. He laughed so much that I could not help laughing too. 8. Now that he is sick we shall have to do the work. 9. What can I say but that I hope you will be happy? 10. Society can have no hold on any class except through the medium of its interests.

LESSON XXI

Numerals. Pronominal Suffixes. ذو. صاحب. Prepositions. Adverbs. Conjunctions. Interjections.

1. The cardinal numbers in Arabic are as follows:

Masculine	Feminine	Numbers	Masculine	Feminine	Numbers
أَحَدٌ / وَاحِدٌ	إِحْدَى / وَاحِدَةٌ[1]	1	أَحَدَ عَشَرَ	إِحْدَى عَشْرَةَ	11
إِثْنَانِ	إِثْنَتَانِ	2	إِثْنَا عَشَرَ	إِثْنَتَا عَشْرَةَ	12
ثَلَاثٌ	ثَلَاثَةٌ	3	ثَلَاثَةَ عَشَرَ	ثَلَاثَ عَشْرَةَ	13
أَرْبَعٌ	أَرْبَعَةٌ	4	أَرْبَعَةَ عَشَرَ	أَرْبَعَ عَشْرَةَ	14
خَمْسٌ	خَمْسَةٌ	5	خَمْسَةَ عَشَرَ	خَمْسَ عَشْرَةَ	15
سِتٌّ	سِتَّةٌ[2]	6	سِتَّةَ عَشَرَ	سِتَّ عَشْرَةَ	16
سَبْعٌ	سَبْعَةٌ	7	سَبْعَةَ عَشَرَ	سَبْعَ عَشْرَةَ	17
ثَمَانٍ[2]	ثَمَانِيَةٌ	8	ثَمَانِيَةَ عَشَرَ	ثَمَانِيَ عَشْرَةَ	18
تِسْعٌ	تِسْعَةٌ	9	تِسْعَةَ عَشَرَ	تِسْعَ عَشْرَةَ	19
			عِشْرُونَ		20
عَشْرٌ	عَشَرَةٌ	10	أَحَدٌ وَ عِشْرُونَ		21

[1] The final *fathe* of the numerals is usually preserved in Persian (and not changed to *e*); similarly the *kasre* of سِتَّة and تِسْعَة preserves in Persian its Arabic value, i.e. it approximates to the vowel in the English word 'bit'.

[2] In Persian ثَمَانِي.

Masculine & Feminine	Numbers	Masculine & Feminine	Numbers
ثَلَاثُونَ	30	مِائَتَانِ	200
أَرْبَعُونَ	40	ثَلَاثُ مِائَةٍ (مِئَةٍ)	300
خَمْسُونَ	50	أَلْفٌ	1000
سِتُّونَ	60	أَلْفَانِ	2000
سَبْعُونَ	70	ثَلَاثَةُ آلَافٍ	3000
ثَمَانُونَ	80	أَحَدَ عَشَرَ أَلْفًا	11,000
تِسْعُونَ	90	مِائَةُ (مِئَةُ) أَلْفٍ	100,000
مِائَةٌ ; مِئَةٌ	100	أَلْفُ أَلْفٍ	1,000,000

2. In the case of the cardinals 3–10 Arabic uses the masculine form with a feminine noun and vice versa. The numerals 20–90 are declined as sound plurals. The oblique form is usually used in Persian, e.g.

عِشْرِينَ twenty.

3. أَلْفٌ 'thousand' has two plurals آلَافٌ and أُلُوفٌ; the latter is used for 'thousands' in an indefinite sense.

4. Compound numbers from twenty onwards are formed by joining the units, tens and hundreds by وَ. The largest number is put first, but the units are put before the tens, e.g.

أَلْفٌ وَ تِسْعُ مِئَةٍ وَ خَمْسَةٌ وَ أَرْبَعُونَ 1945.

5. The ordinals are formed from the cardinals on the form فَاعِلٌ except ٱلْأَوَّلُ (m.) 'first' and ٱلْأُولَى (f.), e.g.

ثَانٍ (m.)	ثَانِيَةٌ (f.)	second.
ثَالِثٌ	ثَالِثَةٌ	third.
حَادِىَ عَشَرَ	حَادِيَةَ عَشْرَةَ	eleventh.

For the higher numbers the cardinals only are used; the ordinals of the units are joined to the cardinal of the tens to express the compound ordinals. If defined both parts of compound numbers take the article.

عِشْرُونَ (m. and f.) twentieth. اَلْعِشْرُونَ the twentieth.

حَادٍ وَ عِشْرُونَ (m.)
حَادِيَةٌ وَ عِشْرُونَ (f.) } twenty-first.

اَلْحَادِى وَ ٱلْعِشْرُونَ
اَلْحَادِيَةُ وَ ٱلْعِشْرُونَ } the twenty-first.

6. The numeral adverbs 'first, secondly, etc.' are expressed by the accusative of the ordinals, e.g.

أَوَّلًا first. ثَانِيًا secondly. ثَالِثًا thirdly.

These are frequently used in Persian.

7. The denominator of fractions when it lies between 3 and 10 inclusive is formed on the measure فُعْل except 'half' which is نِصْف, e.g.

ثُلْث a third. رُبْع a quarter.

The plural of fractions is formed on the measure أَفْعَال, e.g.

أَثْلَاث thirds.

The Arabic fractions are used in conjunction with Persian cardinals, e.g.

دو ثلث *do sols*, two-thirds.

سه ربع *se rob'*, three-quarters.

8. The multiplicative adjectives 'twofold, threefold, etc.' are formed on the measure مُفَعَّل, e.g.

مُثَنًّى (in Persian مُثَنَّى) twofold.

مُثَلَّث threefold; a triangle.

مُرَبَّع fourfold, square; a square.

9. Numeral adjectives expressing the number of parts of which anything is made are formed on the measure فُعَالِّى, e.g.

ثُنَائِّى biliteral.

ثُلَاثِّى triliteral; three cubits high or long.

رُبَاعِّى quadriliteral; four cubits high or long; quatrain.

10. The Arabic Pronominal Suffixes are:

1st pers. sing. ـِى		pl. نَا
2nd pers. sing. (m.) كَ	dual (m. and f.) كُمَا	pl. (m.) كُم
2nd pers. sing. (f.) كِ		pl. (f.) كُنَّ
3rd pers. sing. (m.) هُ[1]	dual (m. and f.) هُمَا[1]	pl. (m.) هُم[1]
3rd pers. sing. (f.) هَا		pl. (f.) هُنَّ[1]

e.g. الٰهِى my God.

مَوْلَانَا[2] our master, lord.

Occasionally an Arabic Pronominal Suffix is added to a Persian word, e.g.

نور چشمی *nure caʃmi*, light of my eye (=my son).

استادی *ostadi*, my master.

Note also the following expressions:

عَيْنُهُ himself (from عَيْن 'self, substance') used in Persian to mean 'exactly like', e.g.

شکل برادرم عينه شکل خواهرم است *ʃekle baradaram âinaho*[3] *ʃekle xaharam ast*, My brother's appearance is exactly like my sister's.

اين مملکت عينه مملکت ماست *in mamlakat âinaho*[3] *mamlakate mast*, This country is exactly like our country.

[1] The *zamme* of هُ, هُمَا, هُم and هُنَّ is changed after ـِ, ـِى and ـَى into *kasre*.

[2] This is the title usually given to the poet Jalal od-Din Rumi.

[3] See Introduction to Part II, para. 12 for the pronunciation of this word.

مُشَارٌ إِلَيْهِ[1] above mentioned, aforesaid (from اَشَارَ إِلَى to indicate).

مُدَّعَى عَلَيهِ the defendant in a lawsuit (from اِدَّعَى عَلَى to enter an action against).

11. The word ذو is used with a following noun to denote 'possessed of' the quality indicated by the noun. It is declined as follows:

Nom. sing. m.	ذُو	f.	ذَات	dual m.	ذَوَا	f.	ذَوَاتَا	pl. m.	ذَوُو	f.	ذَوَات
Gen. sing. m.	ذى	f.	ذَات	dual m.	ذَوَىْ	f.	ذَوَاتَىْ	pl. m.	ذَوى	f.	ذَوَات
Acc. sing. m.	ذَا	f.	ذَات	dual m.	ذَوَىْ	f.	ذَوَاتَىْ	pl. m.	ذَوى	f.	ذَوَات

An alternative masculine plural is أُولُو or أُلُو (nom.) and أُولى (gen. and acc.). The first vowel of أُولُو and أُولى is short. The vowel of ذُو and ذى before the definite article is also short. E.g.

ذُو حَيَاتَيْن amphibious.
ذى رُوح animate.
ذى هُوش intelligent.
ذى نَفْع interested in (an interested party).
أُولُو ٱلْأَمْر commanders.
أُولُو ٱلْأَلْبَاب intelligent, prudent (persons).

12. صاحب is also used to mean 'possessed of', e.g.

صاحب مال *sahebmal*, rich.
صاحب خانه *sahebxane*, owner of the house, landlord.

In the above examples صاحب *saheb* forms part of a compound. In the following example it does not form part of a compound and takes the *ezafe*, e.g.

صاحب تأليفات زياد است *sahebe talifate ziad ast*, He is the author of many works.

[1] The *tanvin* is in this case pronounced in Persian, i.e. *mosaron eleih.*

13. أَهْل is used to denote 'capable of, possessed of, belonging to'. It takes the *ezafe*, e.g.

اهل این کار نیستم *ahle in kar nistam*, I am not capable of doing this, I am not prepared to do this.

اهل فن *ahle fann*
اهل خبره *ahle xebre* } an expert, technician.

اهل کجائید *ahle koja id*, Where do you come from?

اهل انگلستان هستیم *ahle englestan hastim*, We are English.

14. Arabic prepositions are of two kinds: separable, i.e. those which can be written alone except when followed by a pronominal suffix, and inseparable, i.e. those which consist of one letter which is always attached to the following word.

(*a*) Inseparable prepositions:

بِ in, by, with, e.g.

بِسْمِ ٱللّٰه in the name of God (for باسم).

بِاللّٰه by God.

وَ by, e.g.

وَاللّٰه by God.

لِ for, to, because of, e.g.

لِهٰذا therefore (for this).

لِ also means 'for the benefit of' (in opposition to عَلَى 'against') and the phrases بَر لَه and بَر عَلَيْه (عَلَى compounded with the Arabic 3rd pers. sing. masc. pronominal suffix and the Persian preposition بَر *bar*) are used in Persian to mean 'for' or 'in favour of' and 'against' respectively, and take the *ezafe*, e.g.

قاضی بر له او حکم داد *qazi bar lahe u hokm dad*, The judge made an order in his favour.

كَ like, as, e.g.

كَذا such like (like this).

(*b*) Separable prepositions:

إِلَى until, to, e.g.

إِلَى ٱلْأَبَد until eternity.

حَتَّى up to, as far as, even. In Persian it is used to mean 'even', e.g.

همه آمدند حتی بچه های کوچك *hame amadand hatta*[1] *baccehaye kucek*, All came, even the small children.

عَلَى against, over, e.g.

سَلَام عَلَيْكُم peace (be) upon you.

عَلَى ٱلْخُصُوص especially.

See also (*a*) above under لِ.

عَن from, instead of, e.g.

رَضِيَ ٱللّٰه عَنْهُ may God be satisfied with him.

عَنْقَرِيب shortly.

فِي in, e.g.

فِي هٰذِهِ ٱلسَّنَة in this year.

مَعَ with, e.g.

مَعَهٰذَا in spite of this.

مَعَذٰلِك in spite of that (= with that).

مِن from, e.g.

أَعُوذُ بِاللّٰهِ مِنَ ٱلشَّرّ I take refuge in God from evil.

(*c*) Nouns or adjectives in the accusative used as prepositions. These lose the accusative termination in Persian and are used alone or in conjunction with a Persian preposition. They take the *ezafe* in the same

[1] In the phrase حَتَّى ٱلْمَقْدُور *hattal-maqdur* 'as far as possible' the second vowel of حَتَّى is short and so always before a *hamzat ol-vasl*. Cf. also عَلَى ٱلْخُصُوص *alal-xosus*.

way that Persian prepositions which were originally nouns take the *ezafe*, unless they are followed by a Persian preposition:

بَعْد after. This is usually used in conjunction with the Persian preposition از *az*, e.g.

بعد از او *ba'd az u*, after him.

بَیْن between, e.g.

بین من و شما *beine man o šoma*, between me and you.

مَا بَیْن and فِی مَا بَیْن are also used to mean 'between'.

تَحْت under, and its compound در تحت *dar taht*.

عَوَض (for عِوَض) instead of.

قَرِیب near, about.

فَوْق above.

قَبْل before. This is used in conjunction with the Persian preposition از *az*, e.g.

قبل از ظهر *qabl az zohr*, before midday, A.M.

وَرَاء beyond. This is usually used in conjunction with the Arabic pronoun مَا 'what', e.g.

مَاوَرَاء طَبْعِیَّت supernatural (what is beyond nature).

مَحْض for, e.g.

محض خاطر شما *mahze xatere šoma*, for your sake.

مُقَابِل and its compound در مقابل *dar moqabel*, opposite.

بَابَت and its compounds در بابت *dar babat* and از بابت *az babat*, on account of.

جَانِب at the side of, and its compounds از جانب *az janeb* 'on behalf of' and بجانب *be janeb* 'towards'.

طَرَف at, on the side of, beside, and its compounds از طرف *az taraf* 'on behalf of' and بطرف *be taraf* 'towards'.

أَطْرَاف (pl. of طَرَف 'side'), and its compound در اطراف *dar atraf*, about, around.

غیْر and its compound غیر از *γeir az*, other than.

خارِج and its compound خارج از *xarej az*, outside.

دَوْر around, round.

ضِدّ and its compound بر ضد *bar zedd*, against.

خِلاف and its compound بر خلاف *bar xelaf*, against, contrary to.

جِهَت and its compounds بجهت *be jehat* and از جهت *az jehat*, for, on account of.

سِوَی (which becomes in Persian with the *ezafe* سوای *sevaye*), apart from.

Certain Arabic compound prepositions are also used in Persian, e.g.

مِنْ قَبْل before. مِن فَوْق above.

(*d*) The following are compounded with a Persian preposition. They take the *ezafe*:

با وجود *ba vojud*, in spite of.
بوسیله *be vasile* } by means of.
بواسطه *be vasete* }
از جمله *az jomle*, from among.
در اثنا(ی) *dar asna (ye)*, in the course of (=in the middle of).
در ظرف *dar zarf*, in the course of (=within the period of).
بمنظور *be manzur*, with the intention of.
از قرا *az qarar*, at the rate of, according to.
بقرار *be qarar*, according to.
بعنوان *be envan* (with the title of =) as.
بسمت *be semat* (with the mark of =) as.
بمنزله *be manzele* (with the rank of =) as.

15. Stress on the prepositions and their compounds listed in paras. 14 (*c*) and (*d*) above conforms to the general tendencies of Persian, i.e. it is carried on the final syllable (excluding the *ezafe*), e.g.

مقابل *moqa'bel*, opposite.
در اطراف *dar at'raf*, about.
از جمله *az jom'le*, from among.

This is also the case with the majority of prepositions in para. 14 (*a*) and (*b*) above, in so far as these carry the stress, but حَتَّى, مَعَهٰذا and مَعَذٰلِك carry the stress on the initial or the final syllable.

16. Arabic adverbs are of two main kinds, inseparable particles, which are not used in Persian, and separate particles and nouns in the nominative or accusative.

(*a*) Separate particles:

بَل usually compounded in Persian with كه, thus becoming

بلكه *balke*, but, rather, on the contrary.

بَلَى yes.[1]

فَقَط only.

لَا not. This is only used in Persian in compounds, e.g.

بِلَا شَرْط unconditionally.

بِلَا تَرْدِيد undoubtedly.

لَا أَقَلّ at least.

لَا بُدّ of necessity.

لَا يَنْقَطِع unceasingly (lit. it does not cease).

لَمْ not. This also is only used in compounds, e.g.

لَمْ يَزْرَع uncultivated (lit. he did not sow).

بل *bal* and بلكه *balke* are used after a negative expressed or implied, e.g.

نه تنها فردا (خواهد آمد) بلكه پس‌فردا هم خواهد آمد

na tanha farda (*xahad amad*) *balke pasfarda ham xahad amad*,
Not only will he come to-morrow, but he will come the day after tomorrow also.

نه فقط ما بلكه همه مردم بر اثر اين پيش‌آمد متاسف شدند

na faqat ma balke hameye mardom bar asare in piʃamad motaʿassef ʃodand.
Not only we but all the people were grieved at this event.

[1] In Persian this becomes *bali*; the form بله *bale* is commonly used.

بلکه *balke* is also used after a rhetorical question to mean 'on the contrary', e.g.

اشتباه یعنی چه بلکه فی‌الواقع عمدًا این کاررا کرده‌اید

eʃtebah ya'ni ce balke fel-vaqe' amdan in karra karde id,

What do you mean? A mistake? On the contrary, you did it on purpose.

With an affirmative verb بلکه *balke* means 'nay rather', e.g.

این کتاب چهل ریال می‌ارزد بلکه پنجاه ریال

in ketab cehel rial miarzad balke panjah rial,

This book is worth forty *rials*, nay rather fifty *rials*.

In Colloquial Persian بلکه *balke* is sometimes used in the sense of 'perhaps', e.g.

بلکه آمده باشد *balke amade baʃad*, Perhaps he has come (after all).

(*b*) Many nouns can be used in the accusative as adverbs, e.g.

أَحْيَانًا	perchance, at times.	اِتِّفَاقًا	by chance.
جَمْعًا	together.	نِسْبَةً	relatively.
اَلْآنَ	immediately, now.	فِعْلًا	at present.

(*c*) Certain prepositional phrases are also used as adverbs, e.g.

فِی ٱلْفَوْرِ [1]	immediately.	حَتَّی ٱلْمَقْدُور	as far as possible.
بالاخره (for بِٱلْآخِرَةِ)	finally, at last.	مِن غَيْرِ رَسْم	unofficially.

17. Stress is carried on the final syllable of the forms given in para. 16 above, except بلکه *balke* which carries it on the initial syllable, e.g.

فقط *fa'qat*, only.

دائمًا *da'e'man*, continually.

18. Certain phrases compounded of Arabic and Persian words are used as adverbs, e.g.

بتدریج *be tadrij*, gradually.

Stress in such compounds is carried on the final syllable.

[1] See Introduction to Part II, para. 8(*d*) for the pronunciation of this word.

19. Among Arabic conjunctions used in Persian are the following:

وَ and.

إِلَّا if not, except; and وَإِلَّا and if not, otherwise.

أَمَّا as for; in Persian it is also used to mean 'but'.

لٰكِن and وَلٰكِن and its variants لِيكِن and وَلِيكِن but.

20. The following phrases compounded of Arabic and Persian words are used as conjunctions:

وقتیکه *vaqtike*, when.

مادامیکه *madamike*, as long as (مَا دَامَ as long as it continues).

حالانکه *halanke*, although, albeit, notwithstanding the fact that.

هر قدر که *har qadrke*, even if, however much that.

در صورتیکه *dar suratike*, in the event that, although; whereas.

هر وقتیکه *har vaqtike*, whenever.

بمجرد اینکه *be mojarrade inke* } as soon as.
بمحض اینکه *be mahze inke* }

قبل از آنکه (اینکه) *qabl az anke (inke)*, before.[1]

21. Stress is carried on the initial syllable of the forms in para. 19 above, except وَلٰكِن and وَلِيكِن which carry the stress on the second syllable. The forms in para. 20 above carry the stress as follows:

وقتیکه *'vaqtike.*

ما دامیکه *ma'damike.*

حالانکه *'halanke.*

هر قدر که *'har qadrke.*

در صورتیکه *dar su'ratike.*

هر وقتیکه *'har vaqtike.*

بمجرد اینکه *be mojar'rade inke.*

بمحض اینکه *be 'mahze inke.*

قبل از اینکه *'qabl az inke.*

[1] This is followed by the Present Subjunctive. Cf. پیش از آنکه (اینکه) p. 74.

22. Various Arabic phrases are used as interjections. Among them are the following:

يَاأَللّٰه	O God!
اَلْحَمْدُ لِلّٰه	Praise be to God.
إِنْ شَاءَ ٱللّٰه	if God wills.
مَا شَاءَ ٱللّٰه	what God wills.
أَعُوذُ بِٱللّٰه	I take refuge in God.
إِسْتَغْفِرُ ٱللّٰه	I ask pardon of God.
بَارَكَ ٱللّٰه	God bless (you); bravo.

در صفت دبیر[1]

دبیر باید پیش از همه کار و بیش از همه چیز سعی کند که دارای ملکات فاضله و خداوند اخلاق ستوده گردد جمال صورترا بکمال معنی آراسته کند و جامه تقوی و پرهیزکاری بر تن راست نماید و اندام اعتبار را بزیور درستی و امانت بیاراید و گفتار خودرا با راستی و حقیقت بیامیزد و بفصاحت منطق و صراحت لهجه زیور بخشد و زبان و قلم از ناشایست پاك دارد و در نگاهداشت رازها کوشش فراوان بکار برد و اعتماد همگان‌را بسوی خود فرا آورد و عنان قلم از آنچه بر خلاف حقیقت است باز گیرد و کسی‌را بدانچه در او نیست نستاید و از تملق و چاپلوسی که کشنده روح ادب است بگریزد دبیر چون بدین صفتها و زیورها آراسته باشد هر آینه قدر و بهای او نزد مردم بزرگ شود و جایگاه او در جامعه بلند گردد و سخن او در گوشها و دلها تأثیری هرچه بیشتر بخشد و باید دانست که دبیری‌را شرایطی چند است که تا آن شرایط در وجود دبیر و نگارنده جمع نشود نام دبیری بر وی راست نیاید و کار نگارندگی‌را از عهده بر نتواند آمد

[1] آئین نگارش تالیف حسین سمیعی (ادیب السلطنه)

معنی آزادی[1]

برادران و هم میهنان عزیزم

بحمد الله بفضل خداوند در سایه توجه شاهنشاه جوان جوانبخت بار دیگر پا بدایره آزادی گذاشتید و میتوانید از این نعمت بر خوردار شوید البته باید قدر این نعمترا بدانید و شکر خداوندرا بجا آورید از رنج و محنتی که در ظرف سی چهل سال گذشته بشما رسیده است امیدوارم تجربه آموخته و عبرت گرفته متوجه شده باشید که قدر نعمت آزادی‌را چگونه باید دانست و معنی آزادی‌را در یافته باشید در این صورت میدانید که معنی آزادی این نیست که مردم خودسر باشند و هرکس هر چه میخواهد بکند در عین آزادی قیود و حدود لازم است اگر حدودی در کار نباشد و همه خودسر باشند هیچکس آزاد نخواهد بود و هرکس از دیگران قویتر باشد آنانرا اسیر و بنده خود خواهد کرد قیود و حدودی که برای خودسری هست همان است که قانون مینامند پس مردم وقتی آزاد خواهند بود که قانون در کار باشد و هر کس حدود اختیارات خودرا بداند و از آن تجاوز نکند پس کشوری که قانون ندارد یا قانون در آن مجری و محترم نیست مردمش آزاد نخواهند بود و آسوده زیست نخواهند کرد این حقیقتی است بسیار ساده و روشن و هیچکس منکر آن نمیشود اما متاسفانه کمتر کسی باین حقیقت ایمان دارد زیرا که غالباً می‌بینیم مردم حدود یعنی قانونرا برای دیگران لازم میدانند اما رعایتش‌را برای خودشان واجب نمیشمارند اگر هرکس معتقد بود که رعایت حدود قانون تنها نسبت بدیگران واجب نیست بلکه نسبت بخود او هم واجب است تخلف از قانون واقع نمیشد و حال آنکه ما هر روز می‌بینیم بسیاری از اشخاص از قانون تخلف میکنند و کمتر کسی است که متوجه باشد که اگر من تخلف از قانونرا از طرف خود جائز بدانم دلیلی ندارد که دیگران هم تخلف از قانونرا از طرف خودشان جائز ندانند در این صورت تخلف از قانون امری رایج و شایع خواهد بود و همان نتیجه دست میدهد که گفتیم یعنی آسایش از همه سلب میشود متأسفانه بسیاری از مردم چنین اند که هر وقت بتوانند زور بگویند میگویند غافل از اینکه اگر بنا بزورگوئی باشد امروز من میتوانم بزیردست خود زور بگویم اما فردا زبردستی پیدا میشود که بمن زور بگوید پس همین کس

[1] نطق مرحوم آقای فروغی که در روز ۱۰ مهر ماه ۱۳۲۰ در برابر دستگاه رادیو تهران ایراد و پخش شد

که امروز زور میگوید فردا دوچار زبردست‌تر از خود میشود آنگاه آه و ناله میکنند و باین ترتیب دنیا درست مصداق گفته شیخ سعدی میشود که میفرماید

ببری مال مسلمان و چو مالت ببرند
داد و فریاد بر آری که مسلمانی نیست

پس اولین سفارشی که در عالم خیرخواهی و میهن‌دوستی بشما میکنم اینست که متوجه باشید که ملت آزاد آنست که جریان امورش بر وفق قانون باشد و بنا بر این هر کس بقانون بی اعتنائی کند و تخلف از آنرا روا بدارد دشمن آزادی است یعنی دشمن آسایش ملت است یک نکته دیگر هم در این باب میگویم و بمطلب دیگر میپردازم و آن اینست که شما شنوندگان من یقین دارم بسیار شنیده اید که از تمدن و توحش و ملل متمدن و وحشی سخن میگویند آیا درست فکر کرده‌اید که ملت متمدن کدام است و ملت وحشی چیست گمانم اینست که بعضی از شما خواهند گفت ملت متمدن آن است که راه آهن و کارخانه و لشکر و سپاه و تانك و هواپیما و از این قبیل چیزها دارد و ملت وحشی آنست که این چیزهارا ندارد و یا خواهند گفت ملت متمدن آنست که شهرهایش چنین و چنان باشد خیابانهایش وسیع و اسفالته خانه‌هایش چند اشکوبه باشد و قس علیهذا البته ملل متمدن این چیزهارا دارند اما من بشما میگویم بدانید که این چیزها فروع تمدنند اصل تمدن نیستند اصل تمدن این است که ملت تربیت داشته باشد و بهترین علامت تربیت داشتن ملت اینست که قانونرا محترم بدارد و رعایت کند اگر این اصل محفوظ باشد آن فروع خود بخود حاصل میشود اما اگر ملتی قانونرا محترم ندارد هر قدر از آن چیزها داشته باشد نمیتوان گفت تربیت دارد و نمیتوان گفت متمدن است آن چیزها هم عاقبت از دستش میرود پس از این مقدمات که گمان میکنم قابل انکار نباشد میپردازیم باصل مطلب و یادآوری میکنم که وجود قانون بسته بدو چیز است یکی قانونگذاری و یکی مجری قانون و جمع این دو چیزرا حکومت یا دولت میگویند و چون ملتهای مختلف‌را در زمانهای مختلف در نظر میگیریم میبینیم حکومتهای آنها همه و همیشه یکسان نبوده و نیستند گاهی از اوقات قانونگذاری و مجری قانون یکنفر بوده و گاهی چند نفر معدود و بعضی از ملتها هم بوده و هستند که قانونگذاری و اجرای قانونرا تمام ملت بر عهده گرفته است قسم اول حکومت انفرادی و استبدادی است قسم دوم حکومت خواص و اشراف است و قسم سومرا حکومت ملی میگویند که اروپائیان دموکراسی مینامند و هریك از این سه قسم هم

اشکال مختلف داشته و دارد که چون مقصود من این نیست که بشما علم حقوق درس بدهم داخل این بحث نمیشوم و همین قدر میگویم ملتها هرچه داناتر و برشد و بلوغ نزدیکتر میشوند بقسم سوم یعنی بحکومت ملی متمایلتر میگردند جز اینکه ملتها چون غالباً دارای جمعیت فراوان و کشور پهناورند نمیتوانند هر روز یك جا جمع شوند و وظیفه قانونگذاری و اجرای قانونرا خودشان مستقیماً بجا بیاورند بنا براین بهترین ترتیبی که پیدا کردهاند این است که ملت جماعتیرا نماینده خود قرار دهد که بنام او قانونگذاری کنند و مجمع آن نمایندگانرا ما مجلس شورای ملی نامیدهایم و مجلس هم چند نفررا برای اجرای قانون اختیار میکند که هیئت وزیران نامیده میشود و این هر دو جماعت در تحت ریاست عالیه یکنفر هستند که اگر او انتخابی باشد رئیس جمهوری نامیده میشود و اگر دائمی و موروثی باشد پادشاه است شما ملت ایران بموجب قانون اساسی که تقریباً سی و پنج سال پیش مقرر شده است دارای حکومت ملی پادشاهی هستید اما اگر درست توجه کنید تصدیق خواهید کرد که در مدت این سی و پنج سال کمتر وقتی بودهاست که از نعمت آزادی حقیقی یعنی مجری و محترم بودن قانون بر خوردار بوده باشید و چندین مرتبه حکومت ملی یعنی اساس مشروطیت شما مختل شده است آیا فکر کرده اید که علت آن چیست من برای شما توضیح میکنم علت اصلی این بوده است که قدر این نعمترا بدرستی نمیدانستید و بوظایف آن قیام نمیکردید و بسیاری از روی نادانی و جماعتی از روی غرض و هوای نفس از شرایطی که در حکومت ملی باید ملحوظ شود تخلف میکردند شرایطی که در حکومت ملی باید ملحوظ باشد چیست فراموش نکنید که معنی حکومت ملی اینست که اختیار امور کشور با ملت باشد و البته میدانید که هرکس اختیاراتی دارد در ازای آن اختیارات مسئولیتی متوجه او میشود پس اگر بمقتضای اختیارات خود چنانکه وظیفه وجدانی حکم میکند عمل نکند مسئول واقع میشود و معنی مسئول واقع شدن همیشه این نیست که کسی از او سؤال و باز خواست کند مسئول واقع شدن غالباً باینست که شخص گرفتار عاقبت وخیم میشود اگر مخلوقی نباشد که از او باز خواست کند خالق از او بازخواست خواهد کرد باز خواست خالقرا هم همیشه بروز قیامت نباید محول نمود غالباً باز خواست خالق در همین زندگانی دنیا واقع میشود و شخص جزای عمل خودرا میبیند و چنانکه گفتهاند

از مکافات عمل غافل مشو
گندم از گندم بروید جو زجو

اکنون ببینیم اگر ملت در اختیارات خود بمقتضای وظیفه قانونی و وجدانی عمل نکند چگونه مسئول واقع میشود طبقات ملت مختلفند و هر کدام در عمل حکومت ملی وظیفه خاص دارند عامه مردم موظفند که در انتخاب نمایندگان خود برای مجلس شورای ملی اهتمام داشته و نمایندگان صالح انتخاب کنند و پس از انتخاب مراقب رفتار آنان باشند و افکار صالح یعنی عقاید آزادی‌خواهی یعنی قانون‌خواهی یعنی میهن‌دوستی نمایش دهند و معتقد باشند که خیر عموم خواستن بر اعمال اغراض شخصی مقدم است و هر فرد از افراد ملت مکلف است شغل و حرفه مشروع آبرومندی مطابق استعداد خود اختیار کند و در انجام آن بکوشد نمایندگان ملت موظفند که در قانونگذاری و نظارت در اجرای قانون اهتمام ورزند و نمایندگی ملت‌را وسیله پیشرفت اغراض وهوای نفس و جاه‌طلبی ندانند وظیفه وزیران اینست که خودرا مجری قانون و خدمتگذار ملت بدانند و در پیشنهاد قوانین بمجلس و اجرای آن قوانین همواره خیر و صلاح ملترا در نظر داشته باشند وظیفه مستخدمین و کارکنان دولت اینست که در اجرای قوانین از روی صحت و درستی وسیله پیشرفت کار وزیران باشند و موجبات آسایش ابنای نوع خودرا که مخدومین ایشان هستند فراهم آورند وظیفه روزنامه‌نگاران اینست که هادی افکار مردم شوند و ملت و دولترا براه خیر دلالت کنند وظیفه پادشاه اینست که حافظ قانون اساسی و ناظر افعال دولت باشد و افراد ملت‌را فرزندان خود بداند و بمقتضای مهر پدری با آنها رفتار کند و گفتار و کردار خودرا سر مشق مردم قرار دهد روی هم رفته وظیفه جمیع طبقات ملت اینست که گفتار و کردار خودرا با اصول شرافت و آبرومندی تطبیق کنند که چنانکه یکی از حکمای اروپا گفته است اگر بنیاد حکومت استبدادی بر ترس و بیم است بنیاد حکومت ملی بر شرافت افراد ملت است و مخصوصًا اگر متصدیان امور عامه شرافت‌را در اعمال خود نصب العین خویش نسازند کار حکومت ملی پیشرفت نمیکند و بالاخره جمیع طبقات باید دست بدست یکدیگر داده در پیش بردن حکومت ملی متفق و متحد باشند که بزرگترین آفت حکومت ملی اختلاف کلمه و نفاق است پس اگر افراد ملت فقط ملاحظات و منافع شخصی‌را منظور بدارند و حاضر نشوند که یک اندازه از اغراض‌جوئی خودرا فدای منافع کلی کنند و از راه صلاح خارج شده بجای اشتغال بامور شرافتمندانه برای پیشرفت اغراض خصوصی وسایل نامناسب از تزویر و نفاق و فتنه و فساد و دسته‌بندی و هوچیگری بکار برند و اگر نمایندگان ملت در قانونگذاری یا اجرای قانون اهتمام

لازم ننمایند و نمایندگی ملت‌را وسیله تحصیل یا حفظ منافع شخصی بدانند و عوام فریبی‌را پیشه خود بسازند و دسیسه‌کاریرا شعار خود کنند یا معنی نمایندگی ملترا فقط مدعی شدن با دولت بدانند و اگر وزیران وزارترا فقط مایه تشخیص و جلب منافع شخصی فرض کنند و اگر روزنامه نگاران بجای حقیقت گوئی و رهبری ملت براه خیر روزنامه‌را آلت هتاکی و پیش بردن اغراض فاسد قرار دهند و اگر پادشاه حافظ قوانین نباشد وافراد ملترا فرزندان خود نداند و سلطنت‌را وسیله اجرای هوای نفس بسازد و اگر طبقات ملت از طریق شرافت پا بیرون گذارند یا راه اختلاف و نفاق پیش گیرند گذشته از اینکه شخصًا مسئول یعنی گرفتار عاقبت وخیم میشوند باید حتم و یقین دانست که باز اوضاع این سی و پنج سال گذشته تجدید خواهد شد کشور و ملت هر روز گرفتار مصیبت و فتنه و فساد میشود و نه تنها آزادی تباه خواهد شد بلکه بدار فنا و نیستی خواهیم رفت و اگر ملت عبرت گرفته باشد و بوظیفه وجدانی خود عمل کند امیدواری میتوان داشت که روزگار محنت و ذلت سپری شود و دوره شرافت و سعادت و سرافرازی برسد

APPENDIX I

Irregular Verbs.

The following is a list of the main irregular verbs. A few verbs of rare occurrence have been omitted. The verbs have been arranged in alphabetical order. The meanings of the verbs will be found in the vocabulary. Obsolete verbs are put in square brackets.

Present Stem		Infinitive	
(*ajin*)	آجین	(*ajidan*)	آجیدن
(*az*)	آز	(*axtan*)	آختن
(*ara*)	آرا	(*arastan*)	آراستن
(*azar*)	آزار	(*azordan*)	آزردن
(*azma*)	آزما	(*azmudan*)	آزمودن
(*asa*)	آسا	(*asudan*)	آسودن
(*aʃub*)	آشوب	(*aʃoftan*)	آشفتن
(*aɣar*)	آغار	(*aɣeʃtan*)	آغشتن
(*oft*)	افت	(*oftadan*)	افتادن
(*afraz*)	افراز	(*afraxtan*)	افراختن
(*afraz*)	افراز	(*afraʃtan*)	افراشتن
(*afruz*)	افروز	(*afruxtan*)	افروختن
(*afarin*)	آفرین	(*afaridan*)	آفریدن
(*afza*)	افزا	(*afzudan*)	افزودن
(*afʃar*)	افشار	(*afʃordan*)	افشردن
(*agin*)	آگین	(*agandan*)	آگندن
(*ala*)	آلا	(*aludan*)	آلودن
(*ama*)	آما	(*amadan*)	آمادن
(*a*)	آ	(*amadan*)	آمدن
(*amuz*)	آموز	(*amuxtan*)	آموختن
(*amiz*)	آمیز	(*amixtan*)	آمیختن
(*ambar*)	انبار	(*ambaʃtan*)	انباشتن
(*andaz*)	انداز	(*andaxtan*)	انداختن

Present Stem		Infinitive	
(*anduz*)	اندوز	(*anduxtan*)	اندوختن
(*anda*)	اندا	(*andudan*)	اندودن
(*engar*)	انگار	(*engaʃtan*)	انگاشتن
(*angiz*)	انگیز	(*angixtan*)	انگیختن
[1] (*ar*)	آر	(*avordan*, *avardan*)	آوردن
(*aviz*)	آویز	(*avixtan*)	آویختن
(*ahiz*)	آهیز	(*ahextan*)	آهختن
(*ist*)	ایست	(*istadan*)	ایستادن
(*baxʃa*)	بخشا	(*baxʃudan*)	بخشودن
(*bar*)	بر	(*bordan*)	بردن
(*band*)	بند	(*bastan*)	بستن
(*baʃ*)	باش	(*budan*)	بودن
(*biz*)	بیز	(*bixtan*)	بیختن
(*pala*)	پالا	(*paludan*)	پالودن
(*paz*)	پز	(*poxtan*)	پختن
(*pazir*)	پذیر	(*paziroftan*)	پذیرفتن
(*pardaz*)	پرداز	(*pardaxtan*)	پرداختن
(*pandar*)	پندار	(*pandaʃtan*)	پنداشتن
(*pe͡ivand*)	پیوند	(*pe͡ivastan*)	پیوستن
(*pe͡ima*)	پیما	(*pe͡imudan*)	پیمودن
(*taz*)	تاز	(*taxtan*)	تاختن
(*tab*)	تاب	(*taftan*)	تافتن
(*tavan*)	توان	(*tavanestan*)	توانستن
(*jah*)	جه	(*jastan*)	جستن
(*ju*)	جو	(*jostan*)	جستن
(*cin*)	چین	(*cidan*)	چیدن
(*xiz*)	خیز	(*xastan*)	خاستن
[(*xosb*)	خسب	(*xoftan*)	خفتن]
(*xah*)	خواه	(*xastan*)	خواستن

[1] The Present Stem can also be formed regularly, آور *avar*.

Present Stem	Infinitive
(*deh*) ده	(*dadan*) دادن
(*dar*) دار	(*daʃtan*) داشتن
(*dan*) دان	(*danestan*) دانستن
(*duz*) دوز	(*duxtan*)[1] دوختن
(*duʃ*) دوش	(*duxtan*)[2] دوختن
(*bin*) بین	(*didan*) دیدن
(*roba*) ربا	(*robudan*) ربودن
(*rah*) ره	(*rastan*) رستن
(*ru*) رو	(*rostan*) رستن
(*ris*) ریس	(*reʃtan*) رشتن
(*rav-, rou͡*) رو	(*raftan*) رفتن
(*rub*) روب	(*roftan*) رفتن
(*zan*) زن	(*zadan*) زدن
(*zada*) زدا	(*zadudan*) زدودن
[(*zi*) زی	(*zistan*) زیستن]
(*saz*) ساز	(*saxtan*) ساختن
(*separ*) سپار	(*sepordan*) سپردن
(*setan*) ستان	(*setadan*) ستادن
(*seta*) ستا	(*setudan*) ستودن
(*seriʃ*) سریش	(*sereʃtan*) سرشتن
(*sara*) سرا	(*sorudan*) سرودن
(*somb*) سنب	(*softan*) سفتن
(*suz*) سوز	(*suxtan*) سوختن
(*ʃetab*) شتاب	(*ʃetaftan*) شتافتن
(*ʃav-, ʃou͡*) شو	(*ʃodan*) شدن
(*ʃu*) شو	(*ʃostan*) شستن
(*ʃekan*) شکن	(*ʃekastan*) شکستن
(*ʃomar*) شمار	(*ʃomordan*) شمردن
(*ʃenas*) شناس	(*ʃenaxtan*) شناختن
(*ʃenav-, ʃenou͡*) شنو	(*ʃenidan*) شنیدن

[1] To sew. [2] To milk.

Present Stem	Infinitive
(*ferest*) فرست	(*ferestadan*) فرستادن
(*farma*) فرما	(*farmudan*) فرمودن
(*foruʃ*) فروش	(*foruxtan*) فروختن
(*farib*) فریب	(*fariftan*) فریفتن
(*feʃar*) فشار	(*feʃordan*) فشردن
(*kah*) کاه	(*kastan*) کاستن
(*kar*) کار	(*kaʃtan*) کاشتن
(*kon*) کن	(*kardan*) کردن
(*kar*) کار	(*keʃtan*) کشتن
(*kub*) کوب	(*kuftan*) کوفتن
(*godaz*) گداز	(*godaxtan*) گداختن
(*gozar*) گذار	(*gozaʃtan*) گذاشتن
(*gozar*) گذر	(*gozaʃtan*) گذشتن
(*gir*) گیر	(*gereftan*) گرفتن
(*goriz*) گریز	(*gorixtan*) گریختن
(*geri*) گری	(*geristan*) گریستن
(*gozin*) گزین	(*gozidan*) گزیدن
(*gosel*) گسل	(*gosestan*) گسستن
(*gosel*) گسل	(*gosixtan*) گسیختن
(*goʃa*) گشا	(*goʃadan*) گشادن
(*gard*) گرد	(*gaʃtan*) گشتن
(*goʃa*) گشا	(*goʃudan*) گشودن
(*gu*) گو	(*goftan*) گفتن
(*gomar*) گمار	(*gomaʃtan*) گماشتن
(*lis*) لیس	(*leʃtan*) لشتن
(*mir*) میر	(*mordan*) مردن
(*neʃin*) نشین	(*neʃastan*) نشستن
(*negar*) نگر	(*negaristan*) نگریستن
(*navaz*) نواز	(*navaxtan*) نواختن
(*nevis*) نویس	(*neveʃtan*) نوشتن
(*nama*) نما	(*namudan*) نمودن
(*neh*) نه	(*nehadan*) نهادن
(*hel*) هل	(*heʃtan*) هشتن
(*yab*) یاب	(*yaftan*) یافتن

APPENDIX II

Interjections.

The following is a list of some of the interjections in common use:

آفرین	*afarin*, bravo!
افسوس	*afsus*, alas!
به به	*bah bah*, bravo!
حیف	*heif*, what a pity!
خوش بحال او	*xoʃ be hale u*, lucky fellow!
راستی	*rasti*, really!
اینك	*inak*, lo! behold!
زنهار	*zenhar*, beware! have a care! mind!

The two last are used in Classical rather than in Modern Persian.

APPENDIX III

The Calendar.

The Muslim era is used in Persia. It dates from the morning after the flight (or *hejre*) of the Prophet Mohammad from Mecca to Medina on the 16th of July, A.D. 622. For civil purposes a solar year is in use. It begins with the 1st of Farvardin, which falls on the 20th, 21st, or 22nd of March. There are twelve months, the names of which are:

فروردین	*farvardin.*	مهر	*mehr.*
اردی بهشت	*ordi beheʃt.*	آبان (ابان)	*aban (aban).*
خرداد	*xordad.*	آذر	*azar.*
تیر	*tir.*	دی	*dei.*
مرداد	*mordad.*	بهمن	*bahman.*
شهریور	*ʃahrivar.*	اسفند	*esfand.*

The first six months have thirty-one days and the last six thirty days, except Esfand, which has twenty-nine days. Every fourth year is a leap-year (کبیسه *kabise*) in which Esfand has thirty days.

The civil day begins at sunset.

The present year (1952) is, according to the Persian solar year, 1330/31.

The Muslim lunar year, by which religious holidays are reckoned, consists of six months of thirty days and six months of twenty-nine days as follows:

محرم *moharram.*
صفر *safar.*
ربیع الاول *rabi' ol-avval.*
ربیع الاخر (ربیع الثانی) *rabi' ol-axer (rabi' os-sani).*
جمادی الاولی (جمادی الاول) *jomadi ol-ula (jomadi ol-avval).*
جمادی الاخری (جمادی الثانی) *jomadi ol-oxra (jomadi os-sani).*
رجب *rajab.*
شعبان *ʃa'ban.*
رمضان *ramazan.*
شوال *ʃavval.*
ذو القعدة (ذی القعدة) *zol-qa'da (zel-qa'da).*
ذو الحجة (ذی الحجة) *zol-hejja (zel-hejja).*

In a period of thirty years an intercalary day is added to the last week of the year eleven times.

The following formula[1] gives the A.H. lunar year (=Anno Hegirae, or year of the Hejre) equivalent to the A.D. year:

$$(\text{A.D.} - 621{\cdot}54) \div {\cdot}970225.$$

The following formula gives the A.D. year equivalent to the A.H. lunar year:

$$(\text{A.H.} \times {\cdot}970225) + 621{\cdot}54.$$

The present year (1952) is, according to the lunar year, 1371/2).

Popularly the year is divided into a number of periods, which include forty days known as the چله بزرگ *celleye bozorg* at the summer solstice when the heat is at its height, and forty days at the winter solstice when the cold is at its maximum. The *celleye bozorg* is followed by the چله کوچك *celleye kucek*, a period of twenty days when the heat and cold respectively are still considerable. There is also a period at the end of the winter known as the سرمای پیرزن *sarmaye pire zan.*

[1] This formula is given by Duncan Forbes, *Grammar of the Persian Language* (Calcutta, 1876), p. 60.

Public Holidays

The weekly holiday is celebrated on Friday.

A period of three to five days' holiday is observed at the New Year. The 13th of Farvardin, known as سیزده بدر *sizdah be dar*, is also observed as a public holiday. The anniversary of the Constitution, to commemorate the Grant of the Constitution by Mozaffar od-Din Shah in 1906, is a public holiday; it falls on the 14th Mordad.

The official religion is the Ja'fari or the Ithna 'Ashari rite of Shi'ism.

The chief religious holidays are the 10th Moharram, known as عاشورا *afura* or روز قتل *ruze qatl*, the day on which the Imam Hosein was killed[1]; the 20th Safar, forty days after *afura*, and hence known as اربعین *arba'in*; the 27th Safar, in commemoration of the martyrdom of the Imam Reza; the 28th Safar, in commemoration of the martyrdom of the Imam Hasan; the 29th Safar, in commemoration of the death of Mohammad, known as رحلت حضرت رسول *rehlate hazrate rasul*; the 17th Rabi' I, in honour of the birthday of Mohammad; the 13th Jomadi I, in commemoration of the death of Fatima, the daughter of Mohammad, and the 20th Jomadi II, in celebration of her birthday; the 27th Rajab, known as عید مبعث *ide mab'as*, the anniversary of the day Mohammad began his mission; the 15th Sha'ban, the anniversary of the birthday of the twelfth Imam, Hazrate Hojjat; the 19th Ramazan, in commemoration of the day on which Ali was fatally wounded, and the 21st and 23rd Ramazan, in commemoration of the death of Ali; the 1st Shavval, known as the عید الفطر *id ol-fetr*, when the fast of Ramazan is broken; the 10th Zol-Hejja, known as the عید قربان *ide qorban*, the day on which pilgrims to Mecca make a sacrifice; and the 18th Zol-Hejja, known as the عید غدیر *ide γadir*, the anniversary of the day when Ali became Caliph.

[1] The first ten days of Moharram are regarded as days of mourning in commemoration of the martyrdom of the Imam Hosein. The 9th Moharram is known as تاسوعا *tasu'a*.

APPENDIX IV

Currency, Weights and Measures.

1. CURRENCY

The monetary unit is the *rial* (ریال).[1] A *rial* is equal to 100 *dinars* (دینار).

The following terms are also used:

1 *shahi* (شاهی) = 5 *dinars*.

1 *sannar* (صنار) = 10 *dinars*.

1 *abbasi* (عباسی) = 20 *dinars*.

yak hazar (یك هزار) = 1 *qeran* (which was formerly equal to 1000 *dinars*).

1 *qeran* (قران) = 1 *rial* or 1·25 *rials*.

1 *toman* (تومان) = 10 *rials*.

Thus ده تومان و سه عباسی *dah toman va se abbasi* means 100 rs. 60 *dinars*; هفت ریال صنار کم *haft rial sannar kam* means 6 rs. 90 *dinars*.

2. WEIGHTS

16 *mesqals* (مثقال) = 1 *sir* (سیر).

10 *sirs* = 1 *carak* (چارك).

4 *caraks* = 1 *mane tabriz* (من تبریز).

100 *mane tabriz* = 1 *xarvar* (خروار).

1 *mesqal* is equal to 71·6 grains or 4·64 grams.
1 *sir* is equal to 2 oz. 185 grains or 74·24 grams.
1 *mane tabriz* is equal to 6·5464 lb. or 2·97 kilos.
1 *xarvar* is equal to 654·64 lb. or 297 kilos.

The *man* varies from town to town. The one most commonly used in North Persia is the *mane tabriz*. The *mane śah* is equal to two *mane tabriz*. The *mane rei* is equal to four *mane tabriz*. The *mane noh abbasi* is equal to 7 lb. 5⅓ oz.

[1] In 1959 the rate of exchange to the pound sterling was 210 rs.

3. MEASURES

4 *gerehs* (گره) = 1 *carak* (چارك).

4 *caraks* = 1 *zar'* (ذرع).

6000 *zars* = 1 *farsax* (فرسخ).[1]

1 *gereh* is approximately $2\frac{1}{2}$ ins.

1 *zar'* is approximately 41 ins.

1 *gaz* (گز) is approximately 1 metre.

The term *angost* (انگشت) is used for a finger's breadth.

1 *jarib* (جریب) is, in some areas, approximately 1 hectare but it varies considerably in different parts of the country.

In certain parts of the country land is measured in *qafiz* (قفیز), approximately $\frac{1}{10}$ of a *jarib*; the *qafiz*, like the *jarib*, varies in extent in different parts of the country. سنگ *sang*, طاق *taq*, جره *jorre*, سرجه *sareje* and سبو *sabu* are terms used in different parts of the country in measuring water. The quantity of water represented by these terms varies from district to district.

The metric system is also used, and is tending to supersede the local measures.

APPENDIX V

Abjad.

Certain numerical values are assigned to the letters of the alphabet. The arrangement of the letters of the alphabet in numerical order is known as *abjad*, so called from the first of a series of meaningless words, which act as a mnemonic to the numerical order:

1000 900 800	700 600 500	400 300 200 100	90 80 70 60	50 40 30 20	10 9 8	7 6 5	4 3 2 1
ضظغ	ثخذ	قرشت	سعفص	کلمن	حطی	هوز	ابجد

[1] The length of the *farsax*, however, tends to vary in different parts of the country. It approximates in some parts to $3\frac{1}{2}$ miles. It tends to be used to express the distance normally covered by a mule or on foot in an hour. In certain parts of the country the distance of the *farsax* is double the normal *farsax*, i.e. some 7 miles, in the same way as the *mane sah* is double a *mane tabriz*.

A doubled letter (i.e. a letter with a *tašdid*) has the value of a single letter only.

پ has the value of ب. ژ has the value of ز.

چ has the value of ج. گ has the value of ك.

Thus, the death of the poet Ahli which took place in A.H. 942 is recorded as follows:

پادشاه شعرا بود اهلی Ahli was the king of poets (= A.H. 942).[1]

APPENDIX VI

Intonation.

1. Rules for word stress have been given in the relevant sections in the *Grammar*. Word stress is, however, usually subsidiary to sentence stress, as will be shown in the following examples. The sentence can be divided into a series of Intonation Groups, which conform acoustically to certain patterns. It is not unusual to find these groups composed, on the one hand, of a single word, or, on the other, of several words. Each Intonation Group contains one prominent syllable, which is differentiated from the other syllables of the Intonation Group by breath-force or stress. This breath-force or stress is also accompanied by tonal prominence due to a change of intonation direction or glide.

2. If the sense of an Intonation Group is not complete it conforms to a certain tone pattern which indicates that there is more to follow. This can be called a Suspensive Intonation Group. If the sense is complete the Intonation Group conforms to another type which can be called a Final Intonation Group.

3. The intonation of Persian falls between two principal tone levels. There is a rise to the high tone level on a syllable on which there is breath-force or stress, and if the stress is final either there is a downward glide on it to the low tone level or a gradual descent to the low tone level begun on the final stress and continued on the remaining words or syllables in the Intonation Group.

4. Sometimes, in order to break the monotony of an Intonation Group, a glide from the high tone level to the low tone level is introduced; this is usually unaccompanied by breath-force and is thereby differentiated

[1] See Duncan Forbes, *Grammar of the Persian Language* (Calcutta, 1876), p. 24.

from the downward glide on a prominent syllable or word in a Final Intonation Group. Such internal glides are only used, however, on syllables which can carry word stress.

5. There are, of course, many variations of tone in addition to the two main tone levels, and the actual division of sentences into Intonation Groups varies from speaker to speaker. In order to make the general pattern clearer a graphical method has been adopted in the following examples. This, in attempting to bring out the general tendencies of Persian intonation, will inevitably make Persian intonation appear more stereotyped that it is in actual practice. The prominent syllable in each group is marked by a vertical stroke preceding it, thus *kar'dan*. A thick line — represents a stressed syllable containing a long vowel or diphthong and a thick dot • a stressed syllable containing a short vowel. A thick curved downward stroke ↴ represents a downward glide or a final stress; a thick downward stroke equal to approximately half the foregoing, thus ↴, represents a downward glide on a final stress, followed by a gradual descent on the remaining syllables in the Intonation Group. A thick upward stroke ⤴ represents an upward glide to the high tone level used in questions (see below, para. 9). A thin line — represents an unstressed syllable containing a long vowel or diphthong and a thin dot · an unstressed syllable containing a short vowel. A vertical stroke | represents the end of a Suspensive Intonation Group and a double stroke || the end of a Final Intonation Group.

6. The English student should be careful to give each syllable its full value and not to clip his words as is often the tendency in English. Vowels do not lose their quantity in unstressed syllables. A long unstressed passage tends to be articulated more quickly, but the relative length of the vowels remain the same. The English student should also remember to give a double consonant its full value.

7. Final Intonation Groups. In Final Intonation Groups the unstressed syllables preceding the final stress are on the low tone level. There is a rise to the high tone level for the final stress, on which there is either a downward glide to the low tone level or a gradual descent spread over the unstressed words or syllables which follow the final stress. The descent tends to be gradual if the unstressed syllables following the final stress exceed two in number, e.g.

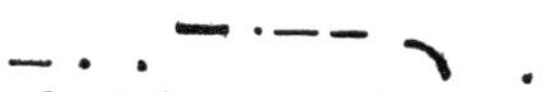

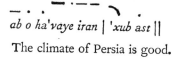

ab o ha'vaye iran | *'xub ast* ||

The climate of Persia is good.

in dokkan'dar | *aj'nase xodra* | *be qe͡i'mate monaseb* | *'miforuʃad* ||

This shopkeeper sells his goods at a reasonable price.

dar tabes'tan | *'namiʃavad inja ʒendagi kard* ||

In summer it is impossible to live here.

If the finite verb is not in a final position there tends to be only a slight rise of tone in the final Intonation Group followed by a downward glide on the final stress, e.g.

ʃo'ru' kardand | *be xandi'dan* ||

They began to laugh.

8. Suspensive Intonation Groups. The unstressed syllables preceding the stressed syllable are on the low tone level. There is a rise to the high tone level on the stress and the high tone level is then maintained to the end of the group, e.g.

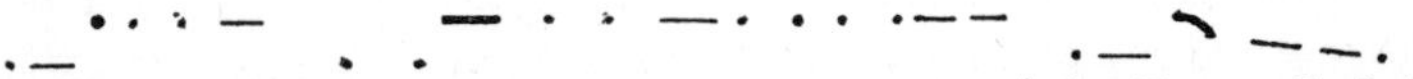

vasa''ele tahsil | *dar ta'mame ʃahrhaye boʒorge iran* | *fara'ham mibaʃad* ||

Facilities for study are available in all the large cities of Persia.

aha'liye esfahan | *dar s̀axtane anva' va aqsame ʒorufe noqre'i* | *os'tad and* ||

The people of Isfahan are masters in making different kinds of silver vessels.

The following would be a possible alternative version if the internal glides in the second suspensive Intonation Group were omitted:

aha'liye esfahan | *dar sax'tane anva' va aqsame ʒorufe noqrei* | *os'tad and* ||

If a subordinate clause precedes the principal sentence, there tends to be a rise to the high tone level on the last syllable of the final word of the subordinate clause and this is accompanied by breath-force, which, even if it would normally fall elsewhere, is moved to the final syllable of the clause, e.g.

har ce aẓ qodrat va qovveye dõulate markaẓi mika'had | *dar at'raf va aknafe*
As the power of the central government decreases people in the distant

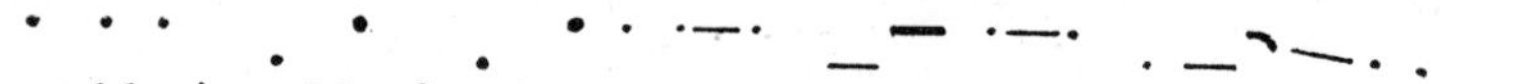

mamlekat | *mar'dom* | *gar'dan aẓ eta'at* | *bi'run kaśide* | *toɣi'an mikonand* ||
parts of the country, having thrown off its allegiance, rebel.

In the above example the stress in the word *mikahad* is shifted from the first syllable to the final syllable.

If a subordinate clause follows the principle sentence, it sometimes begins on the low tone level and gradually descends below that level, e.g.

eśte'ha | *'nadaram* | *ke ciẓi 'bexoram* ||
I have no appetite to eat anything.

In the case of auxiliary verbs such as *tavanestan* 'to be able' and *xastan* 'to want' there is usually a rise to the high tone level on the auxiliary verb while the following dependent subjunctive clause or clauses descend gradually to the low tone level. If the initial syllable of the auxiliary carries the stress, the descent begins on the immediately following unstressed syllables of the auxiliary, e.g.

'namitavanad | *tasmim 'begirad* | *ke 'beravad* ||
He cannot make up his mind to go.

aẓ inke ba adab va rosume mamlekat aśna na'bud | *natavanest jehate*
Because he was unacquainted with the customs of the country, he could not

dõulate matbu'e 'xod | *ahdnameye tejara'ti* | *mon'a'qed namayad* ||
conclude a commercial agreement for his sovereign government.

9. Interrogative Sentences.

(*a*) Sentences containing an interrogative word such as *ce* 'what'. Stress is usually carried on the interrogative word, which rises to the high tone level. There is either a downward glide on the interrogative word to the low tone level or a gradual descent beginning on the syllable carrying the stress and continuing throughout the remaining words or syllables of the Intonation Group. The tonal pattern of interrogative sentences of this type does not, therefore, materially differ from that of statements, e.g.

ko'ja mixahid beravid ||

Where do you want to go?

esme in aba'di | *čist* ||

What is the name of this village?

If the emphasis is not on the interrogative word but on some other word in the sentence, the stress will be carried on this word and not the interrogative, thus

esme 'in abadi čist ||

What is the name of *this* village?

(*b*) Sentences without an interrogative word. In sentences of this kind, the interrogation is marked by an upward glide to the high tone level on the final syllable of the last word in the sentence, or by a rise to the high pitch level on the final stress; the remaining words or syllables continue on the high tone level or there is a very slight fall on the final stress, e.g.

aqabe 'kasi | *'migardid* ||

Are you looking for someone?

aẓ 'in | *'me͡il* | *'mifarmaid* ||

Would you like some of this?

aẓ' in | *baraye ʃo'ma* | *'beyavaram* ||

Shall I bring you some of this?

Questions introduced by the particle *aya* are treated in the same way as questions which contain no interrogative word, e.g.

'aya | *in* | *male ʃomast* ||

Is this yours?

'aya | *far'da* | *'miravid* ||

Are you going to-morrow?

INDEX

PERSIAN INDEX